RESILIENT

MITCHELL
JOHNSON

RESILIENT

ABC
Books

The ABC 'Wave' device is a trademark of the
Australian Broadcasting Corporation and is used
under licence by HarperCollins*Publishers* Australia.

First published in Australia in 2016
This edition published in 2017
by HarperCollins*Publishers* Australia Pty Limited
ABN 36 009 913 517
harpercollins.com.au

HarperCollins*Publishers*
Level 13, 201 Elizabeth Street, Sydney NSW 2000, Australia
Unit D1, 63 Apollo Drive, Rosedale, Auckland 0632, New Zealand
A 53, Sector 57, Noida, UP, India
1 London Bridge Street, London SE1 9GF, United Kingdom
2 Bloor Street East, 20th floor, Toronto, Ontario M4W 1A8, Canada
195 Broadway, New York NY 10007, USA

National Library of Australia Cataloguing-in-Publication entry:

Johnson, Mitchell, author.
  Title: Resilient / Mitchell Johnson.
  Edition: Second edition.
  ISBN: 978 0 7333 3854 0 (paperback)
  Notes: Includes index.
  Subjects: Johnson, Mitchell.
  Cricket players — Australia — Biography.
  Cricket — Australia.

Cover design by Matt Stanton and Darren Holt, HarperCollins Design Studio
Front cover image by Ryan Pierse/Getty Images
Back cover image by Gareth Copley/Getty Images
Internal picture credits: pages viii–1 Gareth Copley/Getty Images; 16–17 Patrick Eagar/
Popperfoto/Getty Images; 40–1 Robert Cianflone/ALLSPORT via Getty Images; 72–3
Darren England/Getty Images; 92–3 Prakash Singh/AFP/Getty Images; 114–15 Cameron
Spencer/Getty Images; 150–1 Mike Hewitt/Getty Images; 194–5 Alexander Joe/AFP/
Getty Images; 228–9 Mark Kolbe/Getty Images; 258–9 Alexander Joe/AFP/Getty Images;
274–5 Matt Roberts/Cricket Australia/Getty Images; 292–3 Michael Dodge/IDI via
Getty Images; 308–9 Ryan Pierse/Cricket Australia/Getty Images; 334–5 Will Russell/
Cricket Australia/Getty Images.
Cricket statistics by Ross Dundas
Typeset in Sabon LT by Kirby Jones
Printed and bound in Australia by McPhersons Printing Group
The papers used by HarperCollins in the manufacture of this book are a natural,
recyclable product made from wood grown in sustainable plantation forests. The fibre
source and manufacturing processes meet recognised international environmental standards,
and carry certification.

To Jess, Rubika and Leo

CONTENTS

1

Redemption

I'M 32 YEARS OLD, I'm at the top of my mark and my heart is pounding. I am so nervous I'm just holding my breath. It's all come down to this. It feels like everything I have ever tried to achieve in cricket is on the line. I get it right now or I limp away with my tail between my legs. I know if I stuff this up I will be written off as a cricketer. It's the second morning of the first Test in Brisbane and we have our first chance to bowl at England. I feel like it's my first Test match. If I could breathe out, I might be able to breathe in, but I can't seem to do either.

A lot of people have already written me off and are wondering how I got back. People are asking themselves which Mitchell Johnson will show up today and have been all week in the lead-up to the game. Will it be the one who was dropped after the last Ashes match in Brisbane when he failed to get a wicket? The one who got 0–170 in that game? Or the one who bounced back in Perth three weeks later and took 9–82 in the third Test?

Will it be the one who broke both of Graeme Smith's hands (sorry about that) and terrorised South Africa, or the one who the Barmy Army wrote that song about? You know the one: *He bowls to the left, he bowls to the right, that Mitchell Johnson, his bowling is shite.* I am asking myself the same question.

Ashes performances define a cricketer. Almost all Australian and English Test players are measured by how they go in the Ashes. What's the thing you remember most about Warne? I'd guess it's the Gatting ball. Or his performance in 2005. Matthew Hayden, Glenn McGrath, Justin Langer and all the legends who retired in 2006–07 are remembered because they won that last series 5–0 after slipping up in England in 2005. Some bloke called Pratt is remembered because he ran out Ricky Ponting at Trent Bridge. He never played a Test match, but he did that. Mark Taylor, Steve Waugh, Allan Border all stood up to be counted on this stage. I am judged by my failure in England in 2009 and my struggles in the years after that. But redemption is possible and now is my moment to prove it.

Ryan Harris has bowled the first over and now I am running in from the Stanley Street end bowling to Michael Carberry. If I am completely honest I am a nervous wreck. I'm shitting myself. I don't know if I have ever felt it this much. Maybe it's because this is my chance to change everything. If only I could calm down and breathe!

I know what the team expects because our plans are clear and simple. I have to bowl fast in short spells. Push the batsman's weight back with short balls. Make sure they are in the wrong position when there is one pitched up to drive. When the tail comes in I rattle their cage.

I have been out of the side for most of the past two years. I've only played four Tests since breaking down in South Africa. I got my body right quickly enough, but there were questions about me and they weren't just about my bowling. Some didn't think I was up to the job mentally. I understood that. They didn't pick me for the last Ashes and I reckon that was part of the reason.

I know I have done the work, I know I can do it, but when you have failed once before there's always that element of doubt. Controlling those negative voices is hard work.

The Gabba was my home ground and it is a place I love to bowl at, but I have never felt tension like this. It's humid like it always is and the sun is belting down. There is never any breeze in this ground; it's almost suffocating at times. I am sweating so much it's hard to grip the ball. There are over 30,000 here at the ground and they've been warmed up by a day and a bit of our batting. I've had some fun with the bat, but that's not my job.

Come on, tough it out, I tell myself. Dennis Lillee has me working on that 'tough' concept. He spells it TUFF; it's to remind me of a couple of little elements – Tall, Upright, Front arm, Follow through – but I have adapted it slightly. There are two marks on the ground that I have measured out this morning. My run-up proper starts at 25.6 metres but I take off from 26.6 metres. Process. It's all down to processes.

When the field is settled and Carberry nods, I run the measured distance to the back crease and let the first one go. Bugger! It's a full toss down the leg side. There's a hint of a groan from the Australian fans, an early cheer from the Poms. The Australian fans outnumber them but seem as anxious as I am and I can almost hear the Barmy Army clearing their throats.

I tell myself it's not a big deal to spray the first one. I am going to bowl bad balls. Everyone in the world knows I am not a land-it-on-a-coin-hit-the-top-of-off bowler. If you want control, get a 'sweat band swinger' (that's what the fast bowling cartel calls them). The scoreboard says it was travelling at 144 km/h, which is good pace. And I want to bowl fast. If I can't do that I don't want to bowl. Back to the top of the mark and I try again. Better line this time, but the third ball is full and down leg again and Alastair Cook comes on strike as Carberry takes a single to fine leg. Fourth ball is full and fast on middle stump and Cook digs it out. Next one is full but drifting down leg and he flicks it away for a couple of runs. I tempt him with one outside off with the last but he isn't interested. I reckon I got through the whole over without taking a breath, but it hasn't gone too badly. Pace is good, line and length are not so great, but I've had worse.

Cook is facing when I start again; I hold him there for two balls then he clips me for a four off his hip third ball. It's not a great delivery and we both know it. Two dot balls follow and I resolve to dig one in and give him a sniff of it on the last ball. This is the key to our plans. It comes out okay, rises at him and he pulls it for four high over midwicket. Absolutely smacks it.

That sets me back a bit and as we change ends I look at the replay on the screen thinking I mustn't have got it right, but it was a good length and he has just had too much time to play it. I'd been relying on balls like this to do the damage and he's destroyed it. I'm back in my shell. The doubts start to circle. My confidence drops and in the next over I don't try anything fancy. The fourth ball swings and beats Carberry. That happens, but it's something I can't control. I can't go searching for it again.

I've pinned him down for five balls, which is positive. I run in, pull the last one down wide and short of a length, and he slashes it over the cordon for four. Gawd, that really was an awful ball. I'm not happy with myself but that's the end of the spell. I have time to think about things when Pete Siddle replaces me. If I can't back myself to bowl short my whole game plan changes. I can't set the batsman up if I don't get him on the back foot. It was only one shot. I tell myself to back my game and when I get the ball I need to start again as if nothing has happened.

I guess I was trying too hard, despite knowing better. I was trying to swing the ball, which always goes wrong, and when I look back later I realise there was no effort in that short ball. It was tentative and it sat up nicely. I know if I am getting pulled over midwicket I am not really putting in. Either that or the bloke has played an unbelievable shot.

The Barmy Army have been on top of every stray ball, but that's okay. There's a long way to go yet. My body language is still good. I think I am looking confident even if I'm not feeling it. In the 11th over with the clock moving towards lunch, Ryan Harris gets Cook to nibble at one outside off and gets an edge through to Brad Haddin. The captain wanders off back to the dressing room and Jonathan Trott makes his way out to the middle. He's my man. Sidds has only bowled two overs, but this has been worked out well in advance and so I am back into the attack from the same end. Sorry, Sidds! He's a good man, Sidds, no ego. That's the way us quicks are. We do our job and work as a team. We're all tight.

There's no secret that we are going to target this bloke. I had him in all sorts of bother in a one-day series on their side of the world earlier in the year. We've heard he's been facing left-armers in the nets and practising against the short ball, so I know he is sweating on me. Unfortunately, Carberry is on strike when I get the ball and stays there for the whole over while Trott gets to watch and wait. When I get the ball again Carberry is facing and again Trott spends the whole over up my end.

The plan is for me to bowl in three-over spells. I've already bowled two of them and haven't got a look at my man. Michael has brought Sidds on to replace Ryno from the Vulture Street end and he keeps Carberry in place so I can have a crack at Trott in the 15th over, which should be my last in this spell. I dig the first ball in and it skids up on a low angle. It hits him hard on the gloves. He's all over the shop just as we thought he would be. He has made a real mess of it. There's a groan from the crowd, but it has nothing to do with my bowling. The groan turns into a loud appreciative noise. I give Trott a long hard stare, because he knows and I know that he is in trouble. It feels good to be putting the pressure on someone else. His problem with my bowling is the worst kept secret in cricket.

The second ball is short and he flicks it over backward square, but it's in the air and far from convincing. He's back again next ball and weaves out of the way of one. You can see this is no fun for him, but somehow he hangs on. I've done my three overs and have only had five balls at my man. Michael and I have a quick chat and decide I will bowl another one if we can squeeze it in before lunch. Everybody is instructed to sprint into position to make sure we can pull it off. It's going to be a tight call, but we can feel something brewing. All I need is another crack at Trott.

As soon as Sidds is done, everyone rushes to their designated spot in the field. Steve Smith runs down to get my cap and sprints towards Aleem Dar, who takes it and then scratches at the crease before looking at his watch. It says 11.59 on the scoreboard – they are 1–55. The umpire moves into position and we are all happy. I swear the clock ticks over to midday a moment later, but we've snuck in another over.

Those few seconds change everything. Michael is yelling instructions from slips. He's not really doing it to tell the fielders anything – they know what to do and are already in position – he's making sure Trott can hear what we are up to. Putting another voice inside his head.

After the one-day series we had talked about how far across Trott got and how he blocked himself off. It's obvious from the five balls he's faced from me that nothing has changed despite his talk that he has worked on these things.

At 1–55 they are building a platform and we only put on 295 when we batted. I've got six balls to change the momentum of the morning. I have to bounce him. When I went to Chennai as a teenager to work with Dennis Lillee he used to wait at the top of my mark and ask me what ball I was planning to bowl next, then he'd say, 'Bowl a bumper, bowl a bumper.'

I suck up a last deep breath and run in. It's not a great ball, it's short but it's heading down leg side by some way. Trott hops across like we know he will and is almost outside off stump when he waves the bat around his hip. He is well inside the line and way out of position and manages to get the slightest nick through to the keeper. Hadds is sure of it and so am I. The slips aren't as convinced, but Trott knows he's done and Aleem puts his finger up.

It wasn't the perfect ball, but it was straight from the game plan and the boys love it when that happens. The crowd goes off and so do we. It's a brilliant feeling. We're all celebrating and I can't get the smile off my face as the umpires shoo us towards the dressing room. I will have to finish the over after the break. England is 2–55 after the first hour, our plans have worked a treat and there's a bloody good buzz among the boys. I know not to get too carried away, but there's a sense among this group of players that this is our time. The boys played well without me in the away series without winning and our preparation has been great.

After the break I launch a series of short balls at my old mate Kevin Pietersen. I've owed him one since the morning he and I clashed before play in the first Test at Cardiff in 2009. If it wasn't for Stuart Clark stepping between us then I may well have hit him for what he said. I didn't, but it's a score I don't mind settling every time we meet.

The first delivery he fends off from in front of his face; the second he tries to pull, but it beats him for pace and sails over his right shoulder before the bat can get there. His eyes go wide and I lock in on him. It has been faster than he'd anticipated and he knows he's been done. I'm pretty confident that if he keeps taking me on I will get him. He has a good eye and is a gun player with a record to prove it, but will take chances and is reluctant to back down. KP's ego is his strength and his weakness.

He starts to mouth off when I follow through a few balls later. I just put my hand over my mouth and don't respond. That surprises him. In the book he wrote after he retired he includes a pretty funny account of it:

> 'He looked at me, just stared at me, he didn't say anything
> back. He kept staring and walked past. Shit. Shit. Shit.
> On so many occasions in the past Johnson has always
> bit back: shut up, KP, fuck off, shut up, big shot. This
> time he didn't say anything, and immediately I knew he
> was different. I would have preferred him to have said

something, to engage with me, but he didn't, and that's
when I knew the series could be tough.'

My vow of silence won't be a permanent thing. A few Tests
later I'll be giving him a gob full at the MCG. It was the end
of the day and I was tired and hungry. When I am hungry I get
angry. We've had some good battles over the years. KP is one of
the world's best players. He's come out on top many times and
hopefully I've won a few times too.

But it's Ryno who gets him this time, just on the drinks
break after lunch. We have them 3–82 and we are feeling pretty
good, but we don't have a lot of runs to defend and the game
can still go either way.

I come on again soon after the drinks; Carberry is still
going and Ian Bell is out there with him. I have a good record
against Bell too. Nothing much happens in my first over but
then Watto comes up when I am finished and says I should go
around the wicket to Carberry. Not a lot of teams were getting
left-armers to go around the wicket to left-handers. It's a bit
of a last resort type thing and not something we've discussed
before the game. I am not that keen and decide against it. But
Watto must have got in Pup's [Michael Clarke's] ear because
he comes up when I am getting ready to bowl the next over
and says the same thing. Says it will change the angle and
make him play.

What can I do? I feel like I've been bowling well, they aren't
scoring off me, but I agree to give it a crack. Pup puts in a
short leg and a third man. Turns out it's a good idea. I've been

dotting them up, putting the ball outside of off stump, but he's been letting them go and this is a more aggressive approach. We're not here for a war of attrition. Well, not if we don't have to be and he's been really patient to this point.

I bang one in short and it hits him. He looks uncomfortable. The next one he takes a swing at, but it's in hope more than anything. The third ball isn't as short, but it's still into the chest area. He tries to get the bat out of the way but only manages to nick it. There's something about the way the ball flies to the slips in Brisbane and Perth that can do your head in. It just hangs there. Floats. It just seems to take forever to get to the fielder. I can get pretty nervous in the moment that it takes to get from A to B. Watto, whose idea it was to come around the wicket, is waiting at first slip. And he waits until it gets right to him before it settles in his big hands.

The boys are absolutely pumped that their plan has come off. It's got us onto a bit of a roll. My confidence has been boosted. I'm into that zone that people often talk about – the ball is coming out exactly the way I want it. We've laid down a marker for the series.

A lot of factors that don't show up on scorecards or in match reports go into getting a wicket. Carberry's dismissal is down to Nathan Lyon as well as Watto and Pup. He's bowled three consecutive maidens to hold him down and frustrate him. Carberry is 40 off 94 balls, then 40 off 113 balls when he walks off. The pressure got to him. We are celebrating our wickets, really enjoying them; it doesn't matter who is getting them, everyone is excited. Something special is happening and we've got a really good feeling in the group. It's been there since the camp at Brisbane the week before.

Nathan gets his reward in the next over when he picks up Bell and Prior with consecutive balls. Everyone is having a bit of fun and in the next over I have a bit more. After roughing up Carberry and Trott, I have Joe Root to contend with. The plan is to get him driving from deep in the crease and we set the field for short deliveries, but I keep it up to him early before I get him on the back foot with the third ball and give him some lip.

I pitch the next one full and a little wide and he chases it. It's a rash shot and the edge flies to Smithy at third slip. They have lost four wickets in three overs. Now it's Swanny's turn. He is not one of our favourite players; he can get lippy when they are on top, but he doesn't have a chance to say a word when I get him caught off an inside edge at bat pad by George Bailey.

We just have this unstoppable momentum. England has lost 6–9 and has no answers. Our plans are coming off. Even my half good balls are taking wickets. It's just one of those days. I take it up a notch and spray Stuart Broad with short balls. He's the first of their tail and I want to let them know they are in for a hell of a time. He cops one off the glove and onto the helmet and weaves inside a few others. He is not having a good time, but does alright to survive half an hour before Sidds gets him and we've bowled out England for 136.

Now I can finally breathe out and enjoy our openers having a bat again. We haven't won the Test yet and my four wickets aren't going to be worth much if I stuff up later on, but I have a really good feeling about this.

Maybe, just maybe, this Ashes is going to be the one where I live up to the expectations that were placed on me when I was discovered nearly 15 years before. More importantly it feels like a series where this team of 11 blokes can do something only the great teams do.

England U-19s v Australia U-19s, Third Test,
Chester-le-Street, 2 September 1999.

2

Marking Out My Run-up

I WAS BORN IN Townsville on 2 November 1981. I began life as Mitchell Harber. My mother, Vikki Harber, was just 17 when I came along. She and Dad, Kevin Johnson, weren't together at the time. It wasn't until I was 17 myself that I realised just how young that is to be having a kid. I could hardly look after myself at that age. It wasn't until Jess and I had our daughter, Rubika, that I realised just how difficult raising a child can be – and I was 30 and married when our girl came along.

There's a scar across my stomach that's a little reminder of just how much trouble I was back then. As a baby I would scream and projectile vomit like something out of a horror movie. I must have been like the devil's child. It was eventually worked out that I had a problem with my stomach and they operated on it and fixed things up. When Rubika was born she had similar problems with reflux that were undiagnosed. She made a lot of noise, which I guess I had been doing 30-odd years earlier. Like Mum, Jess had to deal with that by herself a fair bit. I was away a lot with the cricket, but, like Mum, Jess had a close family to help out.

Mum was one of six kids and she used to leave me and my brother at Nan and Pop's most weekends so she could have a break or whatever. That was fantastic. It was a great place, a big old Queenslander with a built-in downstairs for her brother Jason, who was at high school and still living at home. A lot of my cousins used to hang around the Harbers' and we all had a great time together.

I loved my nanna very much and grew very close to her. Her name was Lorraine. I spent a lot of time with her over the years. She sheltered us and loved us when we needed it most. I think grandmothers have a special love for kids. I know mine did and the memory of her remains with me to this day, although she is sadly no longer with us. Nan used to have this black porcelain panther in her house that I was obsessed with. I would ask her if I could take it home with me, but she would never let me. After she died somebody made sure I inherited it. Years later, when I was about 25, I had a dream where I got a tattoo of the panther. Then I had the same dream again.

I don't know what it was about, but it seemed pretty clear that the thing to do was to get a tattoo of the panther and after a lot of searching I took a photo of it to a tattooist who was good at doing animals and got the panther tattooed on my side. It's something from my nan and it is special to me. It looks pretty cool, too. I wish I could have shown her that.

The backyard was full of cars because Pop, Max, was a mechanic, and I used to spend a lot of time watching him fix them. I would sit in the cars and maybe that's where I got the love of them. We used to make billy carts and my uncle raced go-karts. Max is quite the character. He loves his cars still and heads off to the Gympie Muster (a country music festival) and has a spot at Bathurst where he watches the race every year. All the young people apparently love this old bloke who joins in and gets on the rum with them. I want to be able to do that with him one day.

Mum was caring and protective. We never had much money, even when Dad was around, but I don't remember it ever really bothering us. We got by. Mum did her best to give me and my brother everything we needed. If you saw my dad, Kevin Johnson, you'd realise straight away we are related. He, me and my little brother are almost identical, but then people look at pictures of Mum and say we are alike, too. He was tanned and looked after himself. He used to go to the gym four or five times a week. He was extremely strong, which was quite impressive to me as a boy. You wouldn't have been well advised to mess with him. I tried a couple of times as I got older but realised pretty quickly it was a bad idea. He was a man's man, a no-nonsense sort of guy who'd had an interesting upbringing. His parents were from the outback up near the Atherton Tablelands and they sent him to boarding school in Charters Towers. In the school holidays he would work on his uncle's property, riding horses and fixing fences. Sometimes I used to go up and stay with his parents when I was playing tennis. My grandfather, Jim, had this independent spirit. He used to fly ultra lights around in the bush and just do his own thing. That country up there breeds tough men. He became a bit of a hermit, living out on a 50-acre block by himself. Jim was still climbing windmills and getting into scrapes on the property up until he died in August 2016. Once, he even managed to run himself over with his own car!

Dad had the same independent spirit as his father – which was the way he was with us. He is definitely a Queensland male, but he has become gentler as he's got older and we are pretty close. Well, as close as Australian males can be.

Mum and Dad got married when I was about five years old. They'd been together on and off in between times. I was a pageboy at their wedding. It was good having a mum and dad, but even better because a year or so later my little brother Adam was born.

Dad worked at the *Townsville Bulletin* as a printer. He did the night shift for nearly 20 years. It was a dirty job and the hours were hard. He'd come home tired and covered in ink. Printers don't earn a lot of money and we never had our own home. We moved around a lot, living in different rental properties. When I go back to Townsville I try to remember the streets and houses. It's a bit of a stretch but I can find most of them.

I was living at my grandparents' when I started at school but then with Mum and Dad after they got married. I started at Railway Estate State School, then in Year 4 we moved to Heatley, which was on the other side of town, and I shifted to the primary school there. I was definitely annoyed about having to change schools at the time, but it didn't take too long to get used to it and settle in. I made good friends there, Chris (Dingo) and Kevin (Leonard), and they have been my mates ever since.

Things were always a bit rocky at home. Mum and Dad just didn't get on and they were pretty fiery people. It made life quite unsettled. I have a vivid memory of walking with Mum and Adam late one night from wherever we were living to Nan and Pop's place after Mum and Dad had had an argument. I can only imagine what it looked like to see us wandering around the streets at that hour and I remember it was upsetting. After Dad left, Mum raised me and Adam for about five years on her own again.

Kids are resilient and you get on with things, but I know it used to bother me and I was a bit of an anxious kid. I remember one time sitting there on the balcony of Nan and Pop's house and having what was like a nightmare in broad daylight. I could see all this stuff going on. That really freaked me out. It was soon after Mum and Dad split and it was a pretty unpleasant time for everybody.

Mum had a new partner, Brian, and they had two girls, Jazmine and Maddison, and later a son called Jack. We were living in a house on Churinga Street in Kirwan, near the soccer ground. One Sunday, they announced they were leaving town and moving south. I was supposed to start at Kirwan High with Dingo and Leonard the next day. The decision came out of the blue, and I was pretty shocked. I wanted to stay in Townsville with my mates and go to school with them. I was sick of moving around, so I said I wasn't going to go. Mum wanted to take Adam with her, and I just couldn't let that happen because

I wanted to be able to keep an eye on him. He was my little brother and I had become quite protective. I said, 'He is staying with me; we will go and live with Dad.' I wasn't an assertive kid, so for me to make that stand was out of the blue. Maybe that was why Mum listened and understood. It was a big thing for me to speak up like that.

I dug in my heels and, somehow, got my way. Dad was living with his grandfather in an old house in Pimlico. My great-grandfather was really old – I think he was 90 or something. I was scared of him; he was a pretty cranky bloke, but I was more scared of the house. In my mind, it was haunted. It was on stilts and had a falling down shed out the back with a cockatoo in a cage. It smelled musty, and it freaked me out a bit. I hated lying in bed at night, and I was pretty pleased that we didn't stay there too long.

Dad was a single man with a job and motorbike, a big Kawasaki 1100, which he loved. But now he had us two, and so he got rid of it and bought an old station wagon. It's only later that I realised the sacrifices he made.

Recently, I got to make it up to him. When he turned 50, I went to his place and gave him a bottle of Scotch and a poster of Casey Stoner on a Triumph, which was the bike he really loved. I said, 'It's bad luck that that is the closest you are going to get to a bike again in your life.' He laughed. Then, we took him to the garage where Jess and I had hidden a red Ducati 1098 for him earlier in the day. He got pretty emotional about that gift. It made me feel good to give something back to him and to see him moved like that.

I was a bit of a ratbag in the years that followed moving in with my dad – I guess I was acting out – and we clashed a lot. I was rebellious and gave him a hard time. He didn't have the time or patience for that, but I respected him because he was my dad.

Mum wasn't gone long and she moved into a caravan at the back of her mother's place. We used to see her on the weekends, but we didn't move back with her.

Somehow, despite having two kids, Dad met a woman, Kylie, and she had two kids, Abby and Zac, who were much younger than me, and we all moved in together. I was very much the older brother; I would go and almost supervise when they played in the park or went skating or whatever. It was quite an age gap, but I didn't mind. It was good to have a few people around. Eventually, we moved to a Queenslander in Heatley, near the airport, and they put up a few walls downstairs to make a room for me so I could have my own space. I was a teenager by then, and it was probably as much about not having to put up with my moods as anything else. I had long hair and buckteeth, wore heavy metal t-shirts and looked like an absolute bogan. I acted like one, too.

Around Year 7 people had started calling me Chompers. I'd dived into a mate's pool, hit the bottom and smashed my teeth. I thought my dad would kill me so I didn't tell anyone. I hid it for half a day but the nerve ending was sticking out and the pain became unbearable. By that time it was Friday night and the dentists were closed, so it became a much bigger deal than it should have been. It was a real hassle finding someone to fix them. Dad was more annoyed at me for that than anything else. I was lucky I hadn't snapped my neck when I jumped in the pool. That would have changed a lot of things.

I played a lot of sport as a kid but it took me a long time to get to cricket. Soccer was my first game. I used to go alright. One year, I won club player of the year and was in the Under-8s when I played in the Under-14 side on a day when they were short – I scored in that game and was pretty pleased with myself.

After a year or so our coach left for some reason and they asked Dad to take over. He'd never done any coaching so he got a book from the library and learned all these drills and stuff and took it pretty seriously. Naturally there was a bit of father–son conflict. Dad didn't have a big sporting background. His main interest was a game called Broomball, which was basically played on ice with a ball and a solid broomstick-shaped thing. It's a bit like hockey. He was really into ten-pin bowling and a little bit of golf, but I don't remember him playing too many other sports.

Dingo and Leonard were into golf when we got a bit older and it was surprising I didn't get into it. I used to have a crack. I started as a leftie but changed to right-handed because Dad had right-handed clubs and I remember hitting lots of balls in the backyard at my great-grandfathers'.

Dingo had a good golf set-up at his house. His dad worked for the council and had one of those roller mowers and kept the lawn in good nick. We used to chip the ball from his front yard onto the front lawn. I never once broke a window with the ball, but I did with a cricket ball once.

I spent a lot of time at his place over the years and his mum and dad, Sarah and Chris, were like second parents to me.

Later on in life everyone was playing golf when we were on cricket tours, but I just didn't really get into it that much. Ricky Ponting and Glenn Maxwell are both really good, and Greg Blewett is also a gun. I started taking my clubs to the Indian Premier League (IPL) after I stopped Test cricket, so it might happen, but I don't know if Jess will be all that happy if I swap cricket for another sport.

Leonard's place was on a main road opposite the school. We played cricket on the front lawn and made a rule that if it landed in the school it was six and not out. If it landed in the traffic you were out and you had probably caused an accident as well. We risked our lives chasing balls, but I guess that's what kids do.

Mum played a bit of indoor cricket. I joined in a couple of times as a little fella, but I got scared because they hit the ball pretty hard. Her brother Jason, who raced go-karts, was really good at rugby league. He was ten years older than me, but because he was living at Nan and Pop's I spent a lot of time playing cricket with him and his mates on the front lawn. He was almost like an older brother.

One morning when I was at school I watched some kids playing tennis and I thought I wouldn't mind giving it a go. I was in Year 4 and we had a coach called Mr Osborne at the school who helped me out. I took to it straight away. I was a right-hander with a big serve and I developed quite a power game as I got older. I modelled myself on Pete Sampras. My single-handed backhand was my favourite stroke – I had control of it, but I tried to hit my forehand too hard.

I started playing club tennis at Wests on the weekends; Mr Rowe was my coach and I enjoyed playing. As I grew stronger so did my game and after a few years I started playing in tournaments and doing alright. I am not sure I had the right temperament for tennis, however. I was impatient and tried to hit winners all the time. When I play now I have a bit more control and patience, but of course that has come much too late.

I had a mate called Chris James and we were pretty competitive. We played doubles together and one year we beat the Australian champions at the Queensland Schoolboy titles. When it was match point I hit a ball I thought was out and was really annoyed because it would have meant we'd lost, but then Chris reminded me it was doubles and a legitimate shot. I don't know what I was thinking. Maybe it proved I was a fast bowler at heart!

There was no chance of becoming a tennis brat with my dad. Once when I was 12 and I was playing in a state tournament at Rockhampton, the umpire was the best mate of the kid I was playing against and to my mind he was cheating. I got more and more frustrated as calls went against me and eventually I lost it and smashed my racquet into the court. It bounced so high it nearly went over the fence. Dad grabbed me and said you do that again and you will never play again. We didn't have the money for that sort of carry-on. I never did it again.

I enjoyed being part of the tennis club. I liked the social side of it and started coaching little kids to help out. I guess I must have been going quite well because when I was 14 I was offered a scholarship, which meant I would have to move down to Brisbane, go to school and train down there. I suppose it was my chance to really make a go of it, but I was too shy. I just didn't want to leave home and so I told Dad I didn't want to do it. I just wasn't that confident. He understood.

I played a lot with another kid called Shaun Hutchison. His parents were really good and would give me a lift to tournaments around the state. We had been at primary school together and would train together. I always had it over him on the court, but towards the end of school he worked me out and started to beat me. I was really competitive and it annoyed me, but no matter what I did he kept winning. It should have been a wake-up call to encourage me to work even harder; instead I started to think that maybe I had peaked. Maybe I was right. I was getting a bit older and starting to lose a bit of interest, which I think kids do at that stage. It was one of those fork-in-the-road moments and I took the easier option. I would have them again later in life and the temptation was always to do the same. I had a dream of playing Wimbledon by the age of 18, but I was getting older without getting any closer. In fact, when Shaun started beating me it was a sign that I had stalled while he was getting better. He gave it up, too, a bit later on.

Looking back, it seems strange I didn't play more contact sports. I was drawn to them but tennis took up all my time. I was a pretty physical kid and while I wasn't big I was fearless. I used to love playing rugby league in the schoolyard and I remember playing one game for the school on the wing where

I got really frustrated that I wasn't getting the ball and I just smashed some poor kid. I wish I'd played more but maybe it was better that I didn't, though there was a period when my cricket wasn't working out and I thought about going back to Townsville and playing league.

Now I have finished my cricket I want to get back into tennis; it is just finding the time and a club. The real problem I have with it is if I am going to do it I have to do it properly. I will want to train, I can't just turn up and play, I can't do things half-arsed and so I don't think I will have the time. I just have this perfectionist thing that makes me really sweat on my preparation. It helped when I was at the top level but it is a bit crazy the rest of the time.

We played tennis sometimes on tour with the Australian team. I played Steve Smith when we were in the Windies in 2014. We were hungover after a win in Jamaica, but played three sets. He got me 6–4 in the first one but I turned it around and beat him 6–1, 6–0 in the next two. I won a tournament when I was in the Queensland squad, too. Jimmy Maher was quite competitive and wanted to win at any cost but I eventually got it over him. He did not give up easily, but that was Jimmy, he was a fierce competitor and I still have him on a bit of a pedestal. However, tennis isn't a great sport when you are supposed to be playing cricket and after that day I was so sore I felt like I had ripped the muscle off the bone.

By the time I was 17, I had given up serious tennis and was pretty much just hanging around with my mates and playing some cricket to be sociable. It wasn't anything serious; in fact,

I had to be dragged along a bit at first. I learned to really like cricket slowly. The difference, I guess, between it and tennis was that it was a team sport and I needed that. With tennis you are on the road a lot playing tournaments all over the place and you are pretty much on your own. You do meet a lot of people along the way, but it's very different from competing in a team. I enjoyed the club environment of cricket. All teenagers want to run with a gang or be part of a movement and for me cricket provided that. With tennis you have to pay for everything too and that really stretched us. We were away every weekend and the cost of petrol, accommodation and all those things really added up. Dad worked hard to make sure I had the equipment but when I chucked it in I could understand why he wasn't too keen on investing in my cricket gear.

One of my earliest cricket memories is running past a game my uncle Jason was playing in with his mates at my grandparents'. I got too close to the batsman who was playing a shot and I ended up with the bat wrapped around my head. It was a fair hit and might explain why I have never been fond of batsmen.

We used to play a bit at school and my mate Dylan and his brother Dave started nagging me to come and play at their club. I wasn't really interested to be honest. I just wanted to play at school and have a bit of fun. Tennis was still my main sport and while their club, the Wanderers, was keen for me to play more it was not a priority. At one point Dad stopped me playing in a school rep carnival because tennis came first and that was fair enough.

By this stage we had moved right out of town to a place called Rupertswood, which is about 15 kilometres past the football stadium where the North Queensland Cowboys play. We had a fair bit of space, which I loved.

The Wanderers had their ground out the back of our high school in town. I didn't have any wheels at the time except for a push bike. There was usually nobody at home to give me a lift to games on Saturdays because they had other things on. Cheryl Minear, who was Dylan and Dave's mum, would drive right out to Rupertswood to pick me up and take me to training and games. She was a nice lady, very bubbly and always wanted us to have fun. She would go out of her way to help me. There was always someone at the club pulling up outside to make sure I got to a game or to training if Cheryl couldn't. I guess there was a bit of a conspiracy going on behind the scenes and it goes to show you how clubs operate. They saw something they liked in me and got together to make sure I would show up and play. It didn't take long before I fell in love with the place and the people. I started to move up through the grades. I bowled and batted pretty high in the order.

Things got serious and soon we found ourselves playing on turf wickets. The only problem was that I didn't have any bowling shoes with spikes on them. There was no way we could afford cricket boots so I wore Dad's golf spikes. They were a size or two too big so I had to wear extra socks so I didn't slide around in them. The club eventually took sympathy on me and found me a pair of cricket shoes that were the right size. I didn't like to ask for things but my coach Graeme (Humpo)

Humphries used to look after me really well. There were plenty of really good guys up there at the club that took care of me.

I had no idea I was fast. There was a guy called Clint Kelly at the club who was the same age. He was at school with me and I felt slow compared to him, but I wanted to bowl like that. I used to do my best, but he always seemed faster. I didn't know why I was a left-arm bowler, either. It made no sense. I am right-handed at everything else, but if I try to bowl with my right arm I chuck. I throw left-handed, too, but am good enough on the right side.

After a while I was ruffling a few feathers on the weekends and a few of the opposition tried to take the young buck down. Some succeeded and others didn't. One day I was bowling quick on a spicy wicket and a batsman came out with no helmet and a pair of sunglasses. It was his way of saying that he wasn't worried by my pace. My teammates told him to put on a helmet and I said the same thing to him. I was going to bowl short whether he wore it or not, but he wanted to make a point. It was a pretty crazy thing to do. The second ball knocked the sunglasses off his face. He wasn't hurt, but it was centimetres away from doing some serious damage. He wore a helmet after that.

The same thing happened on my first night training with the senior team. I was not a confident kid overall, but I was pretty confident when it came to sport and thought I could handle myself with the bat. I didn't own a helmet so I went in bare-headed. We had two opening bowlers, Craig Hallett, who was our junior coach, and a tall bloke called Horse. Both of them decided to teach me a lesson by pelting me with bouncers. I'd never really worn a helmet before and didn't think I needed one, but after a few balls I went off and borrowed some headgear.

Looking back, club cricket was a revelation. I enjoyed my time at the tennis club, but as a 16-year-old the dressing room environment in cricket is more attractive. Playing up with the senior sides meant I was mixing with older blokes and getting to hang out after the game. The beers would come out and the young fella might get a couple and the stories would start to flow. You learned a lot on the field with these guys and even more off it. The bowlers took me under their wing. Craig, especially, looked after me. In my first A-Grade game the opposition batsmen gave me a spray, but it was nothing compared to what Craig gave them.

He had my back and it was important because cricket in Townsville was pretty fiery. To be honest, I loved that stuff; it was hard school, competitive and much tougher than the stuff that goes on in international cricket, but it was just men clashing with men. There were no kids watching at home and no interfering umpires. Our club used to go up to what is called the Goldfield Ashes in Charters Towers. We'd set up camp in a paddock and all these teams would be playing all over the place, but I got the feeling it was mostly about drinking.

I loved the dressing room culture of cricket from the early days and never lost it. It was something that was emphasised in my early years in the Queensland and Australian teams. Jimmy Maher and Ricky Ponting were keen on us celebrating wins and locking ourselves in to debrief in the same way clubs around the country do every Saturday night. I was never one for taking it to a nightclub or whatever. That was a poor replacement for a dressing room with your mates.

It is the one thing I held close to me right through my career. I always go back to club cricket. If I am in Townsville I head straight back to the Wanderers; I love the environment. It's where I grew up. I was lucky that when I got to Perth, Dave and Dylan had already moved across and were waiting for me, so I joined them at Wanneroo.

I discovered early that sport was a good way of not having to do school work. I missed a lot of classes because I was off at tennis tournaments, but I would put my hand up for anything if it meant a day off. I did athletics, volleyball, swimming, anything. At one school carnival I decided that if I could throw a cricket ball I could throw a javelin and gave that a crack. Jeff Thomson was a javelin thrower and we were both sling bowlers so maybe there was a connection there. I went alright, threw it about 50 metres and ended up representing the school at a carnival in town. I had the same footwear problem I faced later with cricket, but I went through the lost-and-found bag. I got lucky and found a pair of javelin spikes – they were bright pink. It didn't worry me too much and I threw it 55 metres, which meant I got chosen to go to Brisbane for the big state competition with all the Queensland schools.

I choked. Massively choked. There were all these kids there who had been doing it all their lives and they had shoulders like swimmers and elbows all strapped up from years of throwing. I was so tense I don't think I threw more than 40 metres. It was pretty embarrassing. But at least I got a day off school.

I found some old report cards the other day and pretty much every teacher said that I was lazy and needed to improve, *blah blah blah*. I didn't get too many high scores; most of the time I was 'sound', though there were a few grades of 'limited' and even 'very limited'. I even got a 'sound' in sport but that was because I failed the theory.

I was quite a ratbag then. We were always getting in trouble for smoking behind the sheds. I still can't believe I used to smoke cigarettes, but there you go. We used to get into a bit of trouble for things with the local police, but it was never anything serious. I got caught a few times riding my bike without a helmet. I got dragged in and read the riot act occasionally. No self-respecting Townsville kid wore a helmet in those days. One night I was out with Dylan and another mate called Rob and we got chased by the police. Well, I did.

I didn't have a light or a helmet and I was on my dad's racing bike. I knew if they got me I was in for it as I was on my last warning, so I rode down into an irrigation channel. It was pitch black and I couldn't see a thing, but I knew my way around and managed to get back to Rob's place flying through the dark. I hid behind a trailer in his shed in case they had followed me. I heard a noise and was scared it was the police, but it was those two, they were laughing. The police had asked them who the other kid was, but they said they didn't know me. To be honest, I was a bit more worried about what Dad would say than what the police would do.

We weren't bad kids, but we weren't goody-two-shoes either. We used to go around to another mate's place and drink his dad's whisky. He caught us one day and all he said was: 'If you little buggers are going to drink my whisky, drink it straight, I don't want you ruining it with Coke.' So we started drinking it straight with ice. We'd have a couple on a Saturday night. Not too many.

We used to get up to mischief at Leonard's. He had a pool room below the house and we used to hang out down there, playing heavy metal music and sneaking beers. I remember we were there the day Princess Di died. We were watching it unfold on the television and were just speechless. It was really emotional. We drank a toast to her memory.

Leonard and I had a punch-up once. It was completely stupid. We'd bought a case of beer and taken it to Paluma Beach, then moved on to keep drinking at a local golf course, then into town where we were meant to meet his older brother. We were niggling each other and then, suddenly, we were fighting. I have no idea what it was about; he was banging my head into a car window at one stage, but I know I landed a few good ones.

I went around there the next day with Dingo and Leonard and I were a bit standoffish for a while, but then we both said sorry and that was that. Leonard had a bit of a mark under his eye, but no real damage. I marked him up a bit more one day when they convinced me to play indoor cricket with them. It was his fault. He was wicketkeeping and instead of waiting for the ball to bounce off the net he kept up to the stumps. I bowled one that just missed the stumps and it went straight into his face.

I skipped a lot of classes at school, particularly maths and business. I couldn't cope with maths and I was one of two guys in business and the teacher didn't really want us there because we weren't interested. Our high school had a reputation for being a bit rough and there were some drugs around. I remember once some young kids brought ice to school, which was completely insane.

I wasn't that interested in girls at school. I liked them, but I was shy and that made things hard. There were a couple, but all my relationships were long term. Not that there were many.

I did do the Cha Cha in Year 12 and I got an A for it. Doing a dance was part of sport. I actually used to practise it at lunchtime with the girl who was my dancing partner. I might have done more work on that than most subjects. I know I copped a lot of grief for it from my mates.

I really enjoyed primary school, but at high school I had a short attention span and if I had no interest in something I wouldn't try. I did well at sport and computer skills, which I liked, and that was pretty much it. I used to get quite nervous before tests and I still do.

When I was with the Australian team and we had to do our 2-kilometre time trial or gym tests I would get uptight knowing it was coming up. At school I never felt fully prepared. I think I was always a bit anxious and I brought it on myself at high school because I didn't do the work – I didn't want to fail, but I never made the effort to make sure I passed. I guess I was lazy, that is probably a good word for it.

The same anxiety was good for my cricket up to a point. I could never relax until I knew my preparation was complete. I had to do the work to be in the right place before a game or a series. I would get upset if things stopped me preparing properly because it would play on my mind and I would take that state into the game. The number of times I lost it because I couldn't practise my run-ups in nets that weren't big enough was ridiculous.

I was never going to win any academic prizes at school, but I did win the sports prize in my last year and that was something. I had made it through school, but I didn't really have any idea what I was going to do. Dad came and gave me a kick in the pants after the summer holidays.

Townsville is a defence force town. There are 17,000 at the army barracks and another 1200-odd at the RAAF base. I think 10 per cent of the town is army or army family, so it was part of the culture. We'd go to the sky shows every year at the airbase; I loved the planes. Like all boys, I was fascinated with guns and tanks. If I was really keen I'd have joined up earlier but I was having too much fun at school because they let me play so much sport. I knew I wasn't getting that opportunity if I signed up.

Before I could do anything about getting a job, the cricket club saw something about a Pace Academy down in Brisbane that Dennis Lillee was running. They chipped in some money and bought me a ticket to catch the plane down. It was good they did because I was going nowhere. I had no ambitions in life. I was interested in the military life but I hadn't done anything about it. I had no qualifications to speak of and no real desire to get any. I'd never really had a job. Luckily for me, my life was about to change literally overnight.

*Training before Pura Cup, Queensland Bulls v
Victoria, the MCG, 23 October 2001.*

3

Overnight Sensation

IT'S MONDAY, 12 APRIL 1999, and I'm alone on a plane for the first time in my life. On the way to Brisbane. On the way to meet Dennis Lillee. A legend. He might be the greatest fast bowler of all time. He's certainly the best we've ever had.

I'm so nervous and excited that I am almost calm. Maybe it's because I know that everyone is fooling themselves. I'm not a bowler. I just wang the ball down the wicket as fast as I can. I love playing cricket, but it's just fun. It's not like tennis where there was expectation and pressure – most of which I've placed on myself. Our club cricket is cool, I like it and I give it my absolute best, but things need to be kept in perspective.

Catching a plane is a buzz. I might be 18 but I am not exactly the most worldly person going around. I'm a Queenslander. A Townsville boy. Sydney and Melbourne are foreign countries,

Brisbane is almost the same. I don't know if I ever had any plans to do anything with life but stay in that comfort zone. And the fast bowling thing? Well, I had nothing to lose and I really didn't expect to gain anything apart from a few tips on how to bowl better. It didn't get Dad off my back about what I was going to do next, but it gave me a bit of space.

It is all a bit of a blur now. I was too nervous to take in anything. We were told to do this and do that and we did this and did that. I was too shy to talk to anyone, so I kept my head down and did as I was told. After running around in the morning doing a few drills it came time to bowl. I still hadn't seen Dennis Lillee, which was a bit strange. I guessed he was going to show up a bit later. I didn't have the nerve to talk to him anyway. I wished I did, but I wouldn't know what to say.

Most kids want to be fast bowlers. I liked watching Wasim Akram and Curtly Ambrose bowl on television, but who didn't? I wanted to bowl fast but I was never really sure if I was fast or not. Looking back, I guess kids used to dance around in the nets at club cricket so that was a sign I was generating a bit of heat. Nobody seemed to enjoy it when I bowled, but maybe it was because I was all over the place, too. You were never sure where the ball was going and if a bowler doesn't know, a batsman has no hope.

There was a group of coaches standing around watching us bowl. When it became my turn I ran in and let it go as fast as I could. I think I beat the guy or something. The coaches had speed guns directed at us and I learned later that I was bowling at close to 130 km/h, which was pretty quick. I impressed myself! I hadn't realised I could bowl that fast. It obviously impressed the coaches as I could see them talking and reaching for their phones. Something was going on. Then they called me over and asked me a few questions.

It was only around this time that it occurred to me that one of the coaches was Dennis. In all the pictures he seemed so much bigger. He was always that guy with the long hair, the moustache and the open shirt. The dramatic action. The big appeal. He asked me where I was from and what I was doing. The answer was not much. I couldn't get many words out. Then he asked me if I would be willing to go to Adelaide to the Australian Cricket Academy and I said, 'Oh, yeah.' I mean, I didn't have anything much on at the time.

Dennis smiled and said go home and pack your bags, we want you to go there in two days! I didn't know this but he had apparently rung Rod Marsh, who was coach at the cricket academy at the time, and said he had found a 'once in a generation' fast bowler or something like that.

My head was spinning. Adelaide? Wednesday? It was like some sort of weird dream. Dennis Lillee thought I had potential. I figured he was wrong, but I wasn't going to argue. I can't say all my dreams had come true because I had never dreamed of anything to do with cricket. I wanted to go to Wimbledon, but instead I was going to Adelaide, which was okay by me. There was even talk that I might have to go to England mid-year with the Under-19 team.

I flew home and packed a bag. Everyone was pretty excited. Somehow the local paper, the *Townsville Bulletin*, where Dad worked, heard about it and I had to go in there at midnight to have my photo taken for a story they wanted to do. Dad was more surprised than anyone. He had the golf bug by this stage and played it every weekend so he'd never seen me play. He was excited, but a bit perplexed. The next day I flew back to Brisbane and caught a plane across the country to Adelaide. It was the first time I had ever been outside of Queensland.

I made my way out to the cricket academy where they put me in a room with Damien McKenzie. Macca was a fast bowler from Redlands who went on to play for Queensland. He always tells the story of how this scary-looking long-haired guy in a Slayer or Metallica t-shirt knocked on the door. He thought I was going to stab him. He didn't know what was going on. I certainly didn't look like a cricketer.

I was the one who was the most scared. My eyes were really wide open at that stage because I just had no idea what was going on. My feet hadn't touched the ground for two days and I was not really sure why they wanted me. I just bowled as fast as I could; there was no science or secret to it. There were a lot of better cricketers around. And they had never seen me on a bad day. I figured I'd be there a few days and they'd send me home with my tail between my legs. It would be just like my javelin-throwing career.

I was sent out to Adelaide Oval No. 2 where a few coaches were waiting around. When I arrived they announced that they wanted us to have a bowl and said I should put on my spikes. That was a bit awkward as I didn't have any with me. I had arrived in town with pretty much all the cricket gear I had and that amounted to a pair of old runners. There were a few glances exchanged.

I had to bowl off a few paces but I could tell straight away that they were impressed. I didn't need a long run-up to generate pace with my action. I stayed for a couple of weeks and there weren't that many people around. They were just getting a few young bowlers in to do some work with them and I was one of them. But then all the other Under-19 Australian team arrived. They were due to go on a tour of England. I wasn't part of the squad then and there were a few of them looking sideways at me. No one had ever heard of me. All these guys knew each other from playing in state teams and things over the years, but I was a blow-in and I didn't look anything like them. They used to wind me up a bit because I was a kid from the bush, but not too much because they suspected I was a bit of a psycho or something. It was probably because I was shy and never said anything. Maybe they were scared I would give them a hard time in the nets if they annoyed me. They were all pretty much kids who had grown up with the game. Anyway, I got to know them and we all got on well. There were a few guys in that intake who went on to play Test cricket, including Nathan Hauritz, Michael Clarke and Adam Voges.

We used to go down to the No. 2 ground at Adelaide and I'd bowl to these blokes. I didn't know what I was doing, I just ran in and let it go. If people think my action was strange later in life you should have seen it then. I was a complete sling bowler. I got so low my hand was almost touching the ground before I brought my arm over. But I was obviously doing something right because they let me stay and then they squeezed me into the squad that was leaving for England in June.

There might have been the odd nose out of joint over that. Here were these kids who'd devoted their lives to making it, whose parents had driven them to trials and now this long-haired bloke with no training was taking one of their spots. I heard whispers around the place. Some parents weren't impressed. To be honest, even I felt bad about it. I felt like I had jumped the queue. I was also intimidated by some of the people around. These people I was with were serious cricketers. I would hear stories about Michael Clarke and how many runs he'd made. They were all so professional about what they did. I knew I was out my league. Everyone knew these people and was impressed by what they had achieved already. I'd done nothing but play maybe one summer with the Wanderers in Townsville and even then I hadn't played a lot of A-Grade games.

They let me go home for a while before England so I could get my life sorted out. The Wanderers had adopted me and they were really happy that I was getting this chance. I didn't have a passport and I didn't have any money so the club organised a job for me washing cars at UBD Motors, which was owned by Mal Death who was at the club and whose sons played there. He had a car dealership that sponsored the club. The guys at the Wanderers were fantastic, they organised equipment for me and I had to put a sticker from UBD Motors on my kit bag as part of the deal. I guess they were my first sponsor, but everyone chipped in to help a bit.

When I returned to the academy, I was getting a bit of stick about my hair from the boys, particularly Sean Clingeleffer, and they were on my back about looking like a bogan so I got a buzz cut. The aim was that I wouldn't frighten so many people, but I think it had the opposite effect.

And so they packed me off to England. A few months earlier I'd been excited about going to Brisbane and Adelaide, so you can imagine how exciting this was. I had started to get to know the others a bit better by now and we had a lot of fun on that trip. England was a revelation for a poor boy from Queensland who barely owned a pair of shoes or a shirt with a collar. Our first games were at Eton College and they put us up in the dormitory there. Adam Voges had to be moved up to the next floor because he snored so loudly. We could still hear him though. I had never seen anything like Eton in my life. The students wore suits and ties, the ancient buildings were like something from *Harry Potter* and the sports fields rolled on forever. We were relegated to the second ground, but it was lush and green and maintained like nothing I had ever seen. We even got invited to dinner in the college with the boarders. I half expected us to retire for a game of Quidditch when it was all done.

Nobody had me down as a one-day bowler then because I didn't have much control, so I didn't get named for the official one-day games, but I did get to play a couple of tour matches. We were due to play three four-day 'Tests' and I got my chance to play in the second one in Bristol. I don't remember a lot about the game. I know they told us to be careful going out at night because Bristol was a bit rough. They'd never been to

Townsville on a Saturday night! I went for a few runs in the game and got my first wicket for an Australia age team. It was a guy called Richard Dawson who played in the Ashes series out here in 2002–03 as a replacement for Ashley Giles.

We moved on to Durham for the second game. I opened the bowling and everything seemed to click. Although it took a while to get the first breakthrough, the wickets came easily after that. The ball was swinging, which meant it was my lucky day. (For most of my career I never bothered with swing; if it did it did, if it didn't it didn't.) I knocked over the two openers in quick succession, one of whom was Michael Gough who umpired us in England in 2015. I then bowled Ian Bell for a duck before bouncing Ian Hunter and hitting him in the throat. He couldn't breathe at first and was in a bad way, which I didn't feel good about. He eventually pulled himself together and faced up again but I bowled him next ball. I hit Ian Bell in the helmet, too, but that was in a tour match at Sleaford. I finished with 4–16 from 12 overs and felt pretty good about myself. The wicket was really green. It was overcast and pretty cool as well. Everyone was excited about what I'd done. In an article a bit later Rod said it wasn't 'so much the wickets he took, but the way he took them … it was a beautiful spell', but cricket has a way of dragging you back down. I couldn't get a break in the next innings and finished with 0–68 from 11 overs.

It was a sign of just how unprepared I was. I was so stiff after the first innings I just couldn't get it happening again. My body wasn't used to it. My mind wasn't used to it. I'd never played four straight days of cricket – or even three days for that matter. Rod Marsh, who was on the tour, told me that they needed to get me better at my second innings. He was understanding about it; he knew I was new to the game and had rarely had to back up. Rod was pretty hard on us, but always fair. I liked him and had a lot to do with him over the years, because later he became the chairman of selectors for the Australian team. I definitely needed to play more cricket and I felt like I wasn't up to the same standard as the other guys.

I was feeling my body. The other bowlers told me it was normal. My back had been sore through tennis, playing on hard courts for many years, and serving puts a lot of stress on the spine, and I had gone hard at cricket straight away. The soreness was a warning sign that I didn't know enough to heed at the time. Looking back, I am sure I had a stress fracture even then. It was going to become a big problem for me in future years.

After I returned from that tour I went back home to catch up on my old life, which I'd neglected since that day trip to Brisbane, but cricket had got its claws into me. Rod Marsh decided I should go home and play cricket in Townsville for the summer and then move to Brisbane for the next season. Before that, they wanted me back at the academy as part of the 2000 intake, which meant I would spend the winter in Adelaide.

There's a story about Rod Marsh phoning the Wanderers to talk about some things. I think he got on to Graeme Humphries, who thought it was someone playing a joke and so hung up. Rod rang back and convinced Humpo it really was him and told him that they wanted the Wanderers to come on board with my training and preparation. The academy wanted me to play A Grade that year; of course they agreed. I ended up playing games all over the place, but first of all I got to play with some of the legends of Queensland cricket in Townsville. The Queensland City Origin v Country Origin match came to town in early September and I was picked to play in the Country side with people like Jimmy Maher, Andy Bichel and Wade Seccombe at Endeavour Park. I got to bowl first change after Bich and another local lad, Chris Adams. I didn't get any wickets but held up my end.

Things just kept moving. I was in the system now and had to fly down to Canberra for a couple of games against the Australian Capital Territory with the Australian Cricket Academy side and then on to Perth for the Under-19s state final against Victoria. After Christmas I played a game for the Queensland Colts side and then I finished my first year of club cricket playing for the Wanderers. I must have impressed somebody because I won the award for the Most Improved Player.

It had become pretty clear my pace was unsettling people. We played on uncovered pitches in Townsville, which often meant waiting for them to 'dry' before beginning play. It was hell for batsmen. Our reserves wicketkeeper Barry Emmanuel was a no-nonsense bloke who had no love for opposition batsmen, but I remember on one pitch even he was sympathetic to the poor blokes who were getting peppered by short balls. He was also feeling a bit sorry for himself because he used to have to stand a bit wider to see my arm and that meant if anything went down leg it would be four byes. He was too proud to put in a backstop, but after a while he conceded because my control was not great and the extras total was getting pretty ugly. Our wicketkeeper in the A Grade prided himself on standing up to all the quicks, but he wouldn't do it to me. He says that he had a stumping from every fast bowler he kept to but me.

In January 2000, I was picked to play for the Australian Under-19s in the World Cup in Sri Lanka. We all stayed in Colombo and I loved the place. I loved the freedom of Asia, the ability to zip around in auto rickshaws, the energy that was in the town. It was a long way from where I came from, but I felt comfortable there. I remember we found a little place run by Australians called the Cricket Club Cafe. It was a pub that served cold beer (hard to find) and chicken schnitzel with chips (even harder to find). We had a great time outside of the cricket. Shane Watson and I were starting to become pretty good mates, but it was a good group and we all got on.

Our first match was against Namibia and we smashed them. Watto got a hundred, Ed Cowan, Andrew McDonald and Shaun Marsh all got 50s, then we tore through their batting and won by 266 runs. I picked up 2–9 from 5.4 overs but that was about as good as it got for me in the tournament. I played most of the early games but my back was getting sore. It's no surprise when you think about it. I'd gone from lying around playing club cricket in summer to having the winter at the academy, the tour of England, all those rep games, club games and now this. I skipped a few games through the tournament and came back for our pool game against Pakistan. I was not great but said I was good to go. I had no idea if I was or wasn't.

How do you know these things? I said I was right to go against India in the semifinal but I really wasn't this time and I knew I was in trouble when I got out there. I only bowled three overs before I was too sore to carry on. The spinners did most of the work on that track. They smashed us. Their opener, RS Ricky, got the second hundred of the tournament and was bowled by Watto – the guy who got the only other one.

Playing an international tournament was a great experience. It was like the Goldfield Ashes on another planet. There were so many good players there, players who I would encounter again over the years. Some were more advanced than others. I managed to knock over the Pakistani batsman Imran Nazir in the match against them. A few months later he made a half-century on debut for his country in a Test match against Sri Lanka.

I remember running into the South African skipper, Graeme Smith, in the lift. He was complaining that their games were getting washed out. I think it cost them the tournament because they were clear favourites. Smithy got a heap of runs when they did play. A bloke called Jonathan Trott was also in their side, but the next time I came across him he was playing for England. Jacques Rudolph was with them, too. India's Yuvraj Singh destroyed our bowling in the semifinal, hitting 58 off 25 balls in a display that hinted at things to come. New Zealand's James Franklin tore through us in a game I didn't play and batted pretty high as well. Marlon Samuels played for the West Indies and we went pretty hard against him.

When I was there, Malcolm Conn came to interview me, which was a bit of a surprise. He was a cricket writer with *The Australian*. Dad has the newspaper clipping at home. Rod Marsh said some very nice things: I was, according to him, a 'beautiful athlete. You can tell by the way he runs and coordinates his bowling action. Not only was he swinging the ball both ways, he was hitting the gloves harder than all the other guys.' Malcolm asked me about my most dangerous asset and I told him, 'I'd like to think it was my bouncer, but you can't do it [in the World Cup] ...'

When I got home there was a four-day game between NSW and the Queensland Colts at Allan Border Field. Ed Cowan, who had played in Sri Lanka, played for the Blues. I bowled three overs and I was done. My back was gone. I had my first stress fracture; it wasn't good, but it was late February and wasn't going to cost me a lot of cricket. Nobody thought too much of it because they gave me a scholarship to attend the academy full time.

One of the things they did do was send me to Canberra for some biomechanical testing. They hadn't been too fussed about the way I bowled because I was quick, but I was all over the place. Anyway, they strip you down to your underpants and put all these sensors on your body. The idea was not to have too much counter rotation. It took me a while to even work out what they were talking about, but I was twisting my torso around about 60 degrees in delivery, my momentum was heading out in every direction but down the wicket the way it should. A bit like my bowling. I was low and slingy and my front leg was bent. It looked really odd, even to me – people didn't bowl that way.

There was a lot of sucking air through teeth and a hell of a lot to work on. I became a bit of a project for the biomechanics and the bowling coaches. There was a lot of focus from Marc Portus and Troy Cooley on getting my hips and shoulders in line when I was landing. It took a lot of time and effort to get my action right, but I definitely had to change it otherwise I wasn't going to last.

It's funny, you get to the point where you are good enough to be considered among the elite by running in, shutting your eyes and whanging it, which is about 97 per cent of what you have to do. There's not much thought process or anything, but then the 3 per cent is pointed out and the real work begins. The fine-tuning for me was more like rebuilding the way I bowled.

For a while there I was just doing rehab work because of the stress fractures, but I started bowling again in time for the following summer. It was as much technical as it was physical. I was not strong, I had never really been in a gym and I reckon the best I could bench press was about 50 kg. The real problem – and would be at times throughout my career – was building up strength in my legs so I was upright at the crease. It was something I didn't have at first and something I would lose when I played too much cricket and didn't have the time to get into the gym.

We had a good group at the academy. Nathan Hauritz, Phil Jaques and Chris Hartley were there, and they put me in a room with Paul Rofe, which was funny, because he was pretty sophisticated, a bit of an intellectual, and I was anything but. Michael Clarke sort of came and went; Watto was there as well, which was good. He was a boy from the bush, too, but he was a bit more sophisticated than me. One night we were going out and he decided it was time I lost the black heavy metal t-shirts, which were about the only thing I owned. I didn't have any money to buy new clothes so he lent me a shirt, jeans and shoes. I didn't have anything with a collar. I might have had a VB t-shirt, but Watto didn't think that would cut it either.

There were things about the place that I couldn't get the hang of and one of them was that we had to fill in these diaries every week about what we'd been doing ahead of an assessment from Rod and Wayne Phillips. I was never good at that. At one point Rod got really angry and threatened to send me home. Not doing homework was going to get me into even more trouble in India some years later, but we will get to that.

Apart from the social life and the diaries, my stint at the academy exposed me to the disciplines needed to be a top cricketer. Strength was an obvious thing I was lacking. My fitness was pretty ordinary, my bowling extremely raw and while raw talent got me there, it wouldn't get me much further. At least I was smart enough to have given up the cigarettes before arriving the year before. They used to smash us on the beach in the mornings. Sand running is up there with water boarding. They had curfews and mostly we respected them, but we were young blokes and sometimes we'd sneak off to the local pub. Young and stupid. I think Rod had spies there because he used to find out.

Other athletes came through. There were some golfers, and then some cyclists came in before the Sydney Olympics as it was part of the Australian Institute of Sport. Shane Kelly and Sean Eadie were there. There were also a couple of Russian gymnasts. We played pool and table tennis against them and it was a lot of fun trying to communicate. We got a bit upset about the situation because they were all getting bacon and eggs for breakfast, while we were on strict diets and only allowed cereal and toast. But Rod wasn't having it, he just told us that if we trained as hard as them then we could eat like them. However, it didn't take long to learn that when they'd left you could sneak in and eat the leftovers. It also didn't take long to learn to make sure you got to the food hall before Eadie. We called him Greedy Eadie because that guy could eat for Australia.

I learned just how hard those Olympic athletes work. Their dedication is absolutely incredible and the rewards so distant. These people work with total focus every day in the hope of winning a gold medal or a world championship, maybe just in the hope of making one of these events. They get absolutely no money, but work harder than most professionals. They were obsessive the way they looked after themselves – they wouldn't even go out on the weekend. I did one of the bike sessions they did in a wind tunnel with the proper set-up and was absolutely cooked. Their fitness is incredible. They put us to shame. They made a lasting impression on me and it was a lesson I would draw on a few years later when Queensland cut me from the contract list and I had to work for a living just as a lot of them do.

At the academy they teach you about public speaking, the media and the history of the game. And they make you 'work'. Punter (Ricky Ponting) always told us how he had installed all the plastic seats in one part of the stand at the Adelaide Oval. My first job was as a driver, which usually meant running people to the airport, picking them up from there or running errands. I liked that one because it usually meant I could sneak back and have a sleep after I'd done what needed to be done. Then they got Nathan Hauritz and me working at the Adelaide Oval. It was pretty slack, but we were slacker. On Monday morning we'd replace the divots in the oval after the footy matches, then they would have us doing basic maintenance work. We were always looking for a way to squeeze in a sleep. One day we snuck into the old scoreboard for a nap. Hauri slept in the first place he found, but I was a bit smarter and climbed up a little higher. Someone came in and busted him which gave me time to grab a broom and look like I was sweeping. I came down to find out what all the noise was about and shook my head in dismay at his poor attitude.

It all felt pretty anonymous over in Adelaide, especially as I was in rehab for most of the time, but I had attracted some attention. In October, Peter Roebuck wrote an article in the *Sydney Morning Herald* that started: 'Australia has discovered a new fast bowler. Mitchell Johnson is his name and he's a roughie from the back of Townsville.' It told the story of how I came from tennis, bypassed the usual youth carnival system and was 'discovered'. It was one thing to have been in the local paper, but this was the big time. Rod Marsh said in it that I was

'10 yards faster than Zaheer Khan [the Indian discovery] and quicker than Brett Lee, too'.

There was no time to get a big head. When summer rolled around so did my back problems. It was incredibly frustrating. Having done all that work and committing myself to the game, when it came time to play I was missing. Stress fractures again. It was another setback. There is nothing worse when you are a young sportsman than sitting on the sidelines. At times it got really difficult to deal with, but I'd signed up for cricket and I didn't know what I would do if it didn't work out. I spent the start of summer batting in club cricket, which was just how I had ended the last one. I did manage to get myself right late in the year to bowl a few games.

Late in that summer, the Under-19s played a one-day and Test series against a visiting Sri Lankan side in Adelaide, and then against New Zealand in Perth. I got picked in a PM's XI game with Steve Waugh in Canberra. In April, I was accepted back into the cricket academy as part of the 2001 intake. Most of my mates had moved on, but there was a good new group that included Xavier Doherty, Brett Geeves, Shaun Marsh, Scott Meuleman and Luke Ronchi.

A few months later, there was even bigger news. Queensland called me in and added me to the contract list for the 2001–02 season. I was a state player alongside legends like Andy Bichel, Adam Dale, Joe Dawes, Matthew Hayden, James Hopes, Michael Kasprowicz, Stuart Law, Martin Love, Jimmy Maher, Brendan Nash, Ashley Noffke, Wade Seccombe, Chris Hartley and Andrew Symonds. It was pretty mind blowing. It also meant I had to move to Brisbane and needed somewhere to stay. I moved in with Mum at Tweed Heads and for quite a while she drove me to Brisbane and back for training. I didn't have a licence so it was a big help. Then I lodged with relatives of Mum's out at Mount Gravatt. I didn't have a car and used to have to lug my cricket bag on two buses to get to the Gabba or out to Allan Border Field. It was annoying enough in the morning when everyone was going to work, but even more so after being flogged all day in the heat at training.

Two years before, I had never left Queensland, but already I was learning about living life out of a suitcase. It became a habit that was hard to shake. For the best part of the next 15 years I had one near my bed on the road or at home. It drove a few people mad over the years. Still does. In June, I was on a plane to Madras (they call it Chennai now) to join Dennis Lillee at the MRF Pace Foundation. Basil Sellers sponsored us on that trip. Basil's brother Rex played a Test match in 1964 and played Shield cricket for South Australia. While he only played one Test, it was significant because the brothers were born in India and nobody else born there has ever played for Australia. That will change though. We've already got Usman Khawaja, who was born in Pakistan, doing alright at the top of the order. Basil was a keen sportsman but an even better businessman and now spends a lot of money supporting young cricketers and footballers.

I went to Chennai with Andrew Thistle, a quick from WA, and we stayed in a little room at the ground. For a meat-and-three-veg guy, India was a challenge. All I ate was tandoori chicken and French fries, which you can get used to. It was an introduction to different conditions. Training in that heat is torture, but I started to enjoy the punishment, a personality trait that has helped me a fair bit over the years. You have to be a masochist to be a fast bowler. We are a bit like marathon runners or triathletes, although I could never do that. I hate running!

Dennis worked really closely with us and a lot of the instruction was how to bowl on wickets that didn't have bounce. He was keen on the leg-cutter. Apart from that he just seemed keen on teaching me intimidation.

'What ball are you going to bowl this ball?' he would say.

'I am going to pitch it up and swing it away,' I would say.

'Bowl a bumper, bowl a bumper.'

I'd come back and he would say, 'What are you going to bowl now?'

'Try and get it up there, swing it away.'

'Bowl a bumper, bowl a bumper,' he'd say.

And I would bowl another bumper.

An Indian reporter tracked me down and interviewed me for Cricinfo. I think he'd seen me bowl at the World Cup in Sri Lanka. I was learning to say the right things and it is amusing to see what my main aim was.

'Coming here has been a great experience in many ways. The most important thing is that it's given me a taste of bowling in different conditions and different types of wickets. I've added the leg-cutter to my armoury and worked on swing bowling quite a bit here.

'When I get stronger and reach my peak, I want to be the fastest bowler in the world, there's no two ways about that. I'm not really too concerned about getting hit for runs. If and when I get the chance to play for Australia my first aim will be to bowl a good line and length with pace. If I get smashed around then I'll just have to change my line and length, keep learning and continue!'

When I get stronger, now there's a line that would echo for some time to come, but that desire to bowl fast had been with me since school. Once I realised I could do it, it was all I wanted to do. Later on when I played Test cricket we had a fast bowling cartel that mocked 'sweatband swingers'. It was all a bit of macho carry-on, but pace was all that mattered to me.

I was a fully-fledged member of the Queensland Bulls and raring to go. I got an early start that summer, playing the Country v City game in Biloela, which is up near Gladstone in banana country, then two games for the academy. The first was against the Northern Territory and the second a four-day match against New Zealand. I took a few wickets, including Dan Vettori and opener Mark Richardson. I got Mark again when I made my first-class debut for Queensland against the tourists soon after.

I got to open the bowling with Andy Bichel in that tour match, but maybe the most memorable thing was that my first scoring shot in first-class cricket was a six. Craig McMillan dropped one short on me and I hooked him over the fence. It was probably a top edge, but I will take it. I have never known a batsman who wouldn't.

My first wicket was Richardson; it wasn't a great ball, but I had unsettled him and he popped a half-volley on leg stump straight to midwicket. In the second innings I had a few of their batsmen sweating a bit, so I was pretty happy with my performance and obviously the selectors were too because they named me in the Queensland one-day side to take on WA in Perth a few days later.

I was sore already. I just wasn't used to four-day cricket and while there was a fair break between the two games against New Zealand, there was a three-day turnaround and a flight to Perth before the match. At this stage I remember a lot of conversations with senior players about backs and they were the same for the next few years. People would say I had to work out the difference between good soreness and bad soreness. How would I know? All I knew was I was sore and I suspected it wasn't right. You are always sore when you are a bowler, but it takes a while to work out what matters. I got a couple of wickets on a pitch that had cracks all over it and then landed heavily on the rope when I slid to try and stop a four. I got up and I was gone. I actually couldn't bend my back. We weren't halfway through November in my first season as a contracted player.

Once in a Generation

Three balls was all it took. I had been working, going from state to state, looking at the pick of the Under-17 and Under-19 bowlers, men and women, with a group called Pace Australia for about a decade. There were some very good ones and occasionally a very, very good one. The idea was to identify the best and make sure they didn't get lost to cricket. The main part of the brief was to coach them to reach their potential.

I remember going to the camp in Brisbane, in 1999, very clearly. When you have done it for so long, if there is someone who is outstanding you pick it up pretty early. There were a lot of guys there and most were bowling a pretty similar speed and then this left-armer with long black hair bowled a ball that flew through and the keeper took it on the up and I thought, hmm, that's pretty handy.

That got my attention. He was from Townsville and nobody had seen him before, which was a bit unusual because most of these kids had played in rep sides or something like that. He bowled a second one and again it was a very good ball that went into the batsman, bounced and nearly ripped him in two. The wicketkeeper took it on the up again – a sure sign that this young guy had some pace. The third ball was another fabulous delivery: it either clean bowled the guy or had him caught behind.

I'd seen enough. I stepped away from the centre wicket practice and got on the phone and called up Marshy (Rod Marsh) at the Cricket Academy in Adelaide.

'I've found one,' I said.

'Oh, no, no, I've already picked the side for the 19s team,' he said. There was an Australian Under-19s tour of England in a few months and the squad was going to the academy for a camp sometime around then.

'I'm not talking about that,' I said. 'You've just got to have a look at this guy; he's been playing tennis and stuff and we have never seen him before and I like what I see.'

Marshy ummed and aahhed and I said, 'How many times have I rung you and said this?' and he said, 'Once.' That one time was Brett Lee and this young fellow Mitchell Johnson was the best I'd seen since. I think I called him a 'once in a generation' quick and he was.

So that was the way it happened. The rest is history. They saw him and they actually picked him in the Under-19s side and while he wasn't an instant success he certainly held his own in England. It wasn't a bad performance for a boy from the bush who had just started bowling. It was more than his pace that caught my eye that day. It was the bounce and the ability to swing it in. He'd faded the first one across but the next two really swung. It didn't matter that he was left-handed – if I had seen that in a right-hander I would have been just as excited – but it was nice that he was.

He was raw in that he hadn't played much cricket, but his action was in pretty good shape, though obviously it was different from what he ended up with after I remodelled him in early 2012.

Mitchell was a great kid. He was a lovely, almost shy young man. He was respectful, eager to listen, one of those salt of the earth young men. I couldn't help but like him. (Graham McKenzie was like that.) I have seen quite a bit of him since 1999 and he's never changed in that aspect.

He came to Chennai twice in the following years to the MRF Pace Foundation with a group of academy bowlers. We had a tie-in with the Australian, English, Sri Lankan and New Zealand cricket boards that allowed us to do an exchange program. He trained hard, he listened, he seemed on track from the start. I never worried about him on that level.

I watched him go through the stress fractures: I had been through that myself. In 1973, they found three in my back and I was in a cast for a while. I know how frustrating it is and how hard you have to work to come back. He didn't need a lot of coaching early or changing because he had so much natural talent. I don't believe in change just to justify yourself as a coach. With Mitch there wasn't a lot wrong; it was a good action from the first day I saw him. He was a natural athlete and a natural fast bowler – there are only a few of them around.

Glenn McGrath wasn't a natural. When I first saw him as an 18-year-old he bowled around 125 km/h, he fell away to the offside, he angled the ball in all the time and it often slipped down legside. He made it look easy in the end, but he had to work to get there. That was what I call a significantly remodelled action. He had it totally right in the end. Sometimes he needed a tweak; I would suggest something and he could fix it in three balls because he understood his action.

Mitch didn't have to understand his action through his early cricket because everything worked. The problem with a natural athlete is that it all comes easy to them and when the wheels fall off they don't have anything to fall back on; they don't understand technique and they don't know where to start. If you are a natural and you are then prepared to listen and learn about techniques, as he was, then you will come through and I knew he would if he did the work and he never shirked that.

He wasn't quite an instant success but he was close. Then things started to go bad in that period after the Ashes in England. We did remedial work during the 2010–11 Ashes when he was dropped after the first Test. He came over to Perth before the team for the third Test. I had a session with him at Floreat Oval; I brought in a few things. I got him to take a few steps back in the run-up, to slow down his build-up of speed in his approach.

He bowled beautifully in that Test and took a lot of wickets, but he didn't try to bowl too fast. He just let the ball do the work and it swung for him. That didn't last too long, though. I don't know what was going on, but the message I got back was now that he had his wickets he was going to ramp it up for Melbourne. I said I don't get it, if I'd have got the return he did in Perth I would be happy, what do you want to change? I think he just wanted to bowl fast; I guess that's understandable, but it didn't help, it set him back to where he was and he didn't bowl well afterwards. I think he felt like he needed to bowl 155-plus again. When you are young and can bowl express pace most of us get obsessed by it.

He was definitely in trouble by the time he got to South Africa at the end of 2011. He was trying to muscle the ball and bowl quick and the action was falling to pieces. His run-up was shot – somebody had told him to start off like a long jumper – he was taking off like a rabbit. He was running with long strides and because of that the jump was long and the delivery stride was too long. His front arm and momentum were falling away. It was a lot of work to fix it.

John Inverarity had rung me after that and said, 'Can you help Mitch?' I said, 'I am sure I can, I know his action like the back of my hand. It's gone to pieces; he has to address that but the first thing he has to do is regain fitness.'

I wouldn't touch his action until I was satisfied that he had regained at least 90 per cent of his fitness and that was going to take a lot of hard work. I gave him a program and sent him away to do that. He used that as a base and worked out some other things. I concentrated on running fitness mainly and he did his own thing on core strength. I made him run with a ball in his hand so that it became second nature. I think he did it at night because he felt a bit silly, but he did it.

I wouldn't look at him in the nets for weeks. I wanted to be sure that he was fit again and strong again. The first few weeks he was as tired as hell from the workouts, which was what I wanted, and he persevered with that. I said to him after it that you must now persist with this for the rest of your career.

All I kept hearing from people was, he is bowling all over the shop and bowling wides and double wides and all I was hearing from the experts was his wrist is in the wrong position. Well, when your action is all over the place of course your wrist is in the wrong position!

It was a matter of making his bowling action second nature again. Once you do that you don't worry about little things like where your wrist or arm is, or whether you are swinging the ball. It's a routine and muscle memory that comes into play. You have to practise it, but once it all goes right it seems like it's easy. It's not easy but it looks easy.

I set him this thing called TUFF, which was to write down and keep.

T = Target

U = Upright in your run-up, not too far forward or too far back.

F = Front arm straight up, not across your body and head. And straight down.

F = Follow through: he was pulling out to mid-on for a right-hand batsman, so I wanted his arm to come down straight beside his hip and knee and straight through.

You can't follow through properly unless all the other things are right. He couldn't just fix one part of his action without addressing the lot. Once you understand the mechanics of how an action works, you realise one part is just a component of the whole deal. If you try to fix only one component the action will still fall apart.

I was surprised when he retired. Really surprised, because we'd spoken a few weeks earlier and he was talking about going on a few years longer. In part, I understood why he walked away. The wickets in Australia in recent years have been flat and must be really disappointing to bowl on. You expect better at home. It would have been a shame to see his amazing talent flattened on those roads they were preparing. I have no doubt that had a bearing on his decision. It is okay to say slow down and bowl more swing, but on wickets like that it doesn't matter anyway; most fast bowlers will struggle.

Anyway, he did it and he can walk away with his head held high because he had to work very hard for what he achieved. People talk about comebacks from injury; what about where Mitchell came back from? To me he seemed to be at as low an ebb mentally as you could be. To come back from that alone is as good as coming back from a major injury. Added to that his action had deteriorated dramatically. All of which makes it possibly even a bigger achievement.

I am not surprised Mitch had some difficulties on that level; I am probably surprised more don't. Professional cricketers come straight out of school, often don't have a degree, often don't have any life skills at all. They are picked up at 16 or 17 and are taught a little bit, a few lectures at the academy or in a state squad, but nothing major. Armed with that you are meant to have magnificent mental toughness to compete at an elite level, you have to travel the world and be away from your support network at home. You have to put up with criticism from crowds, press, selectors, people in restaurants as you have your dinner. I think Mitch was a victim of the new era of professional cricket.

To get to be one of the best 11 or 12 cricketers in the country you have to pass mental tests and you have to be tough, but nothing prepares you for the onslaught when you are in a slump at that level. He had a wonderful career. When I saw Brett Lee at 16 I thought this kid will play for Australia and be a bloody good bowler and Mitch was the next one. He has totally fulfilled all the expectations I had of him. In the end, he was the leader of the pack; he was it and once you are it you are a master of the game. You are in charge. When you are as good as him you can almost control the game.

To perform like he did in the 2013–14 Ashes after what he went through was a sensational achievement. Well done, Mitch, you got the best out of yourself and had a career you should be extraordinarily proud of. I certainly am proud of what you did.

Dennis Lillee
Cricketer

ING Cup, Queensland Bulls v Victoria Bushrangers,
the Gabba, 31 October 2003

4

A Young Bull at the Gate

SCANS SHOWED I HAD a stress fracture of the right L3 vertebra, which was not where the first fracture had been. The Queensland doctor, Simon Carter, thought it might have had something to do with trying to correct my bowling action. The summer of 2001–02 was spent in traction. Then it happened again and 2002–03 was a write-off, too. It was incredibly frustrating. Every time the summer came around so did another stress fracture. I guess that's what happens when you go from nought to one hundred like I had. I notice it happens with a lot of the young blokes today and I wonder what we've learned. They say they don't miss as much cricket, but Pat Cummins seems to have taken the same route with his injuries.

Whenever I tried to fix things something else broke. It was back to the drawing board and I had to work on changing things again. It was bitterly disappointing but I concentrated on the positives. I'd knocked over a few world-class batsmen. It was a hint that I was able to cut it at that level and something to hang on to while they strapped me in a brace and sent me back to rehab again. I'd had a taste of state cricket and I wanted more. I knew that this was part of the journey. Dennis had been there and was in a back brace for a long time, Brett Lee, too. I am not sure there are many fast bowlers who don't get them. I promised to do everything I could to get back, but that was another lesson I was yet to learn. It's easy to pay lip service to these things, harder to do them. You do what you think is needed, but it is all so tedious that after a while you just do the bare minimum. I didn't know at the time I was doing the wrong thing – it is just the way I was, a lesson I had to learn. I went back to Townsville and was supposed to wear a back brace and I did most of the time, but it was just so hot and so uncomfortable that I got into the habit of taking it off.

Possibly things were coming to me too easily, I don't know. At the academy they drummed into us the sort of dedication needed and I was up to it, but I should have taken a bit more note of the Olympic athletes because sometimes it takes a lot more to succeed. Getting there is the easy bit, staying there is when it gets really hard. Not that I was there yet.

I really wanted to be part of the Queensland team. If the blokes at the Wanderers had introduced me to the culture of club cricket in Townsville, it was the men at the Bulls who took me under their wing and showed me how Sheffield Shield worked. They were old-school blokes and I may have been one of the last to be introduced to this type of approach. They were proud Queenslanders and their rivalry with the other states was deeply ingrained.

There were no mates on the cricket field as far as these blokes were concerned. It was drilled into me at Queensland and reinforced later by Ricky Ponting, who told us on one Ashes series that we could say 'hello' to the opposition if we saw them in the hallway, but if we didn't that would be good. Michael Clarke was the same in the 2012–13 series. It's about a mindset and it doesn't mean you hate the guys or won't have a drink with them when it is all over, but while the contest is on there's no time for pleasantries. It was Townsville cricket taken up a level and it appealed to me. I know it didn't always appeal to other sides or commentators, but that was the way it was.

My first night at Bulls training was a baptism of fire. I rocked up to the nets at the Gabba and did my thing, which included bouncing everyone, including Matthew Hayden and Andrew Symonds. They took it without a word but when it came my turn to bat it was brutal. Almost every ball was a bouncer and there were mutterings about the 'young punk who thinks he can come in here and bowl bouncers at us'. I loved it.

My state teammates were enormous in every way. Haydos and Symmo had those broad chests and would try and intimidate bowlers by stepping down the wicket and smashing the ball. People weren't used to batsmen intimidating fast bowlers, but these guys did their best. The way Haydos stood at the crease was something else. He just dominated the space.

Michael Kasprowicz and Andy Bichel schooled me in what it means to be a fast bowler. Bich had this big heart and I used to love watching him run in to bowl. He had a way of relaxing and talking about anything on the way back to the top of his mark, but once he prepared to bowl he would summon his concentration and energy. It was a good tactic that stopped you worrying too much about the ball before. It was the heart and the passion he showed that impressed me. He did the job; whether it was Queensland or Australia, he always gave it his best. Bich had a no warm-up balls policy and I took that on from him. Why let the batsmen get an eye in? He also said you should never finish a game or a day on a bad note and I prided myself through my career on always trying to bowl as fast in my last spell as I did in the first.

I had so much to learn. Kookaburra came on board and sponsored me when I got the state contract, which meant I finally had my own bat and a source of boots. I was never one of the guys to back the truck up and I reckon I only took one or two pairs of boots then wore them until they were no good. Again I had to be told that this was a mistake. Bich told me I had to take care of my feet.

Kasper was another uncompromising cricketer. He is a funny guy, who was always up for a prank, but one of the hardest working bowlers in the game. He probably doesn't want to be reminded of this now that he is a board member at Cricket Australia, but he had a fart machine that he loved. He'd be waiting in the line at an airport and it would make a fart sound. He'd look sheepishly at people around him and then he'd do it again. He'd look sheepish again and then apologise. We would weep with laughter. It was childish, but that's what happens when you have too much time on your hands. Poor Kasper got a reputation for being a subcontinental specialist, which meant he was almost always reserved for tours where it was stinking hot and the wicket was flat, but it was an attitude to bowling that he and Bich taught me. You don't complain about the wickets, you try and rise to the challenge.

Andrew Symonds demanded I earn his respect and then looked after me like a little brother. It was Symmo who taught me to wear sunscreen. I was still an idiot from the bush who didn't care about these things and came off every day burned to a crisp. He took me aside and said I had to take more care.

Stuey Law was captain when I started, then Jimmy Maher carried on the tradition. We would sit down at the end of the match, drink beer and talk about cricket. I was privileged to be there and didn't realise at the time how much I was learning. Later, when things would happen, I would remember something that one of the guys had said and realise that was what he was talking about. I must have been storing things away at the back of my mind. Sitting around in the sheds after a match went missing for a little while in Australian cricket, but Darren Lehmann reintroduced it when he became coach of the Australian team and I was glad he did. It is one of the great parts of being a cricketer and more important than many realise.

The bouncers on my first night at training were a warning that you had to earn your place in the Queensland team. It took a lot of effort to earn it but it was worth it; there was a great reward in the end. Once you were accepted, it was almost like being part of a family. I was a pretty quiet young bloke, which probably worked in my favour. I just shut my mouth and soaked it up. I didn't give too much lip, although I kept bowling bouncers.

Of course, Kasper and Haydos were away a lot, but when they came back there was a different vibe at training. I really wanted to learn from those guys. I remember seeing Haydos batting in the nets once on a bowling machine just for hours. And I thought what the hell is he doing? We're done training. What's he doing more for? That stuck with me. He had a single-mindedness and focus to better himself that could almost look like selfishness from the outside, but it was also to better the team. We all have to have that selfishness to get better. In the World Cup in 2007, Haydos pretty much hogged the bowling machine the whole tour and no one else was allowed on it because he would hit ball after ball after ball after ball. What he did through that World Cup got the team to where it was. We won the final so that justified everything.

Sometimes the things the senior players did didn't make sense, but as I struggled to make it as an Australian cricketer it became clearer, especially on those occasions when I was back at state level and trying to get back into the Test team. It was then that I understood the extra work you have to do. You have to become almost completely obsessed to make it to the top. Life, family, everything has to take a back seat. I thought I was getting there. I was never afraid of hard work, but I am not sure that I knew what hard work really was. I had got to this place almost as a result of my athletic ability and natural talent, but that only gets you so far. Staying at the top level requires more work than getting there. The level of commitment they taught me at the academy was a big step up from being a weekend cricketer in Townsville, but the level the Bulls demanded was a step up from that again. It was almost like making that transition from being a boy to a man. Part of me was still that adolescent lolling around on the couch at home.

I was a long way from taking these lessons on board and headed for a spectacular fall. It seemed so simple but proved so difficult. In June, I played as a batsman for a Queensland XI against Pakistan at Allan Border Field, then I did the same in two City v Country origin matches in September. When it came time for the opposition to bat I didn't get thrown the ball. You can imagine how frustrating it was. With the 2002–03 summer a complete write-off I refocused my efforts on the following year. I rested, I did the rehab, and I played club cricket as a batsman.

The 2003–04 summer started more brightly. When Bangladesh played an academy XI in Innisfail in July, I bowled a ball for the first time in almost two years. Then I bowled twice in the Queensland origin match and a two-over spell for the Queensland academy against a NSW second XI. All the hard work was starting to pay off and Queensland picked me for my first one-day domestic appearance in what was then known as the ING Cup at the Gabba.

It couldn't have gone better. I opened with Joey Dawes and took 4–37 from the ten overs, including the wicket of Michael

Di Venuto, who was one of the best batsmen in the domestic game. I got mileage out of that for years to come as Divva became our batting coach in the Australian set-up. I also got Dene Hills, who was no slouch and would have to endure being reminded of that when he, too, joined the Australian coaching staff, as team analyst. It was a relief to be back with the Bulls after so long and also to have some success. I played the next 50-over game against the Vics and then was chosen for the Shield match at the Gabba. It was the first time I was back at this level since November 2001 and the game started on my 22nd birthday.

I knocked over Matthew Elliott early in the match, then Brad Hodge a bit later on, but after 15 overs I was gone again. This time it was a side strain and then there was another stress fracture. I was back where I'd started. To be honest, I probably wasn't ready. I was taking anti-inflammatory tablets and wearing strapping just to get by. It was frustrating and it was humiliating too. If you are picked and break down, you leave the load on others. In that game Joey Dawes and Shane Jurgensen bowled 64 overs between them in the innings while I stood around. It was November, season over. Maybe my career, too.

I couldn't believe it. Every time it got close it got taken away from me again. I'd pushed through three major injuries but broken down every time I got a chance at first-class level. It took all my resolve to keep going. At first I was shattered, but I had worked too hard to give up. Again, getting a taste of cricket at the top level was enough to make me hungry even with the taste of disappointment in my mouth. Unfortunately, it wasn't up to me.

After the summer I got called into a meeting at Queensland Cricket. I walked out devastated and angry. They told me they needed me to be playing cricket and I wasn't, so they weren't going to give me a contract the following season. It was nothing personal, a business decision they said. There had been plenty of down moments with the injuries, but this was the hardest. I was really annoyed, but at the same time I understood where they were coming from. There were whispers around the place that I was putting it on a bit and that I was soft. What I couldn't come to grips with was the fact they called it a 'business' decision. Where did they get off? It wasn't business, it was something bigger than that. I'd thought we were a team. Maybe even a family. I knew we weren't punching any time clocks.

My back was a disaster and around this period we had decided the only way to fix it was to operate. It was a last roll of the dice and high risk. There was every chance it could go wrong and I would be on my bike back to Townsville for the rest of my life, but I felt I had no option. Just before I was due to go in to the hospital they did another scan and couldn't find the stress fractures, just scar tissue. They cancelled the operation and tried another treatment that involved an injection into my spine. The first one didn't work, but the second one did and my back has been fine ever since.

Looking back, I wonder about the amount of running we used to do in those days, a lot of it on the roads. I never liked running and it wasn't great for my back. We were always running here or there and the constant pounding never felt right. In later years any running we did in the Australian camp was high-intensity short stuff. And it was always on grass.

It didn't matter. I was 22 years old and washed up after two one-day matches for the Bulls. I hadn't even played a full Sheffield Shield game. I went home to Townsville when Queensland cut me and was about ready to throw it in. I stayed there for a month stewing on it, wondering what I would do next. I started to have a few conversations with people; the one I remember the most was with my dad, who asked me if I felt I had given it my all. I knew I hadn't. They were wise words, Dad.

It was around this time I got my first piercings. And my first tattoo. Which might have been a reflection of where I was at mentally. I went down with a few mates. We'd decided that now we were moving on a bit we would get the symbol from a Soulfly album inked on us as a sign of our friendship. I was the only one who even bothered to look up what it meant. I was a bit worried it might have been a Nazi sign or something, but it turned out it was the Aum symbol, which is a sacred mantra for Hindus and Buddhists. The piercings and tatt were a sign I was a bit more comfortable in my own skin, but not everyone was so comfortable with it. Symmo called me 'sinker lip' when he saw them and the next year there was talk on radio and even a newspaper column written about them. Looking back, I am a bit embarrassed about the piercings, but only a bit. You are only young and stupid once.

It would have been easy to throw it all in but I had a burning desire to prove people wrong at this time. I was pretty sure that

I could play for Australia. It was a quiet confidence. I wasn't one to mouth off. I knew when I bowled in that Shield game that I was good enough; I had swung the ball and knocked over some top-class batsmen. It was inside me and I thought all I needed was a chance to play a full season and prove myself. The chances of that were looking pretty slim now that Queensland didn't want me, but I resolved to give it one more crack. I knew I couldn't hide up in Townsville, so I moved back to Brisbane and into a house at The Gap with Nathan Rimmington. Our landlord was Brendan Nash, who was at Queensland and later played Test cricket for the West Indies.

I had been offered a spot with the Queensland Academy of Sport squad and went in for a meeting with Richard Done, who had been at the academy when I started. I told him, thanks, but no thanks, that I wanted to do it on my own. He said that was fine and if I needed anything to come back and ask. He said it would not exclude me from selection for any team, which was useful to know. If I was good enough I would play again.

Being cut would turn out to be the best kick in the teeth I ever had. Brett Mortimer, who was the coach at our club, Norths, in Brisbane, had a plumbing supply business called Plumbtech. Brendan had been driving the van making deliveries for him, but he left and I took over his job. I'd never really had a job before. I didn't mind it, even if I was on the absolute bottom rung of the ladder. I had to deliver supplies to plumbers on building sites and I was on my own. If it was a water tank or a spa bath nobody offered to give me a hand. The bad thing was that the job started at about 5.30 am, which meant getting up at 5 am. The best thing was that I was done early in the afternoon and could concentrate on training. Brett was really supportive. I remember watching a Test match with him that summer and he told me I could do it if I wanted to. I just had to work harder and I had to really want it.

I had that absolute focus of getting back into the Queensland team. I'd had the taste and I wanted it back. I trained with Norths and they allowed me to open the batting in the seconds during the bad times with the stress fractures and that was good for me. It kept me in touch with cricket and gave me a chance to work on my batting.

I didn't want to have anything to do with the Bulls set-up going into the 2004–05 summer. I was desperate to be back there but I wanted to prove to them I could do it myself. I didn't want any hand-outs. There was a guy called John Hetherington, who had a rugby union background and was a trainer with the second XI side at Queensland. Grant Sullivan, who was a good right-arm quick and played a few games for the Bulls a bit later on, worked with John and me. John had a contact at the XXXX Brewery and they had a good gym there, which they let us use. I really started to push myself.

By the time summer rolled around I was as fit as I had ever been. I was keen to show them they had made a mistake getting rid of me. I really pushed myself to get fit and strong. I also started watching my diet much more than I had in the past. I'd always been pretty ordinary at that stuff and had a tendency to pig out on takeaway food, but now I was fiercely determined to prove myself. My burning resentment drove me to work harder than I ever had. Whenever I got the craving to hit the burgers and chips I summoned up the hurt of being excluded and made a better call. I am not one for cooking my own meals and never have been, but I managed to take more care with what I bought. I was seriously cranky, and I learned from this that you have to tap into those things and use them to spark that drive. The reason I kept getting back up was that I didn't want to give people the satisfaction of knowing I was down.

I played club cricket with Norths for the first half of the season and found myself fit and healthy for the first time since I was 19. I was fast and I wasn't tentative anymore. I just felt stronger and had more faith in my body. In early January, I played for the Queensland Academy in a four-day match against a WA XI at the WACA. I had a bit of a day out in the first innings and knocked over six of the top seven batsmen. Queensland was watching and asked me to come back.

When I rejoined I asked to train in the group with the best athletes, guys like James Hopes and Chris Hartley, who were gun runners. I wanted to be pushed because aerobically I had never been good. I didn't always keep up with them, but I did my best and I kept improving. I learned about my body when I came back, too. I started to push into new territory; I was still sore in the lower part of my back, but I knew I had done the work and just kept going through it. Being that bit older helped because my body was more mature. Fast bowlers tend to be prone to stress fractures and other injuries until they are in their mid-20s.

Andrew Symonds, Matthew Hayden, Michael Kasprowicz and Shane Watson were all playing One-Day Internationals (ODIs) with Australia when Queensland's next one-day game came around and I got the call-up for a game against NSW out at Homebush. I played four one-day matches in a row. I didn't get a lot of wickets, but picked up 4–45 against Western Australia, opening the bowling with Andy Bichel, and proved I could hold my own. And then I was called back into the Sheffield Shield team. I could not have been happier. I'd never worked so hard for anything in my life. We played three games in about three weeks and while I didn't do anything special, it was just good to be fronting up and proving at the back-end of the season that I was still fit.

In my first game back we played South Australia and I scored 51 not out in the second innings – my first half-century in first-class cricket and considerably better than my previous highest score, 15. I also bowled a bloke called Darren Lehmann, although he would probably want me to point out he was on 104 at the time.

Losing the contract the year before proved to be a big turning point in my cricket career. I'd felt like I was missing an opportunity, like I was stuffing it up. To be completely honest, I hadn't worked hard enough on coming back from injuries. I was just doing the necessary stuff to get through and nothing extra, but I learned to push myself and things changed. More importantly, it had made me resentful. If there was any criticism of me it was that I was too shy. I just didn't have that killer instinct that fast bowlers needed. I never wanted to draw attention to myself and I'd been taught to be respectful to everyone. That was true but it was changing. Still, it would take another decade or more before I really discovered the 'mongrel' that drove me to be the best I could.

People still believed in me, and when Shaun Tait was picked to play the fifth Test of the 2005 Ashes series I was given his place in the Australia A squad to play a series of matches in Pakistan, which was a real buzz. It was a rare chance to see that country and I loved it. It is such a shame that the Australian side hasn't toured there since 1998. There were some pretty big names in that A side, people like Mike Hussey, Phil Jacques, Watto, Brad Haddin, Marcus North, Stu Clark, Nathan Bracken and Mick Lewis. It was good that people were thinking of me in such company.

I was pretty keen to impress and at one of our early net sessions I went really hard bowling to Mike Hussey. By then he was considered one of the best batsmen in the country and even in the nets he was hard to beat, but I dug one in that he tried to hook, but it got big on him fast and smashed into his helmet. He was a bit shaken up by it and I was concerned that I'd hurt him, but most of all I was surprised that I'd actually beaten Mike Hussey.

Watto and I had a good time with the ball in a win at Lahore and I enjoyed the tour but it had its moments. There were huge security concerns about touring Pakistan at that time and while we were pretty excited to be playing cricket, we were all a bit toey about it. The tour was based in two places: Lahore and Rawalpindi. We were supposed to have what they called presidential level security but it wasn't all that flash. I remember driving into Lahore from the airport and the bus being stuck in traffic all the way. You feel like a target in these situations. You are just sitting there with all these people staring at you, protected only by glass. A few years later we were on a bus in India and there was this incredible noise. We didn't know what it was but it shook us up and then we saw a huge crack in the window right near where I was sitting. Somebody had thrown a big rock at the bus and there was quite a kerfuffle. It was pretty disappointing, but I guess it shows you how excited fans can get.

One day on this tour of Pakistan we were sitting on the bus after a game and this random bloke just appeared in the aisle asking for our autographs. We were dumbstruck. Security eventually dragged him off and he obviously meant no harm, but if he wanted to do some he could have. Of course, four years later the Sri Lankan team's bus got shot up by terrorists in Lahore. We were in South Africa that day; we'd just won a game in Johannesburg and were flying to Durban when the news came through. It shook us up.

Back in 2005 our presidential security meant that one night when we went out to this incredible outdoor restaurant in Lahore we had two snipers take up posts on buildings either side of us. You could see the silhouette of one of the blokes on the wall of a nearby mosque. We were halfway through the meal and I looked around and saw that one of them had fallen asleep in his chair. Then I looked at the other one. Guess what? Yep, he was asleep, too.

I reckon it was the next day, or maybe two days later, that a pair of bombs went off. One of them was right near that restaurant and another on a road we'd travelled on. Six people died and 30 were injured. We watched it unfolding on the television and felt sick. We decided we wanted to go home. They pleaded with us to stay and then we were told by management that we had to. The Pakistan side was worried that if we left, a tour by England, which was due a month later, would be cancelled.

Now we really did have presidential security. They started checking every car that came to the hotel and gave us a proper escort on cleared roads to get to the grounds. It was something you got used to on the subcontinent, but you always felt a little uncomfortable. I think we had too many briefings about being careful in this town or that one and about not going out of the hotels without telling security. We weren't allowed to wander around alone. Things like that get inside your head and you get even more sensitive once you start having kids.

My biggest problem on that tour, however, was getting into the bathroom. I was sharing a room with Watto, which was always interesting. He had two toiletry bags and so much stuff that I was barely able to find room for my toothbrush.

We left Lahore in September and I was keen to put in a solid season for Queensland. I'd been around the place for five or six years by then and it was time to deliver. Things were on the move fast again.

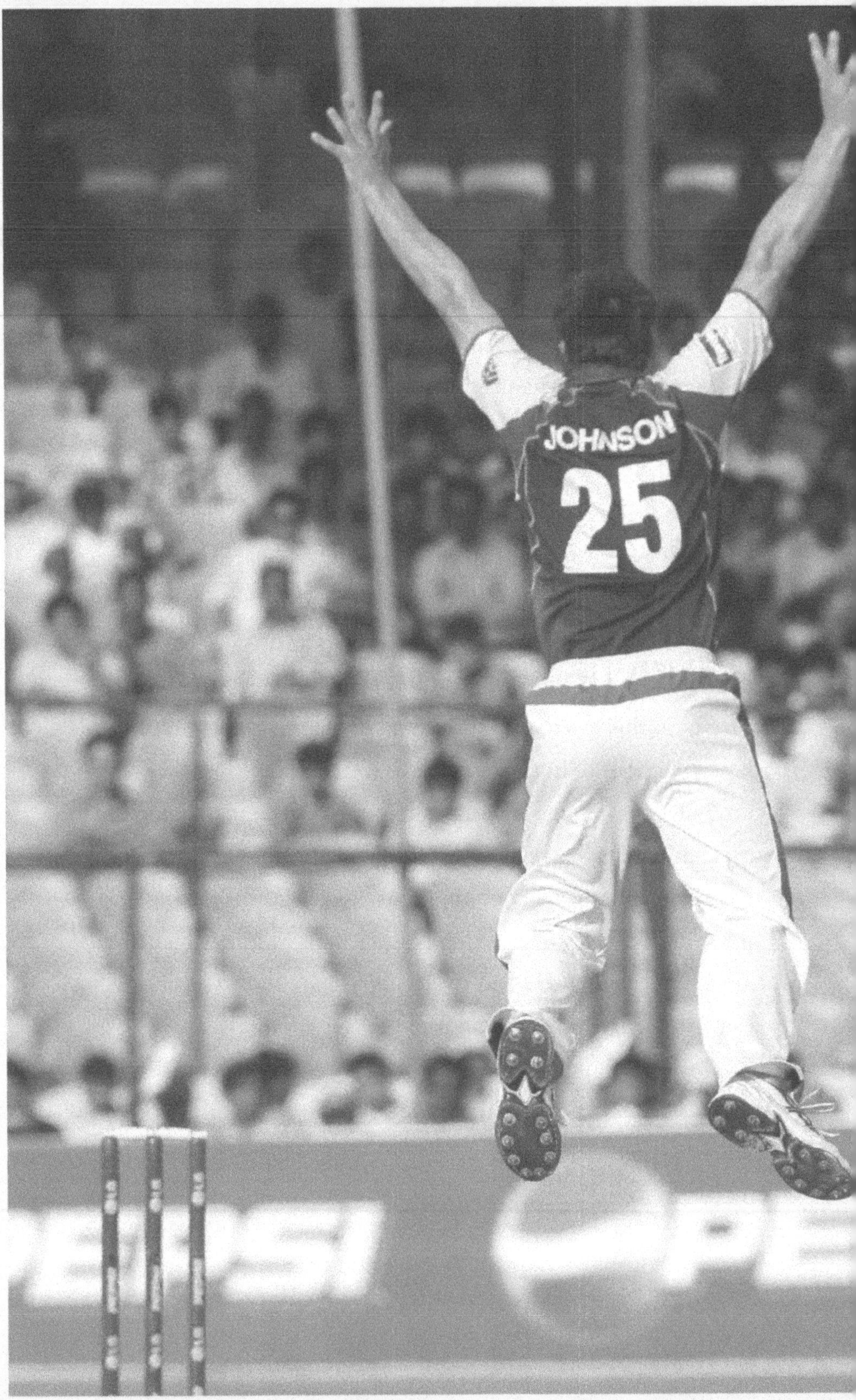
JOHNSON
25

2006 ICC Champions Trophy, Australia v England,
Sawai Mansingh Stadium, Jaipur, 21 October 2006.

5

Playing for My Country

ON REFLECTION, IT'S REMARKABLE how quickly things happened in my career. A season after losing my contract I got a call-up to the national team to play my first ODI and things really got on a roll from there. Many thought they were putting the cart before the horse, just as they had when they picked me in the Australian Under-19s team. There is no doubt there were a hell of a lot of people out there with more experience and more success. There were definitely people taking more wickets.

I was always promoted on potential and in a way that created an expectation around everything I did. I had to manage that myself. I couldn't get frustrated when success didn't come as quickly as selection. I understood, though, why a fair few did get upset and made a bit of noise about it. It was a constant battle. You want to do well but you can't be too hard on yourself for not getting the obvious results or it becomes a negative spiral. I knew I had done the work and I knew that people who were better judges than me thought I had something, and deep down I had confidence I could make it.

Everybody needed a bit of patience, but it was most important that I was patient because I was never going to be a bowler who didn't spray the odd ball or go for a few runs. If I worried about those things, I lost my pace and that was my best asset. I had to spend money to make money, if you know what I mean.

I played the first half of the season with Queensland and managed my best performance in a game against South Australia where I picked up 5–43 in the last innings (previous best 3–23). Even then I felt like a junior player in the group. My more experienced teammates were showing me how it was done. Against Victoria, Andy Bichel took 7–56 and made 84 runs in the first innings, and then Michael Kasprowicz took 8–44. I didn't get a wicket in that match. When Queensland played the West Indies in a tour match early in the summer I only got one wicket: Brian Lara bowled Johnson for one. Still, if you are only going to take one wicket ...

Early in December 2005, I was getting into the car to drive home after state training when the phone rang. It was Trevor Hohns the Australian selector saying they wanted me to fly over to New Zealand, as Brett Lee had a problem and was coming back. I was in shock. I went home, got my things together and then went to the airport. I hadn't had time to tell everyone. I rang Mum from the terminal. They still had Stuart Clark, Nathan Bracken and Mick Lewis in the squad and there was only one match left to play so it was unlikely I would be picked, but I was thrilled even to be thought of as a net bowler. I had only played 12 first-class games – and I'd been around for the best part of five seasons.

Trevor Hohns told the press that they were thinking about the future: 'Mitchell is a young player that we've had our eye on for a while,' he said. 'We felt this was an ideal opportunity, with one game to go in the series, to get him involved. It is certainly a selection with a view to the future.'

It was all pretty rushed. I landed at 2 am and didn't get much sleep before I headed down for breakfast, where I met the team manager and the team. I didn't know what to expect. All the guys made me feel comfortable right away. I hadn't played cricket with many of them before but they were all welcoming. Ricky Ponting was captain and made sure that I was brought into the group.

And then I was named in the side for the next day's game at Jade Stadium in Christchurch. It's funny, I guess I was nervous, but I wasn't that uptight about it. After all, I was a long way from home and I was really the fourth bowler. At least, that was what I told myself to control my nerves. The newspapers pointed out that I didn't exactly have the best record in one-day cricket for Queensland, just 14 wickets in ten matches at 36 runs apiece. My 25 Pura Cup (as the Sheffield Shield was then known) wickets had come from nine matches at 35. To be honest, that didn't really worry me that much because I knew I was learning as I went. If it bothered other people that was their problem.

Playing in New Zealand is an experience for an opposition team; the crowd gets right in your face. Some of the stuff they say is pretty full-on. I really copped it after Jacob Oram hit me for a ridiculously big six. The grounds aren't big over there and they had to send out a search party for the ball. Jacob used to take great delight in reminding me of that when we played together at Mumbai in the IPL. I didn't get a wicket so it wasn't the greatest first game, but I held my head up and enjoyed the moment, I knew it was great experience. I didn't get a bat either, because those were the days when they were experimenting with substitute players and I subbed for Simon Katich.

Back at home I continued on with the summer and got a chance to have a crack at South Africa in a tour match against Queensland at the Gabba. It was the first time I had seen Graeme Smith since the Under-19s and the first time I got to bowl to him. He and I would have some epic battles over the coming decade but I won this one when I got him out in my second over. I also managed to pick up Mark Boucher and Shaun Pollock and finished with 3–33 from my nine overs.

In February, I was named in the Australian squad to go to South Africa. To say I was thrilled would be an understatement, but everyone else seemed a bit underwhelmed. Geoff Lawson thought the selectors could have done better, saying there were 25 bowlers in the country who had done better than me and it was 'an absolute disgrace'. Jeff Thomson said: 'In my day, you got picked for Australia for taking wickets ... you didn't get picked on some selector thinking: this guy might be able to play.'

I could see their point, but I thought they might have expressed themselves a little more diplomatically. The criticism annoyed and motivated me. I am very competitive and like to prove people wrong, which I think I've shown in recent years.

I got a start in the first game at Centurion, but it was rain affected and I only bowled three overs. I had 0–3 at the end of the first, bowling to Smith and AB de Villiers. The second was a bit of a disaster: Smithy hit me for a four first ball then gave AB a turn. After a sighter he belted me for two fours and a six. The third over went a bit better.

And that was my first and last game of the tour. Stu Clark got my spot for the remaining games, including the one at Johannesburg where we got 434 and they chased it down. I ducked a bullet not bowling in that match.

So, I had played two ODIs for my country and had career figures of 0–92. As soon as I took a wicket I would have an average, but it wasn't going to be pretty. When the Tests rolled around, I was sent home, which allowed me to front up for Queensland in the Sheffield Shield final against Victoria at the Gabba. Mabo (Jimmy Maher) had captained the side to five domestic finals in recent years and lost all of them. He was desperate for this and wanted us to go flat-out at the Vics. It was war, he said.

This game was another major turning point in my career. It was the match where I truly earned the respect of my teammates and showed people that I could live up to my potential. The first day was hard work. They won the toss and batted. Ashley Noffke and I got early breakthroughs, but Brad Hodge dug in and the

Vics were 5–269 at stumps. We'd worked hard but they were in a good position. The next morning Andy Bichel got Hodge and we tore through the tail. I picked up the last three wickets cheaply and finished with 4–55. They were all out for 344.

Enter Jimmy Maher, a grizzly veteran, our captain and opening batsman. Mabo knocked up a ruthless 223 that crushed them. Shane Watson matched him, retiring hurt on 201, while Martin Love and Clinton Perren scored 150s. Our batters were just so intent on grinding their bowlers down. It was something to watch.

Mabo joked about us going on to 1000 and he probably wanted to. Two years earlier they had kept him in the field for the best part of three days as they notched up 710. He joked at the time that he understood what a real bull felt like after staring at grass for so long. He finally declared at 6–900 so we could have a crack at the top order before stumps. The Vics had bowled 242 overs and their batsmen had spent a lot of time chasing leather.

I'd had plenty of time to rest and in my second over I got Jason Arnberger and Lloyd Mash. It's funny how that can happen to a batting side after a couple of days in the field. Your legs are like lead and your feet just don't move.

I had my tail up the next day and ran through the Victorians to finish with 6–51 and my first ten-wicket match haul at this level. We'd won the Sheffield Shield final and we were pumped after losing the last three finals. These are the best days you can have in a cricket team and I could see just what it meant to the other blokes. There's nothing better than sharing the experience with friends. I had wanted to hold up the Wimbledon trophy when I was a lad, but that is a lonely triumph; this one created bonds that will last a lifetime. On a more selfish note, I was so proud to have backed up my first innings efforts and to have done it on a wicket that really wasn't that good to bowl on – you don't get juicy decks for finals because they are hosted by the top-placed team, which only has to draw the game to win the Sheffield Shield. Mabo said later that he thought I deserved the man of the match, which was all very nice, but he deserved it. He also acknowledged that it was 'a massive turning point' for me. I hoped he was right.

I was picked in the Australian squad for the one-day part of our tour to Bangladesh in April, but got to watch the Test side play first. I was on hand to see Jason Gillespie, the man that Geoff Lawson thought should have been chosen ahead of me in South Africa, score a double hundred. It was one of those moments and I was glad to witness it. Dizzy had been one of the bowlers I really admired when I first started to get serious about cricket, but that was his last match for his country.

When the one-day series rolled around I was picked to bowl alongside Brett Lee and Nathan Bracken in the first game at Chittagong. On the last ball of my sixth over I knocked out Khaled Mashud's leg stump. It was my first wicket for Australia. I'd been to New Zealand, South Africa and now Bangladesh. I'd bowled 108 balls and gone for 122 runs. Those two numbers were my strike rate and average, but I was on the board. I'd taken a wicket for Australia.

I didn't have any luck on that front in the next game and so my stats blew out even more (strike rate 132, average 146), but I wasn't getting uptight about these things. I was learning on the job, as I would be for most of my international career. Binga [Brett Lee] and Bracks [Nathan Bracken] weren't picked for the next match at Fatullah and I was thrown the new ball. The ball swung and the umpire was kind enough to give the opening batsman, Shariar Nafees, out lbw off my third ball despite a suggestion he might have nicked it onto his pads. It was possible he'd smashed it, but that was the way things went.

We won and I finished the game with 2–24, my best one-day figures, which went some way to improving my stats. The best part of it all, though, was that it was late April and I had made it through another summer without breaking down. The gym work had paid off.

We had a month off then flew up to Darwin with the Australia A side to play a series against India, Pakistan and New Zealand. I played five of the seven games, picked up some wickets and even made another 50.

In September, it was over to Malaysia for the DLF Cup, a triangular one-day series also featuring India and the West Indies. Our first match was against the West Indies and I bowled first change behind Glenn McGrath and Nathan Bracken. Unfortunately, Chris Gayle and Shivnarine Chanderpaul were in great touch and I went for a few runs (4–0–40–0). About 23 overs into the game they were 1–170-odd and 100 behind our total. Ricky asked Glenn and me to come back in to try and get a breakthrough because we were heading for a big loss. Naturally, Pigeon [Glenn] was bowling tight lines and not giving them anything. The only thing I could do was try and blast them out with what I knew best. I dropped short on Shiv first ball. He pulled it. Four. I pitched the next one up. Four. I was in trouble, 0–48 off 4.2 overs. I decided to go double or nothing, pitched short and it was too fast for him. He tried to pull it but just nicked it through to Hadds. Thank God for that. Lara came in next. He flayed a flat-footed drive on his first ball but only managed an inside edge, which should have gone on to bowl him but didn't. Three balls later I swung one back in and had him lbw. Ricky and everyone were pretty pleased. I'd got us back into the game. Watto and Bracks helped clean up the tail and we won a game that we looked certain to lose.

I opened the bowling with Glenn McGrath in our second game against India. It was wet and the ball was swinging and I had a night out, picking up Rahul Dravid and Irfan Pathan with consecutive balls, then Sachin Tendulkar and Yuvraj Singh in my next over. I was flying and felt like I could take all ten wickets in no time. The conditions were terrible for batsmen and that was fine by me because most of the time it was quite the reverse. Unfortunately, it started to rain. Talk about poor timing. The batsmen were the first off and I was last when the umpires pointed to the dressing rooms. I dragged my feet hoping the rain would stop, but it had really set in. The game was called off when I had 4–11 from four overs. I was a bit disappointed, but they couldn't take those wickets away from me. Ricky Ponting was delighted and talked me up big time to the press, who were full of questions about my chance of playing in the Ashes that summer. They got pretty excited about what I'd done.

Ricky said I'd done my chances no harm:

'He got us a couple of vital breakthroughs in the first game, and tonight he was brilliant. He's got the pace, he's a left-armer and he can swing it. That's why we are all excited about him. The idea is to give him a few games under his belt. As far as I can see, he is improving every game, and an outing like tonight will do him a world of good.'

Unfortunately, that was the end of the series for me and a couple of blokes. The selectors had picked an 18-man squad and it was planned that we would play those two games, then go home. Ricky said he would have liked me to stay and I couldn't disagree. Not that there was any shortage of cricket. That tournament was in September, and in October I found myself part of the squad for the Champions Trophy in India. I'd now played games in four different countries but never at home. I didn't mind that, though, I was learning the ropes away from the spotlight. Still, I wouldn't have minded a bowl on an honest Australian deck. Through all of this I was at least learning how to get wickets with an old ball on slow pitches. The early butterflies were gone and I was concentrating on tactics, using the off-cutter and bowling to in/out fields.

We had a fair bowling attack in that Champions Trophy series, but I got called up when they dropped Brad Hogg for our second game against England in Jaipur. I bowled second change with Glenn McGrath, after Brett Lee and Nathan Bracken opened. I took 3–40 from my ten but it was the first wicket that gave me most satisfaction. Kevin Pietersen had just come in; I dropped one short to him that he had to fend off first ball, then nicked him off with an off-cutter next delivery. The old two-card trick. After the game he got a lot of questions about facing short balls. He said he'd never heard of me before the game, but had some kind words: 'He's a good bowler, bowled fantastically well. Good shoulder … I was surprised at the short ball, I wasn't expecting it at all. We'll probably see a lot of him over the summer.' I always enjoyed my battles with KP and there were many more to come.

I went okay in the next two games, including the semifinal against the Kiwis, but was dropped for the final against the West Indies, which we won. It was disappointing to miss out but great to be part of a team that was on such a roll. I'd been in and out of the team for nearly 12 months by then and I was starting to feel at ease with all the stuff that goes with playing and travelling. You have to be organised on a cricket tour. The travel and all that is booked for you, but you have to be switched on and make sure you don't miss team meetings or the bus. You have to find your own rhythm with eating, training and recovery. If you switch off and go into cruise control, things can fall apart quickly. It's a knack that takes a while to pick up, but you are surrounded by people like Ponting who have been doing it since they were teenagers.

The critics were still around and rarely went away, but people were starting to push for my inclusion in the Ashes squad. It was an exciting idea, but with Glenn McGrath, Brett Lee, Stu Clark and Shaun Tait around I was a long shot at best. I also wasn't ready, but that hadn't stopped me to this point.

Allan Border went into bat for me telling the papers:

'He would be in my 12. To me, we are starting to get to a point where we need to take a bit of a gamble with some young guys. We've got steady performers there, but that's just my thinking to throw someone in there who is a bit different. He's a bit raw and all that but, gee, he's exciting. He can bowl 140-plus, he swings it as a left-armer. When you've got that core group of bowling you can rely on – Warne, McGrath, Lee – is there any harm in throwing that young tyro in there? To me, it's worth the risk, particularly at the Gabba, where he might get a wicket that helps him a bit.'

Mark Waugh was another who thought I should be given a chance. Others were wondering what the hell I was doing anywhere near the Australian side. There was a story in one paper that asked just that question and interviewed people from the Wanderers and Queensland. It was actually pretty positive.

Shaun Tait had an edge on me after destroying the Poms in the Prime Minister's XI game in Canberra. I flew with Queensland to Perth for a Shield match the week before the squad was announced. We bowled first on a WACA pitch that was pretty lifeless and I couldn't get a breakthrough in the morning, but after lunch I came back and really ripped into them, knocking over Mike Hussey and Damien Martyn on my way to a four-wicket haul. Three in the second innings didn't hurt either. Watto and Andrew Symonds were both pushing for a place, too, and bowled really well.

When they read out the names for the Ashes squad for the 2006–07 summer I was one of the 16. That should have been the highlight of my life, but in reality there was no chance I was going to play. Don't get me wrong, I was thrilled to be that close and to get to see that awesome team up close.

We were taken on that infamous boot camp before the summer. Warnie hated it and has been complaining about it ever since. Stu MacGill did his knee and was not impressed either. It wasn't exactly their speed, but it was right up my alley and the best bit was being paired with Ricky Ponting, which meant I got to spend a lot of time with him. I was on the doorstep but I had a while to wait yet. The side that played that series was one of the strongest in history and full of stars: Langer, Hayden, Ponting, Clarke, Hussey, Gilchrist, McGrath, Warne, Lee, Clark. When Damien Martyn retired mid-tour, Andrew Symonds took over.

Shaun Tait and I were in the squad but the only way we would get a sniff was if somebody was injured, which is what happened going into the second game. Glenn McGrath had a bruised heel and played with painkillers in the first match. He was still in trouble before the game in Adelaide and it was touch and go. The feeling was I would be picked ahead of Taity because I had more control, which was funny. He must have been the only bowler in the whole country who sprayed them more than me. I was told to get ready. Everyone knew Glenn would play with a broken leg, but they made him take a fitness test on the morning of the game. He passed it and I was allowed to relax.

When they were 3–0 up, there was talk around the place of giving me a go, but Ricky Ponting dismissed it. They wanted to win 5–0 and everybody was doing their job. Every bowler took more than 20 wickets for the series and every batsman averaged over 40 – Huss, Punter and Pup considerably more. Often I was only there for the start of the Tests, as they would send me back to Queensland once most matches started. It was in no way frustrating to be part of the squad because I had the best seats in the house to watch the best team on the planet. At Queensland I had learned about cricket, first at the Wanderers, then at the Bulls, but these guys operated at another level again.

That summer gave me a taste of Test cricket. I was really keen to play, I was around it and I felt I had the trust of the guys. They made me feel like I was a part of the team. Ricky Ponting was really good at making everybody feel part of the group. You had all these strong characters in the team and it would have been hard to manage them. It took a special person to keep them all going in the same direction as they did. I suppose I was doing my dressing room apprenticeship and I watched everyone closely. Watching and learning from people like that is invaluable. I wanted to know how they trained, prepared, their rituals. If they talked, I listened.

Glenn McGrath had that confidence on the field. He could put the ball where he wanted to and he was always totally focused. But off the field, he didn't take himself seriously. Out in the middle he would get fired up and angry with himself and always wanted one more over, but off it he switched off and wanted to have some fun. There was a lesson there. He was a bit of a prankster (I learned from him how to be annoying), but even though he knew he was good he was never arrogant towards any of us.

The big guys like Haydos have that sense of arrogance, which is part of what makes them good. He was the barrel-chested bloke who would go after you as a batter. I got the chance to chat with Warnie on occasion, too. He was always talking about the game in the dressing room. He loved talking tactics and giving opinions about what they should or shouldn't do. He had amazing insights into the game. He was fascinating and I hope I was able to take some of it on board. You could see he wanted to captain, he definitely had that tactical ability. I was signing some gear during the Sydney Test when Warnie looked over my shoulder and announced that my autograph was crap and I had to get a better one. He was serious. He sat down and got me to work on it over and over and over. I filled two pages scrawling my name until he announced that I had something I could work with. The room attendant had been watching and he grabbed the sheets that we left behind. Sometime later, he gave me one back that he'd framed. He'd framed the other one, too, for himself.

Gilly was another fascinating bloke. He was an interesting combination of intense and relaxed. A bit like McGrath. He seemed to bat like he didn't have a care in the world, but he was so focused on his keeping and on the spirit of the team. He could get loose after a few drinks, though, and we had some good nights out. They worked hard but they knew how to have fun. That was not always the case around the team, but I understand how hard it is for people to find the right balance between being disciplined and being constricted.

Gilly was very good. A bowler needs to have a good relationship with their keeper; you need to have a bond. He seemed like a bit of a big brother to me. It felt like he was always there if I needed anything. You felt like he actually cared. We played a fair bit of cricket together in the end and had a lot of good moments off the field. When he went, I struck up a close bond with Brad Haddin.

Binga was an idol because he bowled fast. I studied his preparation closely and will never forget some of the overs he bowled during the series, especially one to Andrew Flintoff in Adelaide.

I remember the first time I met Justin Langer was at the Gabba. I was walking past a room just after he got out and he was in there with the boxing gloves on punching the mitts and going completely crazy. I thought I better stay clear of him. I'd heard stories. He was a pretty intense guy and it could be quite intimidating. As I got to know him I learned he was also one of the more gentle and caring souls in the game and one of the most passionate players you will ever encounter.

Ricky Ponting was a wonderful captain who found time for you, always helping someone out at training, and he never seemed to tire. He set the tone at training, especially in the fielding drills, getting us to lift our standards. I don't know how much time he spent giving me throwdowns and helping me with my batting, but he always seemed to be on hand. He was generally the last person to leave the nets. Captains have a lot on their plate, but he never let it eat into the time he spent at training or with the team. There was a lesson in that. You couldn't leave the nets with something incomplete.

I played six of the one-day games at the end of the summer in a triangular series we had against New Zealand and England, then was picked in the World Cup squad that went to the West Indies but couldn't get a look-in, which was understandable as McGrath, Tait and Bracken did a great job. Hadds was on tour and we trained really hard. I gained good experience bowling to Haydos in the nets a lot. He got furious because he thought I was bouncing him with no-balls. He blew up to the bowling coach, Troy Cooley, about punks who were overstepping. Troy, who is pretty laidback, came and had a look and told Haydos I was behind the line and he was just getting too old to face young quicks. He didn't like that.

There was a bit of a break that winter (a rare thing as I was to discover) before we flew to South Africa for the T20 World Championship, which was won by a young Indian outfit led by MS Dhoni. It was a victory that sparked a revolution in India. We were there waiting for them when they arrived home and rode through Mumbai in an open-topped bus. It was mind boggling how many people turned out to line the route from the airport to Wankhede Stadium near our hotel. I knew there were a lot of people in India, but it still defied the imagination.

Glenn McGrath had retired after the summer and I played all seven games in the series, sharing the new ball with Brett Lee. It was a gruelling series with a lot of travel and only three days between games, but I enjoyed it and was the leading wicket taker, which felt good. All the work I'd done getting fit a few years earlier was paying off. I was strong and ready to go every time another game rolled around. I even managed my first international five-wicket haul up at Vadodara.

The last match in Mumbai was my 25th ODI (average was now a respectable 25) and I was starting to get the hang of it. I was bowling constantly in excess of 150 km/h and felt good about my cricket. The first game in Bangalore was washed out after a couple of overs, but I managed to trap Sachin lbw with my sixth ball for a duck. It was a good way to start the series. Late in the Nagpur match, MS Dhoni and Robin Uthappa were starting to take our attack apart at a critical point in the game. Ricky had shown faith in me opening the bowling and turned to me to try and stop the late rally. I was a bit nervous because both those blokes can hit a ball and they were in a mood but I got Uthappa first ball and Dhoni three balls later. It felt great to do the job the team asks you to do.

There were, however, plenty of lessons to be learned and one was waiting for me in our first Shield game of the summer. We took on NSW at the SCG in October 2007 and Simon Katich, who was out of the Test side at that time, had a point to prove. He hit a triple century – the first hundred came in 200-odd balls, but the next two took 75 balls each. He was in a mood and there was nothing we could do. Brad

Haddin got a hundred, too. Me? I couldn't get a wicket to save my life.

Kat was such a difficult batsman to bowl to because he moved around the crease. I didn't know where to bowl to him. If I put it outside off he was there in a good position to play it and if it was on the stumps he flicked you off the pads. I got on really well with him, but it was always better to be on his side. Bowling to him prepared me a little bit to bowl to the West Indies' Shivnarine Chanderpaul when I came up against him, because he is a bit similar. He was really good, too, and got a lot of runs against us. You would see him move when you were in your delivery stride and it would make you adjust and he would pick you off. He was patient, too.

In November, the Sri Lankans arrived for the first Test match of the summer and eyes turned towards the selectors. They named a 13-man squad for the first match. Brett Lee and Stuart Clark were obvious starters but it was between Ben Hilfenhaus and me for the first game. I hadn't done myself any favours at the SCG and didn't take the opportunity when Queensland played Sri Lanka in a tour game. I vowed to be a bit more aggressive if I did get a chance. I knew there were a lot of people in my corner and Andy Bichel was telling the journos that my time had arrived.

'He's a left-armer, he gives you those options and we haven't seen a left-arm quick for a long time,' he said. 'He's at the right age, he's done his apprenticeship and knows the system; it's perfect timing for him. He's ready to go.'

Well, kind of ...

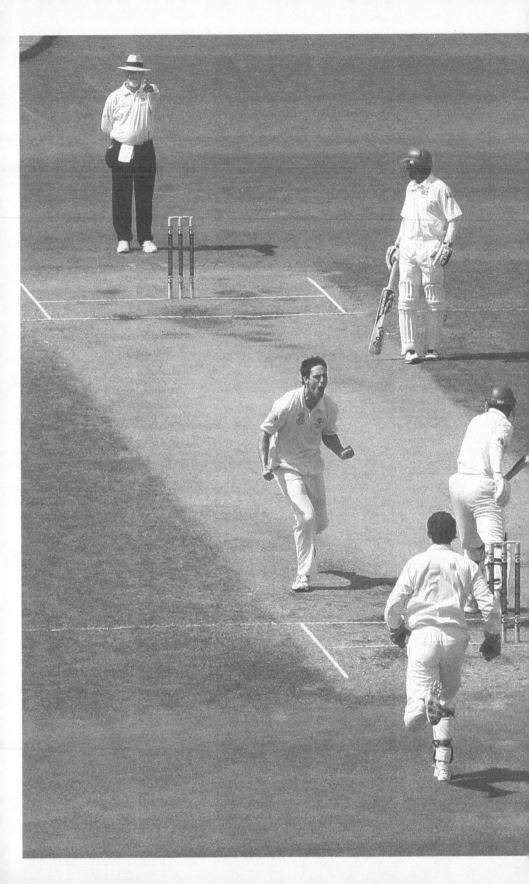

Australia v Sri Lanka, Second Test, Day 5,
Bellerive Oval, Hobart, 20 November 2007.

6

The Baggy Green

THERE ARE A FEW times in my life when I actually think I can't breathe on a cricket field and this is the first of them.

It is late on day two of the first Test against Sri Lanka at the Gabba in November 2007. I've been fielding on the rope for the first over and when it ends Stuart Clark comes down and takes my brand new baggy green. I am almost reluctant to give it up. Ricky Ponting has moved halfway to the boundary to meet me and he's got a shiny Kookaburra for me. Down at the other end the veteran Sanath Jayasuriya is waiting with a bat in his hand. He's playing his 108th Test match. I'm playing my first.

That ball feels like it is going to slip out of my shaking hands. I'm so nervous, I can't seem to grip it. Sweat from the heat isn't helping. It was my 26th birthday a few days earlier but I'm like a kid on his first day at a new school. No, it's worse than that. Worse and a thousand times better at the same time. The Test team has changed significantly from the one I was 12th man for last summer. Warne, McGrath and Langer are all gone. Phil Jaques and Stu MacGill are in the side. Stuey already has 198 wickets so he's not exactly a new kid on the block.

Glenn McGrath presented me with my baggy green on the first morning. I can't remember a lot of what he said but I looked up to where my family were sitting with a big smile on my face. It was pretty cool, nice to do it in front of my home crowd with family there. Dave, Dylan and some mates from the Wanderers also showed up to lend support.

We made 551 in a day and a half. Jaques, Hussey and Clarke all got centuries. I had plenty of time to get ready for my first ball and now the time has come. I suck in as much air as I can, which isn't much, and remember that Pigeon had said that at the top of your mark you should know exactly what you are going to bowl. Jayasuriya is a left-hander, which makes it a bit more comfortable for me and I figure line and length will do: nothing fancy.

The ball wobbles out of my hand and lands roughly where it is supposed to. Unfortunately, it gets to the other end at about 133 km/h, which shows you how nervous I am. He tucks the second delivery away for three, but I am a bit freer and it comes out at about 145 km/h. By the middle of the over I have hit the 150 km/h mark, which is a good sign. I just try to keep the ball full, it is straightening a bit and my line has been alright considering I have a left- and right-hander (Marvan Atapattu) to deal with.

Brett Lee is in control at the other end and has Sanath Jayasuriya out in his second over and Michael Vandoort not long after that. Ricky replaces him with MacGill after five, but keeps me on for one more before giving Stu Clark a bowl. I walk back to the rope at the end of my spell with 6–1–11–0, which is a good start, although I want to get rid of that 0 in the last column. They take the light a little later and we have to wait until the next day.

I don't get my hands on the ball until Binga finishes his spell the following morning. The first delivery of my second over is a stinker, a full-toss wide of off and Samaraweera spanks it to the boundary. The next goes where it is supposed to. It catches the outside edge and flies safely into Adam Gilchrist's gloves.

TI Samaraweera c Gilchrist b Johnson 13

M Johnson 7.2–1–12–1

I had my first Test wicket and was surrounded by the boys rubbing my head, patting me on the back and carrying on like they do in these situations. Matthew Hayden and Andrew Symonds, my Queensland teammates, were the most enthusiastic. I managed to break away for a moment and gave my girlfriend, Jess, a wave up in the stands.

Atapattu hung around for 51, but I got him in my next spell with a short ball that he tried to pull but couldn't control and I had my second Test wicket. How much fun was this? We bowled them out for 211 just after tea and were in a strong position. Ricky asked us if we felt good enough to enforce the follow-on and we all agreed. I'd bowled 18 overs and finished with 2–49 and was pretty happy to have another crack. We finished them off early on day five to win by an innings. I got two more – including Mahela Jayawardene – in the second to finish the match with 4–96.

I figured early in my career that four wickets was a pass mark in Test cricket for a bowler. Three wasn't enough and anything more was a bonus. To be honest, I probably wasn't ready for Test cricket at that stage. I was better at the one-day game; I didn't have much confidence in the longer game. I doubted myself – I guess it was nerves. Still, once I got out there I gave it my all and I think I got away with it.

From there we moved to Hobart for the second Test and I picked up four wickets again without doing anything special. Brett Lee was man of the match in both games and man of the series, so he and Stuart Clark were picking up any slack the new boy left. My lack of experience hurt me a little in Hobart. I had never played there before and was surprised to find that the ground slopes down. I bowled from both ends at various times, but found that it really threw my rhythm out. Things didn't go too well for me after that and I lost my spot in the one-day team to Shaun Tait, which was really disappointing. I didn't see it coming, but when the Indians arrived in town to play a four-match Test series I was called back into the team for the first match at the MCG.

We won the toss and batted in front of 64,000 people. I got my first bat in Test cricket late in the day. We'd gone so well against Sri Lanka I was never needed. I was not out overnight and 15 not out when the innings finished, so I didn't yet have an average.

Nobody remembers much about that series apart from the controversy in Sydney and the whole 'Monkeygate' affair with Harbhajan Singh and Andrew Symonds. Apparently, it had started the year before when we were in India, but I wasn't really aware of it at the time. Talking to Ricky Ponting later, it was obvious that it occupied too much of his time, but I steered clear of it all. I wasn't involved in the hearings and I was the junior member of the team so I wasn't really kept in the loop. I was just aware that Ricky was in a lot of meetings and everyone was on edge about it.

The series was my introduction to the genuine grind of Test cricket. I'd had a taste of it in the Sheffield Shield, but bowling almost 40 overs in an innings to guys like Rahul Dravid and Sachin Tendulkar when they have their eye in is something else. I didn't manage to get Tendulkar with my bowling, but I ran him out with a direct hit in Adelaide where he won man of the match for his 153 in the first innings.

In Perth I hit a half-century as we chased runs without success. Michael Clarke was still in and it was a big deal for me to be out there with a real batsman, so I put my head down and batted carefully, but freed up a bit later on and took Anil Kumble down for three boundaries in one over and a six in the next. I had worked hard on my batting. When I first came to the academy, John Inverarity, who later became the chairman of the national selection panel, used to give us batting drills and he was impressed by the way I hit the ball. I was a natural stroke maker but I didn't have much skill. Rod Marsh used to get us to do work on the short ball where one of us would have to throw the new ball in short at full pace to the other. Some of us handled it better than others. Paul Rofe was hopeless as a batsman and got covered in bruises from my throwdowns. I learned pretty quickly to get in behind them and enjoyed taking on the bouncer. I figured it was an aggressive act and if I could be aggressive back that was a good statement. I would wait for the short ball early in my innings and take it on. If they overpitched I drove hard. If it was a good length I was done because I had no footwork, but not everybody worked this out. It was the way I played for the next decade.

During the stress-fracture years I worked on my batting in grade cricket and had made a few centuries in the lower grades. Making the half-century gave me further drive to be an effective batsman. I already had a really strong throwing arm and I knew if I could start making runs it would be really valuable for the team. Adam Gilchrist had changed a lot of things with the way he batted at No. 7 and I was hoping I could do the same at No. 8, although at this stage they were still batting Brett Lee ahead of me, so I was No. 9.

Adam called it quits during the Adelaide match. It was another significant moment after the big three – Warne, McGrath and Langer – had left the summer before. The old guard was leaving the scene and it felt special to be there when they left. Gilly and I played a fair few games together in ODIs and I valued his company. The summer before, in the lead-up to the Ashes, I had got a taste of just how good these guys were. Gilly batted with Justin Langer in a one-day domestic match against the Bulls and they just tore us apart. JL made a 28-ball half-century and Gilly seemed to take his cue from there. He made a century in 63 balls and was impossible to bowl to. There'd been some idea that he was vulnerable when bowlers came around the wicket, but he'd adjusted and was wearing a squash ball inside the glove on his bottom hand to change his grip. It was the first time he'd done it and it worked a treat.

A month or so after he took us down, he hit a Test century from 57 balls against England at the same ground. I had some sympathy for the English bowlers. Well, that's not really true, but I knew what they were going through. It was an honour to play in Gilly's last Test and a relief to know I wouldn't have to bowl to him again.

We won the series 2–1, but nobody seemed that impressed. We'd been 2–0 up when we took the game in Sydney. Pup got the last three wickets right at the end when it looked like they'd hang on. It was an amazing win, but it seemed certain parts of the media thought we hadn't deserved to win. When Harbhajan got suspended the whole situation became farcical. The Indians were threatening to go home at one point. They bounced back and won on a flat wicket in Perth and we drew the last match in Adelaide. People complained that we celebrated too hard when we won in Sydney, but I didn't see anyone complaining when their tour manager ran onto the ground waving an Indian flag at the end of this match. They were entitled to celebrate a good win and so were we.

I'd taken eight wickets at an average of 30 against Sri Lanka and 16 at an average of 33 against India. And I had a batting average of 56 – boosted by three not outs, that wasn't going to last. Most importantly, I'd played six Tests now and had 24 wickets at an average of 32.

We played nine one-day matches in February through to early March and by the end I was cooked. I started to get pretty loose and I needed a rest. It seemed like I had done enough in the summer to be kept in the side and was included on the tour of the West Indies that followed. Fortunately, there was a month between the last ODI and the first Test, which gave me a bit of a chance to recharge.

The home of some of the world's greatest fast bowlers is not exactly the greatest place for fast bowlers. Bowling is hard work in the Windies because there is no bounce. It was made even harder by the performance of Shivnarine Chanderpaul. He made a lot of runs in that series and was possibly the hardest batsman in the world to bowl to. Fortunately, I'd had a little bit of time batting to Simon Katich, who is similar and knew not to get too thrown off by the batsman moving across the stumps as you bowl. Shiv is just a great player and even when I got him to nick, the wickets were so slow that they rarely carried, so it could be pretty frustrating.

We won 2–0. I wasn't great in that series, but nobody seemed to mind. Playing in different conditions was all part of the learning curve. I stayed in the side for all five of the one-day matches as well, picking up my second one-day five-wicket haul in the last game.

Having done my apprenticeship in the Ashes the year before I felt comfortable around the boys. Some made you work for your place harder than others but it was for a good reason.

When we were in South Africa for the World T20s the year before (2007), I skipped an optional training session and was given a bit of a hard time by Damien Martyn. It seemed if you weren't playing you were expected to show up to these things, especially by the batsmen who wanted to work out in the nets. I took it personally at first and was pretty annoyed by his attitude, but realised after a while that this was how they set standards. Roy and Haydos were pretty demanding, but I had been well trained at Queensland by men like Jimmy Maher and Andy Bichel. I always thought of myself as a bit old school in my approach anyway and I realised that the old bulls need to teach the young bulls a few harsh lessons. Roy became like a big brother to me when we toured and Haydos was great. He would order feasts in his room and invite you in. He loved to talk deeply about the game and life in cricket. He was a bit of a thinker and one of the best prepared batsmen I ever saw.

We had a bit of a break and then moved on to India and had a really tough tour. Brett Lee had bowled magnificently in the lead-up, but was struggling; he had personal issues off the field and was not as fit as he could be. His pace was down and there seemed to be tensions between him and the captain. In the last game, things got controversial with over rates. I stayed out of all that stuff but could see this was not a happy tour. At one stage it looked like we could win the last game to tie the series but it slipped away and we lost 2–0.

It is a challenge bowling in India, but one that I always looked forward to in my career. You earn your wickets on those pitches and in that heat. It takes a lot of resolve to keep bowling quick and I set myself the task of doing that. We were really put to the sword when Gautam Gambhir and VVS Laxman both made double centuries in the first innings in Delhi, but if Test cricket was easy anyone could do it, I guess. I bowled 166 overs on that tour; it was more than any of the other seamers or spinners. This was maybe setting a precedent, but if it was I didn't mind. It showed that I was becoming an important part of the side. Brett's problems meant that the side was looking to me more often.

I made another momentous decision when we got back to Australia. I'd met Jess during the Shield season the summer before. I'd headed out with a few of the boys for a beer in Perth. I was with Shane Watson, Andy Bichel and Chris Hartley at the Leederville Pub where we ended up drinking with a few of the locals. I fell for one of them straight away but I didn't have the nerve to talk to her – she was too good-looking for me. A few drinks would have helped, but I was being disciplined now that I was a chance to make the Australian team. We eventually chatted for a few minutes and somehow I found the courage to ask her for her number.

The boys always used to joke that we were all going to move to Perth because the girls there were fit. Funny how life turns out. I rang her up later and asked her out for dinner at the team hotel. I was rooming with Martin Love and he saw us and said, 'You will be living with her in 12 months,' and I said, 'No chance.'

Nine months later, she was living with me in Brisbane. An accomplished sportswoman, she had come across with her dad to compete in a karate tournament soon after, and I went to Caboolture to watch. I thought it was fantastic. I really enjoyed watching her. Karate is a great sport. I invited her and her dad, Branco, out to dinner after that and I paid. Branco always says to me, 'That was the smartest thing you ever did.' After that we spoke every day on the phone and when I got the chance I flew over because I wanted to meet her mum, too.

One of us had to move. So she came over to Brisbane and moved in with me. We were pretty young and very happy, but it was a big sacrifice for her. Her family was on the other side of the continent and Branco had been her coach so she had given up a lot. In the West Indies I had started to think that maybe I would move across to Perth and live with her. I was starting to be away a lot so there wasn't much for her in Brissie alone.

Jess is an amazing athlete. Karate was her life. Before she moved to be with me in Brisbane, Jess was in her club for 21 years and taught six classes a week. She won 15 national titles, 18 Australian Open titles and 17 international medals. At the world titles, she won bronze but was very close to fighting for the gold. The girl she lost to went on to the finals and won; she said Jess was her strongest opponent in the tournament.

We went to New York after the Windies and I said to her that I thought we should move to Perth. She was really shocked. She had never pushed for it or anything. I told her I was going to go back and play for Queensland in the summer, but it would work out. I'd even done some research and I showed her some houses I was looking at. I don't think she was sure I was serious at first, but I was.

It was hard for me, too. I had my family in Queensland. When the Bulls heard there were all sorts of stories floating around, I assured them I was going to play for them and it was all okay. But then I realised it was all too hard. You can't be half pregnant as they say. So I had to leave the Bulls. The hardest thing was telling the guys. It was pretty emotional.

I had won a Shield at Queensland and that gave me a great bond with the group. That was the biggest thing I had achieved in cricket. Even today I look back at those men and think they were all better cricketers than me. They were giants of the game. Blokes like Andy Bichel were enormous. The way he did a little circle around the top of his mark, grunted and then ran in ... he had a huge career. Him, Kasper, Joey Dawes, Noffers ... they were guys I had always looked up to. They were the old hands and I felt like their little brother.

That said I was still a bit wary of the administration after they called me in and said it was a 'business' and they were cutting me from the contract list. It just never sat well with me. It still doesn't (I do tend to get stuck on things a bit). It wasn't a business. I loved those blokes and I was leaving because I loved Jess. If that's a business decision ...

It took me a while to settle with WA. Because I was away a lot, I didn't play many games and I didn't feel like I was a part of the group. Later, when I did a half pre-season with the guys – that helped. The set-up was really different; for me, Queensland was organised and in a good place, but it wasn't like that in the west. It was a bit laidback – it didn't feel focused. We used to get whipped at Queensland, but things were much more relaxed in the west. Things changed over the years, and when they appointed Justin Langer coach he made a real difference. It's a great set-up these days. Focused and disciplined.

New Zealand was waiting for us at the Gabba when we got home from India in November, and I was happy to be back on a pitch that gave me some assistance. I celebrated by picking up nine wickets for the game (4–30 and 5–39). I was awarded man of the match and was pretty pleased to start the home summer like that. I think every wicket I took in that match was from good length bowling. If you pitch it up in Brisbane, you give yourself the best chance. The short ball – or the threat of it – was what did the damage, though.

Everyone was pretty pumped by my performance. I now had 56 Test wickets at an average of 30.5. I wasn't there yet, but I was working my way into a good place. Five more wickets in Adelaide helped us wrap up the series 2–0 but the real test was going to be in the six Tests we had scheduled against South Africa – three at home, three away – to finish off the summer.

We were a team in transition by then and the Proteas were out to win their first series in this country. They achieved that, beating us in Perth and Melbourne. That frustrated us and our captain, who was rightly concerned with our inconsistency. I have to hold myself up for some blame here.

Ricky kept backing me, as he did right through my career, and I wanted repay his faith. I'd chatted to Dennis Lillee before the Test and he drilled into me that you have to make the batsmen play at the WACA otherwise they can let the ball go all day. We batted first and put on 375. I started okay when we bowled on the second day, getting Neil McKenzie early, but the South Africans dug in and started putting together some partnerships. I then picked up Graeme Smith with a full toss that he played on to his stumps. Coming into my 15th over they were 3–226 with AB de Villiers and Jacques Kallis well set, but the ball was reversing a bit.

I got AB with one that moved away and kissed the outside edge, was denied an lbw against JP Duminy two balls later, but then nicked Kallis off in the next over. I'd gone up a notch and the next chance I got I aimed a bouncer at Duminy, which he could only fend up into the air. Morné Morkel was next. I bounced him and then followed up with a slow ball and he lobbed up an easy catch. Then Paul Harris was caught at backward square. It was a crazy wicket but I took whatever came my way.

What can I say? Everything clicked. It was one of those spells where you can visualise the wicket and it happens. There aren't too many times that happens, but when it does you go with it. I'd taken 5–2 in 21 balls and finished the innings the next day with 8–61. The statisticians pointed out that it was the best haul ever by a left-armer. There aren't many of us, but I will take it. Eventually we set them 414 to win. It was a record chase and everyone figured we would win. They got the runs easily. I picked up McKenzie early, then Smith after he'd got a century and Kallis when they were 300, but they were four down when they chased down our total. It was a pretty disheartening experience to not win a game when you've taken 11 wickets.

I suppose I wasn't inconsistent in that game, but five days later in Melbourne I never really looked like troubling them and they won again. We came to Sydney weakened by injuries to Andrew Symonds and Brett Lee. Watto was also unavailable. Andrew McDonald and Doug Bollinger both came into the side to make their debuts. It turned out to be a great Test match. In fact, it was one I will never forget.

In Melbourne Dale Steyn had frustrated us by scoring 76 and I was determined to return the favour in Sydney, which I did by hitting 64 in the first innings. They had Steyn, Morkel and Makhaya Ntini bowling so I was pretty happy even if I was dropped on 18. I reckon bowlers deserve a break when batting because we have so many dropped when we are doing our job.

I got one to rise sharply on Graeme Smith in the first innings and he had to retire hurt with a bone broken in his hand when he was 30 not out and flying. It was a critical moment in the game. Cracks opened up in the wicket as the match went on, making it harder for the batsmen. On day five we had South Africa nine down with half an hour to go in the match and that should have been it. We only needed one more to win, but Smith decided he would come out and try to hold on for a draw despite not being able to use his bottom hand. It was an incredible effort and the crowd rose to applaud him to the middle. We were all tingling with excitement. We'd had a tight finish the year before at the SCG against India and another beckoned.

We'd bowled more than a hundred overs by that time and were all pretty exhausted. Ricky brought me back on for what

I thought was one last shot at it and I was aiming at a big crack outside his off stump, but not having much luck. I was taken off after a couple of overs so I could come from the other end. I remember people in the crowd yelling, 'Just hit his fucking wicket.' I was trying! With two overs to go I got one to pitch in the crack and jag back through Smith's defences. Nobody could have kept that one out.

We were over the moon. The win meant we kept them from stealing our No. 1 Test ranking and restored some dignity after we'd already lost the series. We didn't know it at the time but it was Matthew Hayden's last game for Australia. I had a bit of a session with him in the dressing room that night and we had front row seats for the famous fight between Michael Clarke and Simon Katich, which came out of nowhere and was ultimately a pretty disappointing thing to happen on Haydos's last night with the team.

I was sitting near Kat on the steps just inside the dressing room and I noticed Michael was urging Mike Hussey to sing the team song so he could get out. I think some of the others might have been going out with him. Everyone was in a good mood, but Kat didn't think that it was right to rush the song and told Huss to do it when he was ready. Words were exchanged and things escalated quickly. Michael didn't back down and the next thing you know Kat had him by the throat.

When it was broken up, Michael stormed off and I went to sit with Kat to make sure he was alright. He asked me if I thought he did the right thing, I said, 'Yeah, but maybe this wasn't the right place for it.' I had a lot of respect for Kat. He was a great cricketer and was always good to me.

The incident changed the mood of the evening. Andrew McDonald was playing his first Test with us and I remember Ricky Ponting apologised to him, but Macca said something along the lines of 'Don't worry, this happens after every match with the Vics.'

I suppose, in the interests of full disclosure, I should confess to being involved in a similar incident between myself and Shane Watson that never got out. Admittedly it happened before anyone had heard of us. It was around 2000 when we were all at the academy. Every night we'd pile into the common room and watch *Neighbours* before dinner. It was always a bit willing as every time there was an ad break there would be an all-in wrestle on the floor until the show started again. In one wrestle I was dragged through the door and into the bathroom by a heap of guys and somebody pushed my head into the toilet. I wasn't impressed and the red mist descended. Somehow I managed to break free and I grabbed whoever it was by the front of the shirt as I got up and someone grabbed mine. I raised my right fist and he did the same. Then we looked at each other.

It was Watto. I think we both looked at each other and thought: nah, I'm not going to hit him, he's my mate, and put our fists down at the same time. I can't say I wasn't angry. It took me a few days to get over it. We eventually started to talk to each other again and Watto remains one of my best mates in cricket.

Before we could get across for the rematch with South Africa we had to play a five-match one-day series against them and another one against the Kiwis. I got a break from two of the games, and was feeling ready to go when it came time to fly across the water to South Africa. We landed in Johannesburg and drove straight up to Potchefstroom, a university town that seems to be a bit of a sports centre, and played a pretty dull tour game there. Almost the entire team got a bad dose of food poisoning from the local caterers, which caused more than just a headache and was pretty funny on reflection. There weren't enough toilets in the dressing rooms and when we were fielding you would see blokes lining up at the gates to get off and get some relief. It was a pretty uncomfortable experience for a few and not very pleasant for all of us who had to share their rooms. Such are the indignities of life on the road.

There's absolutely nothing to do in Potch so we bought radio-controlled cars and raced them around the car park. That became a bit of a thing on subsequent tours and when we were there in 2014 we bought a model helicopter, but it got taken by a gust of wind and we lost it on the roof somewhere. We needed some distraction and had to make our own fun without wasting too much energy. Different fads emerge on different tours. As a group we have trivia nights and things like that; sometimes a few people will get into something like a Scrabble app on the phone, which Ben Hilfenhaus was a gun at. Not that he was smart or anything. I think his trick was to just punch in letters until it accepted a word. Quite a lot of the boys get into PlayStation and that stuff but I am not too keen on computer games.

Phil Hughes and Marcus North both made half-centuries in that game, which was enough for them to earn their baggy greens for the first Test at Johannesburg alongside another debutant, Ben Hilfenhaus. Hughesy got Haydos's place and Marcus came in as a batsman who could bowl a bit of spin. Brett Lee was injured, which meant we had no experienced bowlers. Hilf and Pete Siddle had exactly three Test match experiences between them. I was the senior man, having played 18 since making my debut 14 months earlier. When you consider all-rounder Andrew McDonald had only played one game it made us a pretty inexperienced unit. Having lost the previous series, nobody gave us any chance of pulling off a win on the South Africans' home turf. Mickey Arthur, South Africa's coach, and Graeme Smith had started talking about how they were going to build a dynasty that would rival that of the Australian team of some years earlier. The South Africans even arrived home to an enormous crowd at the airport after beating us.

Ricky won the toss and decided to bat in Johannesburg under heavy skies. It was the sort of conditions I wouldn't have minded bowling in, but he wanted to make a statement and chose to bat. It almost went wrong as we lost three quick wickets, including Hughesy, who made a fourth ball duck. The captain and Michael Clarke rebuilt the innings with a gutsy counterattack and we pushed on into the next day. When I came out to bat, Marcus North was in his 60s and we were close to 300. I could see he was pretty settled for a guy in his first Test and at some point I decided to stay there until he got his hundred. I was about 35 when he got there and it was pretty special to be around to celebrate it with him. It's not often you are up close when a mate does something like that.

Marcus and I put on 117 before he left me. Sidds came out and I figured it was time to get a move on. I was 53 when Paul Harris started the next over and 79 when he finished it. I hit him for two fours and three sixes and blocked one in the middle just for the hell of it. When they replaced the spinner with Dale Steyn I took him on and peeled off three fours from his over. I was 96 by then and so close to a hundred I could taste it. Sidds was facing Morkel and he must have felt the pressure. He nicked the third ball to slip. Fortunately, it was a no-ball and he survived. Unfortunately, the next ball was an exact replica (both were caught by Kallis) but without the overstepping.

I was four runs away from a hundred and I just needed to get on strike. We were nine down when Ben Hilfenhaus came out to face his first and only delivery. He made a golden duck and I was stranded four runs short of a maiden Test hundred. I can't say I wasn't disappointed but it was a confusing emotion as I was more than happy to have got 96 in a Test match. I liked making runs and I was keen to make more. Just so long as it involved a lot of boundaries. Running between wickets was not my thing.

Someone was going to pay for me missing out and it wasn't going to be anyone I shared a dressing room with. The sky was low when we started bowling with a session to go and the lights were on. Smith, whose hand had healed after the Sydney Test, had said before the match that they were ready for me this time. We were ready for him too because I'd been swinging the ball over there and that was something I hadn't been doing in Australia as much, so we figured there was an element of surprise.

He came on strike to the fourth ball of the first over. It swung away from him late and I saw his eyes grow wide as if to say, 'What the hell is happening here?' We knew he was flat-footed at the crease and we thought we could get him to nick off if it was pitched up and moving away. He aimed a cover drive at the second ball and nicked it through to Haddin just like we'd guessed he would. It's always nice when a plan comes off and even nicer to knock over the opposition captain early. If I was tired in the legs after batting three hours I wasn't feeling it. We had them three down at stumps for not many and worked hard the next day to have them all out for 220. I picked up 4–25 from 18.1 overs, which was a fair indication that they weren't willing to take me on.

We set them 454 to win and had to work a bit harder in the last innings to get the wickets, but we got home with 162 runs to spare. I'd picked up another four wickets and was awarded man of the match. The 'new' team was in a good place and so was I. I always enjoyed South Africa – the conditions were similar to home, the South Africans played hard, were competitive and we could go at each other without fear. We moved to the coastal town of Durban 1–0 up, knowing we had them on the back foot. Australia has never been beaten in a series over there and they have a habit of tightening up at home.

The game at Kingsmead (Durban) was incredible for a number of reasons. Hughesy got off to a bad start with the duck, in Johannesburg, but bounced back with a good 75 in the second innings. He was the youngest bloke in the squad, a bright-eyed country kid you couldn't help but like. He had a quiet charisma about him and a determination that we all recognised. He had already made more first-class hundreds than most blokes make in a lifetime. His whole family had come over from Macksville to watch him and they were wide-eyed at the whole thing. They ran a banana plantation over there and were really nice people.

In Durban their young fella went beserk; he hit a four to move into the 90s off Paul Harris and a few balls later banged him over long on for six to move to 99. It was a brave shot and we were all on our feet. Next ball he hit an even more audacious lofted drive into the crowd and we just went crazy. It was one of the great moments. His NSW captain, Simon Katich, was out there with him and they enjoyed the moment, then Kat got his own ton. Hughesy backed it up with a hard-grafted 160 in the second innings that proved the first was no fluke. Nobody who was there will ever forget that effort. A star was born in that game.

Durban is the strangest place to play cricket. One minute nothing is happening and the next thing the pitch becomes unplayable. They say it has something to do with the tides. I don't know what it is but I can tell you it happens. On the second day the tide must have changed because we went from 4–329 to all out for 352. I watched it change and have to admit I wasn't all that keen on having a bat. The ball was just flying around everywhere and I made a first ball duck.

Our tail had surrendered meekly, but we would see what South Africa's batsmen could do under the same circumstances as we got to bowl at them straight after lunch. Neil McKenzie opened with Smith, and I got the first one to swing back in to him, the second held its line a little and the third moved away – taking an edge with it. Hashim Amla walked out and walked back to the dressing room two balls later. I'd got one to come back into him that trapped him dead in front lbw.

Graeme Smith was on strike when I got the ball for my next over and I knew I had to nail him back in the crease. I banged one in short and it bounced off his gloves and he scurried off for a single. He always struggled to get out of the way of the one that followed him. It had hit him hard and after two balls at the non-striker's end he called for some treatment then reluctantly went off. We found out later I had broken a bone in the right hand this time. You don't want to hurt blokes, but at the same time it felt good to know that he could not handle my short-pitched bowling.

We were on a roll now and kept it up when Hilf got AB de Villiers in the sixth over. Things got worse for the South Africans when I came back on. I got one to bounce off Kallis's chin in my second spell and he had to be taken off for stitches. It was a nasty blow and there was blood all over the place. Mark Boucher came out to replace him, but I took out his off stump with a yorker and they were 4–62 with two blokes taken away for medical treatment. Bad light saved them some embarrassment, but we had them all out for 138 the next day – well shy of what was needed.

All the chaos of their innings put into perspective how good Hughesy's 160 was. He worked hard for it and thanks to him and Punter (81) we had them chasing 546 to win. Maybe the tide had changed again because the wicket settled down a bit and they were a bit harder to roll in the second dig. They hung on until halfway through the second session on the last day. Simon Katich was called on to bowl his chinamen. His three wickets cleaned up the tail.

We were 2–0 up in a three-Test series. We were supposed to be a team in transition; we had a lot of inexperienced blokes and South Africa were supposed to be establishing a dynasty, but we'd knocked them off. Ricky Ponting said it was one of the best wins he'd ever been involved with, and coming from him that was high praise indeed. Just a few years earlier he'd been captain of the side that beat England 5–0. The party in the hotel that night was one to remember. Mike Hussey comes out of himself after dark and he was hilarious. The match was on television in the bar and at one stage he was commentating his own innings. The South Africans showed up a bit later and joined in with us, but we'd quietened down a bit by then.

There was a fair break between games, which was good as we had moved to Cape Town and the girls had arrived. It's a great place to chill out, but some of the younger guys continued the celebration like the tour was over and eventually had to be pulled into line. The single boys were making a lot of noise and living it up. Jess wasn't too impressed when one of them took to banging on our door and pranking us. He was lucky he didn't cop the full force of her karate training, but I managed to restrain her. When the last Test started we batted first and not that well. By the time they'd had a go we were trailing by nearly 450 runs.

Marcus North was taken to hospital with food poisoning and Bryce McGain came in for his first match. He took a fearful punishment on what is a small but beautiful ground. His 18 overs cost 149 runs. I am not sure he had fully recovered from a shoulder operation that had kept him out for a while. I had to bowl 37 overs and I finished with 4–148, which was just plain hard work on a surface that didn't offer much. At least I got to have some fun when we batted the second time. I joined Andrew McDonald when we were 6–218. I got to 50 at a run a ball and had a bit of fun after that. I pulled Dale Steyn for a six then Paul Harris for one in the next over.

I got to 95 when Ronnie was out for 68 – we'd put on 163. Sidds came out and made a golden duck and suddenly we were eight down with Bryce McGain walking out to the middle. With only two wickets in hand I knew I had to get a move on. I'd been robbed of my hundred once before and wasn't going to let it happen again. He held out for two balls and now I was on strike. I decided to hit Steyn for six and get it over with before anything else could go wrong. I could only run the first ball to point. There was probably a single in it, but I was focused on my milestone and selfishly turned it down. Steyn dropped the next one short and I was waiting for it. Bang. Got it. High over midwicket. Six. Job done!

It's funny, but when I decided to go all out I started to wonder how I would celebrate. I wasn't getting ahead of myself or anything. I wasn't really sure what to do, then I remembered the batsmen always kiss the badge on their helmet so that's what I did. I waved the bat to the dressing room and sheepishly towards where Jess was sitting with the girls. We'd had an argument before I left for play that morning. It wasn't anything major, just the sort of squabble that can happen when you are tired and living in a hotel room. Being really mature I told her she was not allowed to come to the ground that day because she would irritate me when I had to concentrate. Jess being Jess took absolutely no notice and came. When I saw her after play she announced that she was going to make sure she annoyed me more often in the future.

Bryce was out two balls later, but only because I ran him out trying to run a second so I could keep the strike. I had a bit more fun hitting Steyn for another six and four later before Harris got Hilf and it was all over. This time I was stranded on 123 not out and the only mixed emotions were because we'd lost the Test by an innings and then some.

I won player of the series, which was amazing. I had played 21 matches and taken 94 wickets at an average of 28. I'd also topped the batting averages, thanks to the two big innings where I was undefeated, and the hype around me was something else. People were making all sorts of comparisons. There was more talk that I would be the new all-rounder; even Punter said it at the press conference while I was sitting next to him. I was happy to make runs but as I said earlier, they were dreaming.

This story in *The Australian* gives you an idea of how worked up the journos were:

'The search for Australia's all-rounder ended the moment Mitchell Johnson put his foot down the wicket and pulled Dale Steyn into the crowd to bring up the first century of his career. The Test match may have been a lost cause, but the bowler's exuberant form with bat and ball was enough to bring a smile to his captain's face. Australia has searched for decades in the hope of finding somebody who can really do damage with bat and ball. There had been Keith Miller and later Richie Benaud, but little since.

Now there was Johnson.'

Ricky was leading them on a bit and joked before the T20 match to the press that he was considering opening the batting with me. When they asked me, I said I was happy to keep batting at eight. Or nine. There wasn't time to dream about the future. We had a five-match one-day series and a T20 to play before we could even think about our next task.

No Better Feeling

Mitchell isn't the same man as the one I met in 2006. It seemed like something clicked once we were married. When you hear women say that, it's almost always a complaint, but I'm not complaining, as the man he has become is a more confident and content version of himself. I loved him straight away, but he had a lot to learn about himself and life. I suppose we all do.

We did some really hard yards. At times when we sat in a hotel room in some strange place it felt like the world was crashing down on us. At times when I sat in the stand and heard the booing and those awful, awful things crowds would sing and say, I wanted to scream. At other times, when we were going out for a quiet dinner and they were said again, I was ready to use the lessons I learned from years of karate training, but he would whisper to me to move on and it was probably a good thing I did.

I know that dealing with the constant criticism was at times really hard on him, but sometimes it's just as hard on families. It's awful to see the one you love being treated like that; it breaks your heart. You just want them to do well and when people are trying to tear them down it makes it that bit harder.

Fortunately, we came through it and it made us stronger individually and as a couple and when he retired at the end of 2015 I was so proud of what he had achieved.

There was no better feeling than seeing him lift himself up and achieve his full potential. To sit in the stands in South Africa in 2009 or the 2013–14 Ashes was the greatest feeling in the world at the time. Nobody apart from Mitch and me really knew what he went through to get there and nobody felt as proud as I did. He won the ICC Cricketer of the Year for both those years and that was great, but it was best the second time around. We weren't there when he won it for 2014 but we were when he won the AB Medal and I was so happy and so proud of him.

I wish the world knew the Mitch I know, but being in the public eye opens you up to judgement based on what others portray you as, not necessarily what you are.

We met at the Leederville Hotel in Perth when he was playing for Queensland in 2006. I was driving that night and he was playing cricket so neither of us had our beer goggles on. Something clicked and we exchanged numbers. We were in contact every day and caught up several times while he was in Perth. He went back to Brisbane and we started chatting on the phone and didn't stop talking. We still haven't …

Five months later, when I had a karate competition on the Sunshine Coast in Queensland, he came and watched me compete and I stayed an extra week so we could spend some time together. That was the start of our long-distance relationship. Dad was my coach, so he was with me and they met and hit it off. Then, a couple of months later Mitch flew over and met my mum.

It was a challenge dating from the other side of the country, but I had the world karate championships at the end of the year and so I had to concentrate on that. `

I had never watched cricket before I met Mitch, but we had sport in common and I think it has helped both of us. I understand the dedication it takes when you are competing at that level and the sacrifices you have to make. The hours and hours training and travelling were never an issue for me or him. We got it but it can be harder for somebody who doesn't know the discipline involved. From the outside it might seem selfish sometimes to put sport ahead of the ones you love, but I completely understand that. That's the part of the sacrifice that most people don't understand. The kids can be sick, or it's your best mate's birthday, maybe even yours, but they can't be your priority – unless of course it's something very serious.

When I trained for karate it came ahead of everything else and with Mitch it's cricket.

He's a great guy and an amazing athlete. There's not much he can't do – he is just one of those people who are talented at whatever they try. He has different sides: that aggressive persona you see on the field, while the soft side you see when he is playing with our kids or with friends is something he doesn't give away on the field. He has become a wonderful dad who would do anything for his family.

In the early days, he seemed to struggle in relationships and he never quite understood the dynamic I had with my family. The Bratiches are a close group and we spend a lot of time together and I was always at Mum and Dad's place, especially when he was away. He just didn't understand that. He had a different view on relationships from me. He told me: 'I never want to get married,' and I said, 'Well I don't do kids without marriage.' He wanted kids much earlier than I did and I wasn't going to commit to children unless he committed to marriage. It's always been my view that kids are a much bigger commitment than marriage.

In my life everyone around me had close families, they were all married with children, but I think he had a different experience and he had the perception that everyone who got married got divorced.

We got married in 2011 after being engaged for two years. It was a great weekend. We only invited really close friends and family. There was no one from cricket there, but these days we have some great friends from the game.

He's happier as a person inside himself now, so he is much easier and more enjoyable to be with. He didn't have that confidence when we first met. He was either really clingy or he'd push me away – he would always sabotage things. He thought if he kept people at an arm's length he wouldn't get hurt.

A family friend who has known him since he was a child said recently the day Mitch got married it was like he had a weight lifted off his shoulders. It wasn't so bad after all! It was a long road to get to that point, but once he did it was like he had flicked a switch.

It's funny, for all his resistance, he is such a homebody. Before he left to go on tour he would change. He just got tense and couldn't communicate. He would obsess about getting ready and it was almost like he was steeling himself to leave. Early on, we battled with that leaving and coming back. He didn't want to know me when he left or in the first weeks when he was away because he was getting his head into a cricket space and then just before he was ready to come home he would be on the phone all the time in this excited space, but by then I was in a different zone. I would be like yeah, yeah because I had finally got into a place where I was operating fine without him.

I think we'd just worked it all out before he retired. I am really happy to think about a life where he doesn't have an open suitcase in the corner of the room ready for the next trip. When you have kids, that coming and going gets harder. It started to become a challenge with our daughter, Rubika, when he left, as she began to understand he was going away and every time we'd Facetime she'd say, 'Daddy come home.' I think this started to get to him.

The strange thing about Mitch is that all the tough times have actually made him more confident. You would think it would be exactly the opposite, but that just goes to show you something about his quiet determination.

He is a completely different person from what he used to be. In life and in general. When we met he was indecisive, I would say, 'Do you want to go to dinner Friday night with some friends?' He would be like, 'I don't know, maybe.' Making a decision would be really hard for him, as was committing to it. They were little things to me. It was just dinner.

I think he was scared of the consequences. He didn't want to make the wrong decision, whereas I throw myself into things, some things probably a bit too quickly, and I don't care if I screw up.

As I said earlier, I did get cranky when he was abused by the Barmy Army and other crowds especially when I knew he was struggling personally. The English fans were really full-on; it was frustrating when we'd go out to dinner and they would start chanting in the streets. I always thought to myself, I wonder what it would be like if I turned up at their workplace and swore at them while they were trying to do their job?

Some fans seem to think they are entitled to say what they want whenever they want – I get that to some degree at the game but never away from it. I would never belittle a sportsman who had stuffed up. Mitch has copped some really nasty stuff, although I remember he told me once that a guy in New Zealand called him a 'wife beater'. He just smiled at him and said, 'You haven't met my wife, mate.'

The good times, however, made it all worthwhile. I am so proud of what he achieved in his career because of all the crap that he went through to get there. When he rang from South Africa in 2011 I could hear in his voice he was in a really bad place and I knew I had to get there to be with him, so I surprised him and turned up at his door. He was cooked and he wanted to quit. I talked him through it, but I knew at this point he was in a bad place. I was so proud of the way he batted in the last innings to help them win the match in Johannesburg; I knew what was going on in his head and so I knew better than anyone what a good effort that was.

He was copping a pounding from the press at that time and he needed to get away. I think he must have been the only sportsman in the world who can say an injury was a positive thing. He actually said to me, I hope I get injured. I had warned him that he needed to be careful about what he wished for! His toe injury became a blessing in disguise.

For a guy who was so reluctant to be married he has turned out to be a great husband and father. He knew more about my first pregnancy than I did. He was looking up articles and he downloaded a pregnancy app on his phone and would be telling me how much she had grown that week. He was all over it. It was nice.

It was an emotional day to be there in Perth when he finished playing. I waited on the sideline with Rubika and when he came over I think we all had a bit of a cry. I was happy for him and, the way he'd been feeling over the last year, I knew it was coming. I went to that game thinking this could be it even though he hadn't verbalised it to me yet. After he bowled his first spell I had a gut feeling that it just wasn't in his heart anymore. I messaged his best friend, Dylan, and said, 'I think he's done', and as soon as the game finished my phone rang straight away (which is unusual) and he said, 'I'm done.' I knew it was the right choice for him and he bowled well for the rest of the game because he'd made that decision. I think it was a relief for him.

I am really, really proud of what he has been able to achieve more so because of the hardships he's been able to overcome. It would have been easier for him to give up but he didn't, he put in a lot of hard work to get back on top. He was written off by many people but he proved his critics and himself wrong. It took a lot of heartache and hard work but to me what he has done is incredible.

Soon after that our son, Leo, was born. I think we've got some great days ahead.

Jessica Bratich Johnson
Designer

7

It All Goes Wrong

IT LOOKED LIKE I was hurtling towards a hundred wickets. I was the leader of the pack, one of the fastest bowlers in the world, a man not to be messed with and I was feeling really good about myself, but it turns out I was heading for a brick wall. Or a cliff. Whatever it was, it wasn't good. Something came loose, a wheel began to wobble and my cricket became a slow motion train crash.

Things started going wrong when we arrived in England in 2009. From there it was a long, drawn-out decline. There were false dawns, games or innings where things clicked, the odd good series, but poor performances were never far away. Unfortunately, they started to become more regular than the good ones.

My decline lasted until something snapped in my foot in South Africa in late 2011, but I think something snapped in my mind first. By then I was a shell. I had lost confidence and form. To be honest, I just didn't want to play the game anymore. I longed not to be on a cricket field. The thought of standing at the top of my mark filled me with dread. It would have been a relief to be dropped. I fantasised about being injured and not having to do it anymore.

Some years after the Ashes 2009 series I was talking to a journalist who admitted he'd written an article to celebrate my hundredth wicket. It was all about how quickly I'd got there and how I was now one of the best fast bowlers in the world. I had it all in front of me, he said. He'd written it before we left for England so it would be ready to print the moment I got my hundredth wicket. I got it in the second Test at Lord's by trapping Alastair Cook in front. It was the perfect scenario, but they never ran the story because in a couple of games I had gone from being a hero to, well I don't know, but it wasn't good. People could smell that something wasn't right. By the time that milestone came around the journos were writing very different stories about me. They started to wonder if what had come before might have been a fluke. Maybe I was like a Tiger Woods who raced towards the record number of major wins only to falter and never win another.

In the lead-up to the Ashes I became the go-to guy, especially after those efforts against South Africa, but things tripped me up. After Glenn McGrath retired, Brett Lee became the leader of the pack, then he started to have problems. His marriage broke down, he lost fitness and the grind of bowling more overs than anyone else in cricket started to tell. He got injured and slowly all the attention turned to me. It went well in the two series against South Africa. Everybody was raving about me as the next best thing. I was not only the great hope as a bowler, I was a batsman too. It turned out that these achievements were built on a flimsy foundation.

It was another turning point in my career. When I had lost my state contract as a younger player I learned how hard I had to work physically to get myself out on the field, week in and week out. That wasn't my problem this time; in fact, the opposite was true. My fitness became my enemy. I never broke down, but I was still to some degree relying on my natural talent and didn't have any strong foundations to fall back on when things went wrong. I just bowled. I didn't know how it worked so I didn't know what to go back to when it didn't work. If I didn't try to swing the ball it would swing, when I tried to it didn't. There were lots of little mysteries. To make matters worse I was given nowhere to hide. I kept getting picked even though I was unravelling. Not that all of it was about technique.

None of this was on the cards when we arrived for the 2009 Ashes. We were a good enough team and we were there to make up for what had happened in 2005 when England had ambushed a great team. There was no McGrath or Warne or Gilchrist or Langer this time. Brett Lee was in the squad, but it seemed like they were hanging all their hopes on me, Ben Hilfenhaus and Peter Siddle. Stu Clark was in the squad but had fallen out of favour. He only played two of the Tests. The side was on a high after the away win against South Africa, but we were not settled and were soon found out.

There are times when you do a job and don't get wickets and the stats don't tell the story. The stats from the 2009 Ashes show I took 20 wickets at 32. They are not great figures, but they are not bad. As I said before, I think four wickets a game is a respectable return. The stats don't, however, tell the story of how bad it was. Things started to go wrong when we travelled to Cardiff for the first Test. I had no idea how much media scrutiny and crowd pressure you are under in an Ashes series. Their guys say the same thing about a tour of Australia, but some of the stuff that went on was insane. I got a taste of how big the series was for them when we first arrived and were sent to do interviews in a room where different journos waited for you at tables and you just went around answering questions.

That was pretty intense, but there was worse to come and it started back in Australia. Having raised me on her own, Mum was having trouble with the fact I had left Queensland to be with Jess in Perth. She was naïve about the media and said something in an interview. They made a big story about a rift between us. It became huge news and a bit of an issue at team level. The worst of it was that the story was out the day before the first Test. Cricket Australia likes to manage these things and there were meetings between the coach, the media person, Ricky Ponting, the team psychologist and a host of other people trying to work out how to deal with it.

I was really taken aback and just didn't know what to do. I didn't need something like this on the eve of the biggest series of my life and my head was scrambled by it. I am a private person. I don't seek publicity and I didn't seek publicity about this. I was very protective of my mum. She had raised us single-handedly when she was young. It had never been easy and I appreciated that. I had never dealt with anything as public as this before. I hated seeing my private life played out in the press. Unfortunately, Jess and I had signed a 12-month deal with a women's magazine when we got engaged and I think I was obliged to give them some quotes in reply, which only served to keep the matter burning.

That was a learning curve for us and we learned not to enter into those arrangements again. I didn't really want our relationship to be played out where everyone has opinions about you. Earlier, Jess had done the cover of a men's magazine in a bikini. I didn't mind that at all. She wasn't earning any money from her sport and this raised her profile and was a way of covering some of the costs of competing. She's fit and beautiful and should be on the cover of magazines anyway. I remember Branco saying he couldn't understand what all the fuss was about since the bikini was invented in the 1950s. I denied the rumours at the time, but there is no doubt the whole thing affected the way I played in the series. I just didn't know how to cope and the English media and fans were ruthless. They latched on to any weakness they could find and ran with it. If all of that stuff about the engagement and Mum happened late in my career, I think I would have been fine with it, but I didn't know what to do then and I was totally shocked by it. I am still pretty private now that I am older and wiser, but I have social media accounts and I stir a bit of trouble now and then, but I keep it well away from my home life.

Things got out of hand during the warm-up for the Test and what happened probably indicates where my head was at. Kevin Pietersen is a guy who likes to stir things up and I can appreciate that. He knows how to get under people's skin and when we were bowling in the morning he played a few pull shots in our direction. It wasn't exactly harmless because we could easily have stood on a ball in our run-ups. I threw a ball back to where he was and I suggested he stop it. Of course, he didn't. When he hit another one towards me I kicked it as far as I could in the other direction.

Words were exchanged and KP crossed the line in what he said. He got really personal and I'm not going to dignify his comments by repeating them. The red mist descended and I stormed in his direction with every intention in the world of hitting him. This was all being played out in full view of spectators who had arrived early and the media. Stu Clark saw it all happen and came rushing over just as we came together and jumped between us. KP is a big guy, but I was very worked up. Fortunately, Stu is bigger than both of us because it took a bit to convince me not to go through with what I planned.

I am so glad Stu was there. A few years later there was a minor scuffle between Davey Warner and Joe Root in a bar at Birmingham and that had serious ramifications. I can tell you that this wouldn't have been a minor scuffle. I have rarely had a fight in my life, but when I have had a chance to pull the gloves on I've loved it. During the boot camp ahead of the 2006–07 Ashes series we had to get in the ring with a professional cage fighter. He was a scary bloke and I landed a couple of good hits.

Hardly anyone else touched him. If KP and I had gone toe to toe, life might have taken another strange twist.

I was pretty disappointed with what he said and it stayed in the back of my mind after that. We had conversations off the field and he seemed okay, but I wouldn't say he was the sort of bloke I would ring up or send a text congratulating him on his career. There are limits to what you can say. I am sure everyone knows the line. You can't bring family or stuff like that into it and I am sure he knew he had gone too far, but he did it on purpose because he wanted to get me going.

We should have won that first Test. Cardiff is a damp place, you don't get much bounce or carry, but you do get a lot of swing. I would trade the latter for the former every time. Despite the lack of bounce I managed to get Andrew Strauss to take evasive action and glove a short ball that ballooned to the slips cordon. I even got Ravi Bopara with a slower ball that deceived him into playing on the up. I got a ball to go through Stuart Broad and finished with 3–86. It looked good on paper but didn't tell the story. I got wickets early but struggled for control later and the batsmen realised they could cash in. I only lasted two overs with the second new ball, which was a warning bell. I was struggling to concentrate on the job at hand. There were further signs things were going wrong early in the second innings. The second ball I bowled to Strauss stuck in my hand and almost hit me in the foot. It was a shocker and a hint that I was maybe overthinking things. It showed how uptight I was. Wayward was a word that was bandied about a lot. I know that I almost missed the pitch with one delivery.

The crowd sensed I was struggling and locked in on it. If I strayed wide they delighted in it and seemed to get louder every time I bowled a bad ball. We arrived on the fifth day with victory in our grasp. England was 2–20 and still 219 behind. They'd made 435 in the first innings but we had countered with 674 thanks to centuries from Simon Katich, Ricky Ponting, Marcus North and Brad Haddin.

I had knocked over Alastair Cook late on the fourth day to set us up for a win. There'd been a bit of time lost to rain on the third and fourth days, but if you can't get eight wickets in a day … We started well and had them in real trouble at 5–70 and when I got Andrew Flintoff after lunch they were 6–127, but Paul Collingwood dug himself in and started a series of small but valuable partnerships with the tail.

We took the new ball with about 20 overs to go in the day and they were 7–200-odd. I should have accounted for the lower order but I just couldn't get the job done. If the atmosphere was tense, the tension was broken every time I bowled a bad ball. England were eight down with an hour to go and nine down when we finally got Collingwood with a little over half an hour to go, but Stuart Broad and Monty Panesar held us out. We just couldn't get the breakthrough. I don't know if we had arrived overconfident, but we believed we should have won that game and that became part of our problem.

I felt like something was wrong with my technique, but I didn't know anything about my technique really so I didn't know what to do. I became a little obsessed by my action and you don't want to be thinking about how to bowl when you are trying to win a Test match for your country. Cardiff was an omen for me and the team, but even if I did sense what was coming, the side still felt like it was in a good place.

Jess was there and we were trying to keep a grip on things, but one story led to another (thanks to the magazine deal) and it wasn't a good time on or off the field. The Barmy Army had a sniff by now and they weren't going to let go. They love a song and at Lord's I gave them plenty to sing about. An Ashes match at the home of cricket is never going to be just another game. Everybody wants to do well here; to get your name on the honour board at this place is a big deal. I needed to do well because everybody was relying on me, but there was so much going on. The journos who were firing up their 'Johnson gets his hundredth wicket' pieces were ready to go because I was on 99 after Cardiff. Everyone had seen what I could do before this and it was just a matter of finding that groove again. But, to be honest, I wasn't feeling right.

The distance between 99 and a hundred proved greater than anyone thought. It wasn't that it took a long time so much as the time it took proved that what had happened in Cardiff wasn't an aberration. Suddenly, I wasn't the bowler everyone thought I was.

Lord's was a debacle. It sounds like an excuse and it is, but I could not get my head around how to bowl on that slope. For Pigeon it was a gift; for me it was a nightmare. One line sent the ball too wide and allowed the batsman to score freely behind square; the other line was too straight and I was taken for a ride off the pads. If there was a happy medium I could not find it.

The pitch was, as the English say, a pudding. I was bowling at over 144 km/h early in the innings and the ball was barely carrying through to the keeper, but that was not the problem. You know that song: 'He bowls to the left, he bowls to the right.' That was a perfect description of how I bowled that day. I don't think I have ever had less control and the more I tried to gain it the more it eluded me. My first ball to Alastair Cook was struck wide of slips for four and it set the tone. A couple of overs later I strayed short and wide to Andrew Strauss and he punched me square for a boundary. When I straightened up, he clipped me off the pads for four more. He did the same two overs running and Punter had to take me off. A captain can't set a field for someone who is bowling both sides of the wicket.

When I came back on later nothing had improved. The batsmen were just carving me up, picking off a boundary or two every over. I was dying out there. As my bowling got worse the crowd got louder. They jeered and they mocked me, and I can't blame them. I remember going wide on the crease at one point to try and spear one in, only to fling it so wide down leg that it went for five wides. The noise was something else and there was no escape.

Instead of relying on what I knew, I started to run through checklists that I hadn't really bothered too much with before. I started to think about my front arm and then my release point and then my wrist position. Sure I had done work on my technique before, but not like this and not in the middle of a match. I was fiddling with things I really didn't know anything about, wondering if this was the problem or that was it.

I didn't know what I was doing mentally. I was thinking about everything but what I was doing. I didn't have any processes to fall back on. It was all jumbled, nothing was clear. Later I learned little cues that worked for me and, if things weren't going the way I wanted, I could go back to them and get on track again. I just didn't know what I was doing with my bowling and I was still trying to find what wasn't working.

In my third or fourth spell one kept low to Cook and trapped him in front. It was my hundredth wicket, but there wasn't much to celebrate, England was 1–196 in the 48th over and we were already chasing the Test like a fielder chasing a ball down the slope. I was going at almost seven runs per over.

I had taken the same time as Warnie and McGrath had to get to the hundred-wicket milestone. Dennis Lillee had done it in 22 Tests. I was in good company. One interesting thing was pointed out to me later. My 23-Test career had spanned one year and 250 days. Only Graeme Swann had got to a hundred in that short a period. Dennis took nearly five years, McGrath took over three years and Warnie a bit more than two. That shows how much cricket we were playing at the time and how little time I had before finding myself the senior bowler in the team. If Brett Lee was playing I would have deferred to him, but despite his protestations that he was fit and ready to go they wouldn't pick him.

The thing with being a bowler is that there is nowhere to hide. A batsman who is in atrocious form soon finds himself in the dressing room, a bowler finds himself down on the boundary at third man or fine leg. There's not even the relative comfort of fielding close to the bat. And down there you are at the mercy of the crowd. They were ruthless and they had picked up on the stories about my mother, which were all over the tabloids in England. The Barmy Army started to sing a song about it. I understand that you cop it as a sportsman from opposition crowds, even from your own, but I thought bringing my mum and Jess into it was crossing a line. I still think that. You can't stop people, but you wish people had a bit more decency. Criticise my bowling, my haircut, whatever you want, but leave my family out of it.

Unfortunately, now they had two songs and they were not going to let it go because they could see it was getting to me. I got so down that I believed them when they told me I was shit. It got to the point that Ricky Ponting saw I was suffering so much in the outfield that he kept me up close to the wicket to spare me being abused on the fence. When the agony ended I had 3–132 from 21.4 overs, which meant they had scored more than six runs an over off me. That sort of economy rate is just unacceptable. Then we were rolled for 215 and I was bowling again. No place to hide. The second innings was no better than the first. I didn't get a wicket but at least I tidied up and was only going for four runs an over when they declared. I managed to score a half-century in the second innings, but it was no consolation and not enough to get us over the line. We lost by more than a hundred runs and were 1–0 down in the series.

England knew they had their foot on my throat and they weren't going to let me up. When I batted, the close fielders sang the Barmy Army songs. I found out later that Matt Prior had texted the leader of the Army and told them to keep at me because they could see it had got under my skin. He was right. The songs had got into my head. Even though I hated them, I found myself singing them. It was almost like I was taunting myself.

And then there were the problems with my bowling. I was working with the coaches and doing what I could between matches, but I never felt right at the crease and the ball never felt right coming out of my hand. I wanted to hide in my room at night but I couldn't, which was probably a good thing. Jess was travelling with me and she forced me to get out; she also worked hard to keep me positive about things, but even when we went out for a meal or a coffee we would cop it in the streets from fans. I didn't like it, but it made her really angry and she would have a go at people. You don't want to mess with my wife. Jess is confident, protective and a trained martial artist. She is not a person to back down.

I did a lot of work with Ross Chapman, our team psychologist, trying to learn ways to block these things out and get on with it, but I just kept hearing those songs. On the field. Out in the streets. And as I lay in bed in various hotel rooms and wrestled with nagging doubts.

I was at a really low ebb after Lord's. I was sure they would drop me for the third Test but they didn't, and that probably didn't do me any favours. I guess I was glad they didn't because they showed faith in me and that made me feel a little better. Ricky didn't trust me to open the bowling, though, and I didn't blame him. If I thought the crowd was loud at Lord's I was fooling myself. In Birmingham they are all over you and they had plenty to work with even if I didn't bowl as badly in the one innings where we fielded. The match was rain affected and we could not get a result.

We all got back in the groove at Headingley and managed a convincing win; I even got a five-wicket haul in the second innings, but England sealed the series at the Oval and that was that.

You can accept being beaten if you know you have done your best, but that was not the case here. I had been anything but my best. The expectation had got to me. It had built up over time. I'd always been a bit nervous about Dennis crowning me as the next big thing in cricket, and, while he had apparently been proved right in those early days, my doubts were now justified. The voices in my head were doing a victory lap and I felt terrible for letting everybody down.

There was, however, no time to lick wounds or fix what had gone wrong. The one-day series immediately after the Ashes finished on 20 September and six days later we were playing the West Indies in the opening match of the Champions Trophy in Johannesburg. In Johannesburg, I was announced as the winner of the Sir Garfield Sobers trophy for the ICC Cricketer of the Year 2009. It was quite an honour but I didn't feel like the best cricketer in the world. I said the right things at the ceremony – it was crazy to be among some of those names in world cricket and it meant a lot to me. I had no idea I was getting it and was seriously shocked when I did. The way I had been performing I thought I was no chance and when they read out my name I was like a deer in the headlights. I have the trophy somewhere; it drives my mates mad when they find that stuff lying around somewhere in our house. One day, I might get it all sorted out, but trophies still don't mean much to me, which isn't to say I don't respect the award. When I accepted the prize I thanked everyone and put in a special thanks to Jess for being there through the hard times.

This was a time when the cricket just never seemed to finish. We'd played the summer in Australia, then gone to South Africa for the Test and ODI series, had a brief break, then headed to England for the ICC World T20 and then gone straight into the Ashes series and now we were back in South Africa again. I was shot.

At one point early on the tour of South Africa, the coaches asked Ross, our psych, to go and talk to me because I couldn't work out my run-up at training. I just looked at him and said something like I don't care about run-ups or cricket, I just want to go home. I was emotionally and physically cooked from seven months on the road. He was so worried he went to management and told them they had to give me a break. We were going to get a couple of weeks back in Australia after the Champions Trophy but there was barely time to catch your breath before we were expected back in India for another one-day series. It was like trying to walk up a descending escalator.

Ross told them I should be excused, but I heard talk at the time that they wouldn't do it because there were tensions with host countries when key players were rested. I understood that. I couldn't leave anyway because I didn't want to let the team down.

Somebody did the sums for 2009 and found that we were not at home for something like 300 days that year. Even when we were in Australia we were rarely home. A week or so after coming back from the series in India we were back in camp as there were only three weeks before the first Test of the next summer.

And so it rolled on. I hit 74 not out in the first match of the Champions Trophy but took four wickets from five matches in the tournament. Getting myself up for ten overs at a time wasn't too much of an ask, but my bowling just didn't feel right. We won the tournament, though, and that was the most important thing. I then played five of the six ODIs in India, rushing from Vadodara to Nagpur, to Mohali to Hyderabad to Guwahati to Mohali and then the airport for a flight home.

A problem with all this endless cricket is that you lose strength. I needed time in the gym to build up my legs and my core strength, but there was never an opportunity when the schedule was so relentless. I felt like everything was building up, personally and professionally, and I needed to know how to deal with what I was copping on the field. I sought out a psychologist when we got home; I just wanted some direction and we spoke a lot about being able to communicate. I just bottled stuff up and talking was good for me both on the field and off. I was pretty nervous about doing it, but I knew I needed some help. I eventually learned how to switch on and switch off. The drama with my mum in the media was part of the reason I sought help, but I think I also wanted to see what I was like as a person as well. I wanted to make sure I was okay, that there was nothing wrong with me.

Back at home we played the Windies, we won the three-Test series and nothing much happened except for a big clash between me, Brad Haddin and Sulieman Benn, which saw me and Hadds fined and him suspended. I was only trying to stop the fight, but I guess I was just in the wrong place at the wrong time. It caused quite a stir that business, and when Watto got himself into trouble in the same match it looked really bad. Anil Kumble chirped up with allegations that Australians always got off these things, but that wasn't what it felt like to us. We were judged to the same standards and if someone else got a harsher penalty I reckon it was because they deserved one. Chris Gayle said it was my fault. Thanks, Chris!

The best part of playing the West Indies was that my old housemate from Brisbane Brendan Nash had gone over there and worked his way into their Test side. It was pretty odd to be bowling to him and I had a bit of a laugh, but I went at him pretty hard, just as he knew I would.

Around this time, Brett Lee, Peter Siddle, Ben Hilfenhaus and Stuart Clark – the other four bowlers during the Ashes – were all injured, which meant I was the senior bowler and carrying a fairly heavy workload. It was amazing how far I had come. A few years earlier I could barely play two games in a row; now, I seemed to be the only bloke holding up. Then Pakistan showed up and we played a three-Test series against them, which we won. Then the West Indies showed up and we played three Tests against them and won again. The Tests finished and we played a triangular one-day tournament against Pakistan and the Windies.

By now I was a first-change bowler and just getting by. My rhythm wasn't great, nor was my confidence. I kept getting picked, which says I was doing enough, but it wasn't very satisfying. I was given a couple of the early games off, which was nice, but not enough time to do anything apart from slump in a chair at home with the suitcase lying by the door ready to go again.

While the Ashes were not good, 2009 was on the whole a productive year. There was an article in the paper that pointed out I had become the first Australian to take 50 wickets and make 500 runs in a calendar year. In fact, I had 63 wickets at an average of 27 from 13 Tests. I wasn't counting, but someone else always is!

As soon as we finished the last one-day match against the Windies we flew to New Zealand in March for two T20s, five ODIs and two Tests. I played all but one of the T20s. The five ODIs were squeezed into an 11-day period, which was just nuts.

I only took two wickets in the first Test at Wellington, which was memorable because it was the windiest game of cricket I have ever been involved in. At one point the heavy roller started to get blown across the ground. When the ground staff tried to put down the covers, the wind caught them and one of the guys was picked up in the air and blown all the way to the boundary while hanging on for his life. Somebody said a spectator was blown over standing on a grass bank.

The other memorable thing about that match was Phil Hughes's batting. We only needed 106 to win in the second innings and he nearly got a century opening with Simon Katich.

He finished on 86 not out from 75 balls, while Kat was 18 from ten fewer deliveries. Hughesy only got a game because Watto was injured and he batted with absolute abandon.

The light-plane ride out of Wellington to Hamilton was horrific. It was so windy they had tied the wings down on the tarmac. The take-off was like a rollercoaster ride. Some of our staff refused to board and took a car instead. It was a smart move. We entertained ourselves by watching Nathan Hauritz go from pale to white to green before losing his stomach repeatedly – and that was about two minutes into the flight.

We were pretty happy to get to Hamilton and I got ten wickets for the match, which wasn't a bad way to end the summer. We had played eight Tests between late November and March. I bowled 298 overs and took 41 wickets at about 26, but it wasn't quite enough to get the taste of failure in England out of my mouth. In the 18 months I had played 25 Test matches in five different countries, bowled 991 overs and taken 121 wickets at 26.67. It didn't end there. There were 40 ODI matches in five countries, where I bowled 343 overs, and took 63 wickets at 28.04, not to mention the eight T20 Internationals in four countries where I bowled 26 overs and took nine wickets at 18.52.

There were a couple of tour matches, too, but who's counting.

One thousand three hundred and sixty-odd six-ball overs is a fair bit of work and my body was feeling it. I had various niggles but no real injuries to speak of. You never play free of pain, but there was nothing to keep the doctors or physios occupied. I couldn't complain about the aches, because I knew what it was like to be unable to bowl through injury and I was watching a lot of others around me break down or push on through. Niggles are something you live with. If you don't like hurt you are never going to be a fast bowler because it hurts.

Fortunately, I wasn't playing IPL at this stage for the very reason that I needed to look after myself and so I had a short break after New Zealand, but the tours kept rolling on. We played the ICC World T20 in the West Indies in May and then against Pakistan in two T20s and two Tests in England mid-year. The visit to Lord's didn't go well again. I only got one wicket, but at least we won that match. I got two wickets at Headingley but Pakistan won that game. England was becoming a bit of a bogey place for me. I just couldn't work out how to bowl at Lord's and it was nagging at me a bit. You want to prove yourself everywhere. I can accept that I was never going to be outstanding on the subcontinent, but I was proud of my efforts. I know the English conditions didn't suit me, but at this point I couldn't say I was proud of my efforts. It made me cringe a little.

Young Mohammad Amir bowled out of his skin, but it wasn't long after this that he got tied up with bookmakers and found himself in jail. I'd been really impressed with him. He obviously had a huge future in the game. It was so unfortunate what happened to him. I am not condoning it, but Australian cricketers can't conceive of the sort of stresses he might have been placed under by people older and wiser than him. I have sympathy for him. He was under pressure from his captain. He did the wrong thing, but I think he was dragged down by the senior players. It is good to see him pick up from where he left off. He has that relaxed, almost easy, action, but it generates a lot of pace and a late swing. I remember he bowled me first ball at Lord's. I tried to go legside, which was where the ball was tracking, but it swung and took out my off stump. I was way out of my depth against a delivery like that.

After England, it was India (again) for a couple of Tests in October, although I was excused from the ODIs. We missed winning the first match in Mohali by one wicket. I had taken five in the first innings and was proud of that effort on a track that gave me nothing, but could not get a breakthrough in the second. It was enormously frustrating, especially as we lost the second match in Bangalore.

Even though I took the new ball with Hilfenhaus in Bangalore I wasn't really trusted with it anymore and I have to say, despite the psychological advice, I had become really sensitive after the 2009 Ashes. If I had a bad game it would get to me, I would start obsessing about it. For six months I lost the love of playing. There were times I just didn't want to be out there. I got to the point where I started hoping something would happen so I wouldn't have to play.

A bad seed had been planted; I became quite harsh on myself if I didn't play the way I wanted to. I had always been a hard marker, but it got out of hand. If I bowled a loose ball I would crack the shits and you could see it – my body language wasn't great. I noticed that and others did, too. I couldn't shake the feeling that I was letting the team down and letting myself down. I took it too far. I was fine if I had a good game – that was great and I would have no worries – but most of the time I was struggling and looking for answers. To some degree things had changed; I had come into the game without expectations but now I was weighed down by them. I started to notice it with articles about me becoming the leader of the pack. I was reading what was written and that was a mistake. I wasn't used to getting so much attention.

It was on my mind a lot. At first I wasn't looking for it but it was hard to ignore. There were stories about me everywhere. They started off all being pretty positive, but slowly and surely they changed their tone. My bad performances became big news. Sometimes the journalists just didn't get it; they are often driven by stats, so if you get wickets you've bowled well; if you don't you are bowling badly. I always bowled for the team; there were times when the journos didn't know what was going on in the game. I might have been asked to bowl a different way, to dry the scoring up or to bowl short and keep the batsmen on the back foot, but they didn't know that and would say I bowled too short or something. Don't get me wrong, there were times when I bowled absolute shit and I would hold my hand up. But when I was bowling for the team and nobody knew it, that really frustrated me. It shouldn't have, but that was the way I was getting. I eventually learned a lot from it, though. It was a good lesson for cricket and life.

When England came down for the return Ashes bout in 2010–11, I was feeling okay. I'd scored a century and taken five wickets against Victoria in the second round of the Shield and was looking forward to playing against them on my home turf, but I didn't take a wicket in the first Test at Brisbane. Peter English, a Brisbane journalist who had seen a lot of me, wrote this about my performance for Cricinfo:

> 'Johnson is the attack's front man who can't lead. He has no wickets for the game while giving away 131 runs in 33 overs. The lack of faith in Johnson's bowling, and himself in his action, even seems to be seeping slowly into Ricky Ponting's mind.
>
> 'After Jonathan Trott cut him over gully, Johnson kicked the ground in frustration. In his next over it was Cook's cut for three that sent Johnson's hands to his hips before his right hand rested on his forehead like the first tingles of a migraine. When Trott drove through cover Johnson waved his arm away and turned around without a mutter.
>
> 'Every bowler loses their way, but at the moment Johnson doesn't even know how to return to solid ground.'

The match finished in a draw and the selectors faced a problem. They hadn't picked Doug Bollinger for Brisbane because they thought he needed another round of Shield to prove his fitness and had sent him off to do that in Perth, but the penny had finally dropped that I was struggling. They dropped me and pulled Doug out of the Shield game and told him to get to Adelaide and take my spot. I suppose they expected him to get fit on the plane.

I am not making an excuse, but there is a bit of a ridge at the Gabba and when you land, your back leg is lower than the front leg and rather than pushing through the crease you are breaking. It was really getting to me on this day. By that stage my action was really going and the ridge made it worse. I was dropping on that back leg and had no momentum. So I had to adjust further. Looking back at any video from that match makes me cringe. My leg was collapsing and my arm was low. I was given a program of remedial work with Troy Cooley and Stu Karppinen in the nets at Adelaide during the second Test, which we lost by a long way. While the boys were out in the middle we were out the back just trying to get my momentum going down the wicket and not out towards square. I then flew to Perth early to do a few sessions with Dennis Lillee. You can't change a lot in such a short period, but we got back to the basics and Dennis got me feeling a bit more confident. I also managed to get a little bit of strength work done.

I resolved to be more relaxed with it and was feeling alright. I accepted that I had to miss out, I understood why, but I was getting really annoyed by what people were writing and that fired me up. You know how they say cricket is a funny game? Well, it is. My action was exactly the same in Perth, but I swung the ball and had a blinder. I batted well in the first innings. When I came in we were 6–137 and struggling, but the bounce was true and I was seeing the ball well. My 62 runs helped us get to 268, which wasn't a lot, but it was better than where we had been.

I am not exactly the only person in an Australian dressing room who has had a run-in with Jimmy Anderson, but I have to say that he came out on top in one embarrassing exchange I had with him when we were batting. It's all Ryan Harris's fault and I still haven't forgiven him for putting me on the spot like he did. Jimmy was not having a good time of it when I was batting and I could see he was getting really frustrated as we got out of the hole we'd been in. He just couldn't get a wicket and was going for a few runs. When he was at the top of his mark I was at the non-striker's end and he started mouthing off. I said to him: 'Why are you chirping now, mate, not getting wickets?' Unbeknown to me it was all heard on stump mike. Of course he ran in and bowled Ryno with the next ball, turned to me and raised his finger to his lips to tell me to shut up. He had me to rights. Thanks a lot, Ryan Harris!

I didn't get the new ball, but when I did get my hands on it there was a fair bit of shape back into the batsman and a bit of bounce in the pitch. I bowled okay in the few overs we had at them before stumps on day one.

When I started again on the second morning, everything clicked. First, Cook was out caught by Hussey in the gully. In the next over Trott and Pietersen were both on their way lbw, my old mate KP for a three-ball duck. Then Collingwood was also gone trapped in front. I'd taken 4–7 in five overs and felt fantastic. I finished the innings with 6–38 and backed up with 3–44 and we won easily.

Punter was pumped after the match. 'Mitch's spell was probably one of the all-time great Ashes spells,' he said. 'Him coming into the game under a bit of pressure as well, it was an amazing achievement and set up this victory and the series for us. The spell has transformed him and transformed how they think about him in the English dressing room. Some of the deliveries he bowled will have them seriously thinking about how they play him. I heard rumours coming into the game that they had Mitch's type of bowling worked out – I am not sure they think that now. You don't end up with the record he has by fluke, you have to have a lot of skill and commitment.'

I was feeling pretty good and wanted to take that feeling with me to Melbourne for the next match, but in truth we had papered over the cracks and I'd had a good match, nothing more. Nothing fundamental had changed. Truth was, the stars had lined up. The Fremantle Doctor had done most of the work for me, blowing at the right times and allowing me to swing the ball more than usual. I had not bowled at full pace, but I had bowled better than I had previously and had had a good game. But I knew it was going to be hard to repeat.

I decided to be confident about what had happened and resolved to try and regain a bit of the speed that I had slowly lost over the past 18 months. We batted appallingly on Boxing Day and were all out for 98. By tea England was 0–157 and that was about it for the game. My transformation had been short-lived.

England's batsmen destroyed us in Sydney and there wasn't a lot I could do about it. I bowled 36 overs and took 4–168 as they compiled 644 runs. I had never conceded so many runs in an innings and never would again, but then again I rarely bowled that many overs in an innings either. Fortunately, they didn't need to bat again. We'd lost the Ashes and the team was in a bad place. There were calls for reviews and all sorts of hysteria around our performance from the media, former players and the public. Australians don't like losing and they especially don't like losing to England. I couldn't argue, because I didn't like it either, but we didn't have time to stop. There was the home one-day series and then off to India, Bangladesh and Pakistan for the 2011 World Cup. I started well, picking up 4–19 against Zimbabwe and 4–33 against New Zealand but dropped off after that. I didn't get a wicket in the game against Kenya and I didn't get one in the semifinal against India, which was our last game. That was a pretty flat feeling and I have to admit the whole tour is somewhat of a blur.

Glenn McGrath had come and spoken to me at one stage and said I was being too hard on myself. He said that you bowl the best ball you can and if it goes for four so be it, just go back and try to bowl the best ball you can again. I tried to do that in Bangladesh. It was good advice. Admittedly it was easier said than done, but it was something I worked on.

We were playing so much cricket in this phase and I was bowling a lot. I read somewhere that I bowled the most overs, more than the spinner even. My body was wearing down like my mind, but maybe at a slower rate, which wasn't ideal. I'd had enough of cricket. I just wanted to go home and be away from the game. I kept waiting for them to drop me but it didn't happen. Every time they named a squad I was part of it, every time they named a team the same.

Later in the year, we played three Tests and a one-day series in Sri Lanka. Nathan Lyon and Trent Copeland made their debuts in the first match. Lyno got a wicket with his first ball thanks to a great catch by Pup at slip. It was Michael's first match since he officially took over the captaincy from Ricky. I struggled through the series. I had quite a dry spell on wickets that are never fast-bowler friendly. They weren't all bad performances, but I wasn't getting by and just not going great.

Then it was on to South Africa in November 2011 for one of our – and my – more erratic performances. The one-day series went alright and I even had a bit of fun. In Durban, we had a local policeman looking after us; he was a good guy and well known. One night we hit the town and he was driving us home when we got hungry so we pulled up at the local burger joint to get some takeaways. Everyone was in pretty high spirits and Davey Warner noticed a motorbike waiting behind us with two people on it. He asked this policeman if he could borrow his badge and jumped out of the car to front them. It was totally crazy and could have gone really wrong. Over there, you can get shot for looking sideways; everyone has a gun. Davey demanded to see their licences and flashed them his badge. They were confused for a while about this Australian passing himself off as a copper, but fortunately they thought it was funny and laughed instead of getting angry. Davey was a bit wilder in those days than he is now.

The first Test in Cape Town will never be forgotten by anyone who saw it. We were 188 ahead on the first innings thanks to a good innings by Michael Clarke, and Watto and

Ryan Harris picking up nine wickets between them. Then everything came tumbling down. We were bowled out for 47 in what was the most dramatic batting collapse I have ever witnessed. It was the most incredible day of cricket. At the start of play we were eight down; when stumps were called they had lost one wicket. You might think that three wickets had fallen, but in fact 23 had. And I hadn't taken one of them. It was the seventh time in the past 17 innings where I had failed to get a wicket. Those collapses are just crazy; first of all, you are stunned that a few wickets fall, then shocked that it keeps going and then you realise you are going to have to bat soon. It's a slow-motion car crash. Everything is happening slowly and quickly at the same time. The dressing room is a strange place when it happens. People are all trying to keep out of each other's way. You don't want to go near a batsman who has just got out – they need space – and as wickets are falling quickly, the guys who haven't batted are running around getting their gear on. It's hardly a good environment.

By the time we got to Johannesburg I was sure they were going to drop me. At this stage I was reading whatever was written about me. Wallowing in it. I was withdrawing from the team, too. I didn't want to speak to anybody; I spent a lot of time in my room with the headphones on listening to music and surfing the net to see what the journos and experts were saying.

I developed a hatred of the people who were writing the stories. I would give them filthy looks when I saw them. Everyone knew I wasn't happy. I didn't understand what it was all about, why it was being written that way. I was too sensitive to any criticism. I actually liked a lot of the journos, to be honest. When I saw them around the hotel they were always friendly, but at this time it annoyed me more because I would think they were hypocrites, smiling to me in person but knifing me in the papers.

When I first came into the team the senior players had relationships with certain journalists and there was a trust there, but by 2011 I had the feeling things had changed. It was a weird period. Maybe it was the changeover of people in the team and maybe among the journalists.

I didn't have the communication skills at the time. If I'd had the confidence I could have talked to them and maybe understood why things were said the way they were. When I came back I talked to them a lot more and that made a big difference. I felt like I had a relationship with a few. They explained to me that they don't necessarily like writing negative stuff about players, but if you are failing what else are they going to do? I would read it and think they hated me, and I responded in kind. One of them told me how much he didn't like seeing me in the state I was in, that he could see I was struggling and had lost my smile. That was interesting. I didn't think they cared. I don't hold any grudges anymore, but I did then.

On other tours I would go out and have fun with the boys, but by this stage I just wanted to be alone. It wasn't good for me – I just couldn't face my teammates. I felt like I was letting them down and didn't have the confidence to be around them. I suppose I was depressed, but I am sure it wasn't clinical or anything. I was just in a dark place, which can happen on the road. In my mind I wasn't doing the job for the team and that was certainly what was being written. I know the boys wouldn't have felt that way and that they would have wanted to help. Looking back, I know I should have socialised more; it would have made things easier. It may not have changed the way I was bowling, but you never know.

All the cricket writers wanted me to be dropped, former players were lining up to have a crack at me, but maybe the worst of it was a poll they ran in the *Courier Mail*, the daily newspaper out of Brisbane in the state where I had grown up.

Q: Should Mitchell Johnson be dropped for the second Test?
Yes: 83%

'Yes, he's a loose cannon, too inconsistent. Bring on young blood.' – *Bluedog, Alton Downs*

'Yes. Johnson knows he's out of form and should put his hand up for his mates.' – *Marty, Annerley*

'Yes. Most overrated player by a long way. Someone buy him a bag of marbles!' – *Jeff, Victoria Point*

'Yes, he should be for sure. It's time for the young guys to step up.' – *Skip, Woodridge*

'Mitchell Johnson is too inconsistent.' – *Tom, Ferny Hills*

'Yes, he has been bowling fruit.' – *Dilt, Mansfield*

'Yes. He's been dropped before.' – *Patricia, Gaythorne*

The cricket writers said I was 'underwhelming'. They said I didn't know where the ball was going. That I had to be dropped. Had to be. One who had known me since I was a teenager wrote: 'Johnson is more of a follower than a leader. He does not even take the new ball anymore,' and said that my career looked like it was finished.

In later years I tried to do other things in hotel rooms. I started an online business course and I dabbled in a bit of photography, just something to occupy myself, but I found it hard to concentrate on anything else when I was playing cricket.

When Jess was on tour it was good; we had found a really good place with our relationship by this stage. Jess understood what was going on and what I needed to do because she has competed at the top level, too. She's always been fantastic. There'd be times when I felt I had to go to the gym on a day off and I would apologise, but she would say, 'Don't be silly, the reason we are here is for you to play cricket so do what you have to do.' We've got a great relationship, it's been hard at times with being away from each other so long, but we have been able to go through a lot together and she has been really understanding.

Jess is mentally strong and that is why she got to be one of the world's best at karate. She was extremely good physically, but psychologically she would have it over them, too. You can see that in her everyday life; she handles things so well. I have watched her compete and her focus is incredible. When she was younger she fought with the orthodox stance, which was her dominant side, but opponents started to work her out and mid-career she changed to southpaw and caught everybody else out. She is really switched-on like that.

She used to take my focus off the cricket when I got back to the hotel. If I needed to talk about it, it was good to have her there because then I didn't bottle it up, but she wasn't there in South Africa and that's exactly what was happening. I could talk to the team psychologists and they helped a lot, but there's some things that you can only share with your partner. Hotel rooms are very lonely places at times.

I was stewing on everything and reaching that point where I was going to explode. If somebody had advised me to bowl with the other arm around now I would have done it. I started walking around with my head down because I didn't want to catch anyone's eye. I had no confidence. I felt like everyone was judging me. My shoulders were slumped all the time and I was playing my cricket that way, too. I was consumed by my own thoughts and troubles.

I was asleep the morning before the match in our hotel at Sandton in Johannesburg when I heard someone trying to get in my room. It was about 4 am. I was freaked out. You don't mess around in South Africa, especially not in Jo'burg. Crime there is pretty serious. It was our security guy Frankie and he had Jess with him. She'd woken him up so she could sneak in and surprise me, but he'd had a problem with the key. It was a relief to know I wasn't about to be murdered and more so to see Jess. I had no idea she was coming. We'd been talking on the phone and she'd sensed how bad things were getting and just jumped on a plane. I'd told her I didn't want to play anymore. She said later she could hear I was cooked. I told her I wanted to get injured so it could all stop and she said, 'Be careful what you wish for ...'

My bloody body was proving more resilient than my mind, but it too was going. My core and legs actually felt weak and I wasn't able to hold my body up in the delivery stride. I could feel that and knew the only way to fix it was to get a good spell in the gym. I was losing weight, too. I was down to about 90 kg, whereas my best playing weight is about 94 kg. The game was dragging me down, draining me. I felt like I couldn't play my best cricket. I couldn't even remember what that was.

If I learned anything, it is if you are in that position you have to talk to your teammates. I see it with Mitch Marsh at times – he just wants to do the best he can and do the job for the team, but occasionally you can see that he feels he is letting the team down. If you communicate that with people and talk about it you realise you aren't. Everyone is trying to do their job, everyone is trying to win out there and nobody is being blamed when you lose. It's a team effort in the end.

I just didn't want to go out and bowl in the second Test at Jo'burg and it showed. After the first innings someone suggested I shorten my run-up and I said, 'Yep, whatever's going to work.' I had practised a lot off a short run so it was no big deal. I'd thought about doing it many times before because I thought it would help me get through more overs as my run-up really was long. It's embarrassing now to think I did that in the middle of a Test match, but I was embarrassed by the way I was bowling anyway. I had definitely cracked. I think I was worse in England possibly, but this was body and mind. I'd become a proper sling bowler; I had no front arm, I was dropping on my back leg. The other problem was my mind. I had no concentration when I was running in to bowl. I didn't know what I was doing or what I wanted to do with that delivery; I was just trying to get through.

We batted last in the game and needed 310 to win. History said it was going to be hard. It was only a week or so earlier we'd made 47 in our second innings, but Ricky Ponting and Usman Khawaja batted really well in testing conditions and built a good foundation for us. When the clouds lifted batting became a lot easier. After Mike Hussey got out I came in at 6–215 and joined Brad Haddin. We both had a bit to prove, too, I guess. Hadds had copped a caning for his shot selection in Cape Town and was smarting. Me? I don't know, maybe I was smouldering with resentment about my predicament. We are both aggressive batsmen and were going to play our shots, but I was in no hurry.

It was about the third over after tea when I took off for what should have been two runs and felt this sharp pain in my foot. It felt like a spike had gone through it. I couldn't get back for the second and just ripped my boot off expecting to see that one of the spikes had come through and pierced the skin. I was surprised there was no blood, but it started to swell up. Our physiotherapist Alex Kountouris came out and gave me a tablet. I couldn't put any weight on the foot, but there was no way I was going off. A switch had flicked in my mind and I thought, 'Fuck this, we are going to win this.' I was only on seven at the time and we still needed another 90-odd runs. I guess I was in a dark place and was looking for a fight. The pain was a good distraction from the crap going on in my head. I had to concentrate hard just to get to the other end when we ran a single. It hurt like hell and it was hard to keep balance. The problem was I couldn't run properly; I had to run on the side of my foot, which wasn't good. I was half expecting to roll my ankle as well and it was surprising I didn't.

When I got to about 14, I played a wild swing at Morné Morkel and I lost hold of the bat. It wasn't a good look. A few words were said, but he shut up when I hit the next ball for four. Then Pup sent a message out with Alex at the end of the over, which went something like: 'If you are not going to fucking bat properly, get off.' I sent one back saying, 'I am going to win this fucking game.' By now my anger and pain had made me absolutely determined. Maybe Pup knew that would be the effect when he sent the message.

Hadds was out when we were about 23 runs short of victory, Sidds didn't last long, and it started to get really tense.

Then, 18-year-old Pat Cummins, playing his first Test match, came out to join me. He'd picked up six wickets in the second innings and was thinking this Test cricket caper was pretty easy. Nathan Lyon was our last man in. He's nervous at the best of times but he was almost sick with nerves by then.

They kept showing shots of him on the video screen with his head in his hands, which was pretty funny. The other amusing thing was that Pat had hurt his leg and he was limping, too. We were a pathetic sight and no chance of a quick single. In fact, we were turning twos into ones.

When we needed four to win, Imran Tahir went up for a big lbw appeal, which was referred under the Decision Review System (DRS). It was bloody close. Pat was too young to get nervous. He handled it all well and two balls later he hit a four to win the match. We were pumped to win. It was huge and it was fantastic to be out there with the bat when it happened. Pat was 13 not out and I was 40 not out and we limped towards the boundary knowing we'd done something really special. Little did we both know that we were not going to be playing cricket for some time. Frankly, I couldn't have cared less, but my young mate would be out for years due to the fast bowler's curse – back stress fractures – and that was cruel.

I went for scans that night and they found a bit of metal in my foot, but they couldn't find anything else, so they put me in a moonboot and we went home. The metal in my foot was a total mystery. It must have been there from the Townsville days. There was plenty to think about on the plane. When we got home I heard talk that certain people in cricket didn't want me in the team again. The media had written me off, too. I wasn't sure how I felt about that. Part of me agreed. But part of me wanted to show them how wrong they were.

A Natural Athlete

I first met Mitchell around ten years ago. I was working with a few cricketers including Ricky Ponting, Michael di Venuto and Andy Bichel at the time and running a property consultancy business. Andy suggested that I come down one day to watch Queensland play because there was a young quick he wanted me to think about taking care of. He knew there are a lot of managers out there who are in it only to take the percentage of deals, but elite sportsmen often need more than that.

Andy thought Mitchell had all the potential in the world. When we met we hit it off straight away. He was a humble, shy and respectful kid who had come down from the bush and was obviously a little unworldly, but he had this gleam in his eye. He was also one of the most natural young athletes I had seen. This was well before he played for Australia, in the summer when he won his state contract back.

The athleticism I saw that day was obvious and I think a lot of people don't realise just how strong and fit he is. He played cricket at the top level for a decade and never once missed a match with a soft tissue injury. It is an incredible achievement.

I was there for his first Test at the Gabba and his last at the WACA. I have been there for games in many parts of the world. We have developed a relationship where we talk regularly. He needed someone to protect his interests and that's what I did, but other times he just needed someone to talk to.

Like everybody I have loved watching Mitchell bowl and like everybody I think the series that gave me the most pleasure was the 2013–14 Ashes. I knew better than most how low he got before that both physically and mentally and I knew how hard he had worked to get back. His resilience, determination and class made it all the more thrilling for me.

I will cherish seeing him lead his country to that Ashes win. We were all a little surprised by how well he did. Funnily enough, I had been telling journalists who wrote him off that they hadn't seen the last of him and they hadn't seen the best of him. At least two of them rang me later and acknowledged that I had been right.

I knew what an athlete he was, I knew how determined he was, I knew he would do well, but I didn't expect him to be the ICC Cricketer of the Year – again. Only three Australians have won that award. Ricky Ponting won it twice, Mitchell won it twice and Michael Clarke won it once.

People still don't understand his real achievements. There are only 13 players in the history of the game who have taken 300 wickets and scored 2000 runs. Mitchell was the 12th and Chris Broad is the 13th.

I might be a bit close to this, but the other thing that sticks in my mind is the number of catches dropped off his bowling. I think it was because the ball would come at awkward angles and so fast that it was often too hot for fielders. There are no statistics on that, but I would love to see them if there were.

Mitchell was thrilling to watch. The way he could get players jumping with the delivery that reared off the back of a length. I called it the Smith ball. It just reared up at you and jammed into the gloves of players who were trying to protect themselves. Unfortunately, it broke a few bones but it was quite a spectacle to see people jumping around like they did. He was faster than his 150 km/h because of the way that ball came up at you out of nowhere. It reminded me of Jeff Thomson. Adam Gilchrist told me in 2007 that nobody had ever hit his gloves as hard as Mitch did.

Obviously there were sponsors more than keen on getting involved with us, but from the start we had some really clear guidelines: we would never have anything to do with hard alcohol or fast food. Mitch was always about health and wellbeing. He was so keen on his own fitness it seemed like the right thing to do.

We knocked back some very considerable offers outside his Cricket Australia agreements where he had contractual obligations. That philosophy has paid off now because he has great relationships with Powerade and Swisse Vitamins who are good brands and good partners. His relationship with Blackwoods has been enduring and he has agreements with Spartan and Fox Sports.

Mitchell obviously had a bad time in England in 2009. It was like a whirlwind at that stage; he was playing so much cricket and playing it so well that he ended up ICC Cricketer of the Year, but he hadn't had a break for a while and things just caught up with him. It was a hard tour for him; he was a bit lonely, things went wrong with the business surrounding his mother and it made him anxious. It was a difficult situation. He doesn't wish ill on anybody and he is a very gentle man who only wanted to play cricket for his country.

They made him first-change bowler after a few bad games and I think that confused him about his role. That caused self-doubt: at that stage he wasn't as confident as he is today. He was new to the game. They fixed that up in the 2013–14 series.

He remains an unassuming and gentle bloke to this day. Everybody who meets him through me is blown away by this. They assume he will be arrogant or bristling with confidence, but he is just an easygoing man.

What we all love about Mitch is that he is a really, really good young bloke who happens to be a really, really good cricketer and not the other way around.

Sam Halvorsen
Manager

*Playing for Mumbai Indians, Group B Champions
League T20, Wanderers Stadium, Johannesburg,
20 October 2012.*

8

Limbo

THEY DID FURTHER SCANS when we got back to Australia in late November and I'd done quite a job on my big toe. There was ligament torn off the bone and fractures on top of that. I was on crutches for two weeks, but I stayed in the moonboot for over a month. For most of that time I had no interest in doing anything. Jess had said be careful what you wish for but she was wrong. It was a blessing in disguise to have that injury. My injured toe gave me space and time to restore my mental and physical strength. It would have been interesting to see how I would have coped if I wasn't incapable of playing. I would have been dropped from the Test team, but then I would have gone back to Shield cricket and the summer was already starting so it would just be more of the same. More cricket. More half-good performances at best.

Madness is doing the same thing over and over and expecting a different result, isn't that what they say? I made my debut in Brisbane in 2007 and played 47 of a possible 48 Test matches before breaking down. The only one I had missed was the Ashes game in Adelaide when I was dropped.

I went to Melbourne for the operation. They saw a large bone spur in my other ankle and wanted to get onto that, too, but our physiotherapist Alex Kountouris told them not to go messing around. The bone spur wasn't hurting me, so he didn't want to take any risks. As I was being wheeled in for the operation somebody said, 'Good to have you back again, Ryan.' They thought I was Ryan Harris. The old man must have been a regular customer.

In that month after surgery I had no interest in cricket. I think I said to Jess I didn't want to play anymore but I didn't really mean it. I just didn't think about cricket and slowly the fire in the belly came back. I had a good chat with Jess and worked out that I wasn't finished, that I didn't want to have any regrets because I felt like I hadn't given my best yet. I was 30 and still felt I was young enough. It was a bit similar to the conversation I'd had with my dad and a few others when I lost my contract with Queensland. I definitely would have regretted it if I'd walked away then and would have if I'd done the same this time. I hadn't found that place where I could play my best cricket consistently. I thought that if I could take a deep breath and start again I might get there. There was something unfulfilled in me and that was a good sign.

I had been playing cricket for four years at the top level

without a break and my body started to crave some action. Towards the end of the month I started to get the itch and began swimming even though I was still in the moonboot. Later, when I retired, I took seven weeks off and my body said what's going on here, so I had to go back to training. It's like an addiction.

I'd got my head back together a bit, too. It was a learning experience. When I had a bad game later in my career I knew not to be alone. It was a trap that was too easy to fall into. I don't regret what happened or anything; it was a life experience and I was able to learn from it, but it was tough. I learned how to handle the media better after that, too. I didn't obsess over their coverage and if I did read a bad article I understood that it was only the way somebody else saw it from where they sat. I became confident enough about what I did and what I needed to do.

I was mentally refreshed but I needed to do heaps of rehab on the toe; there was a lot of scar tissue and I had to do constant stretching and physio. It had really stiffened up. It is strange, your big toe is just there at the end of your foot and you don't notice it until something goes wrong. But once it does, you realise how much it is involved. It was quite painful at times. It hurt to walk. It really hurt to do anything like a push-up or a lunge and it continued to hurt a lot for about 12 months after the operation. I had to strap it up a certain way when I did any activity and I strapped it for the rest of my career. It still gets stiff now, but it's only a toe and if I complain nobody is going to give me much sympathy. I have a bit more respect for my big toe now. Even if nobody else does.

The cricket rolled on without me. New Zealand came over and upset things by winning in Hobart. The team was unsettled at the time after retirements and some strange decisions like cutting Simon Katich from the contract list. They dropped Phillip Hughes and Usman Khawaja after that game. Davey Warner made a hundred and started to show the world that he was a Test cricketer. It was an interesting time. Michael Clarke batted out of his skin in the series against India that followed and then they were off to the West Indies and I wasn't on the plane for the first time in years.

You can become a former cricketer pretty quickly if you aren't careful.

You don't have much contact with others when you are out of the team. It is just the way it is. When you are in it you are so focused on what you are doing. You live in a bubble and you don't even realise it until you are outside it. It's not a bad thing; to some degree as a professional sportsman you have to be almost obsessive about the task at hand. I was happy with that arrangement for the moment, but obviously I'd stayed in touch with good mates like Sidds, Ryno, Hadds and Watto.

I've mentioned there was talk that some people didn't want me back in the team after South Africa. I could understand it, but that only motivated me further to prove they were wrong. I knew I had to come back stronger, fitter and more determined than ever before. I had always been one of the fittest blokes in the squad, but I wanted to take it up another notch.

But I was also learning that sometimes it is just as important to let your hair down. Jess and I had a joint 30th birthday at our house, an '80s dress-up party. I did the moonwalk in my moonboot. I really enjoyed that, seeing all our friends and relaxing. I had to go to a Scorchers game the next day. I was contracted to them for the 2011–12 Big Bash League season, but I was injured and never got to play a game. In this case, it was lucky I didn't have to play because I was pretty hungover.

I did some work with Rob Naish, who was our physio at WA at the time. He is a running coach so that worked out well. Cricket Australia sent Stu Karppinen over to make sure I was on track. To be honest, I was never too keen on the programs they set me. I get bored doing repetitive stuff and so I tend to do things my way a bit. The older I got the more confident I got to do what I thought was right and not what they thought. That's not being arrogant or disrespectful, I just knew my body and I knew what would keep me interested. And fit. If they gave me a set number of balls to bowl in a week I would accept that and not go silly. Sometimes I did a bit more, sometimes I did a bit less. They understood that I ran my own race because they knew I always turned up in good shape for the next tour. Nobody had bowled as much as I had without breaking down, so I was obviously doing something right – at least up until the bit where I broke down, but even then it was while I was batting.

Around this time Cricket Australia introduced this wellbeing app on our phones, which we were supposed to fill in every day. It was stuff like how you slept and what work you'd done and how you felt. I was never good at my homework – that story is coming – and I was never good at filling that thing in. I've always been that way. Sometimes I'd get a call saying I had fallen behind and would resolve to make a better effort. I was doing the work. I just wasn't filling in all the boxes.

I knew if I was going to come back I had to be absolutely bulletproof physically and mentally. I made an enormous leap with my fitness and rehab in that period where I'd lost my Queensland contract because I knew I needed to do that to get back and give myself a chance of playing Test cricket. I was one of the fittest cricketers in the period that followed but it hadn't been enough to stop me wearing down, so I resolved to be even fitter.

I started working at the Mill Gym, which is run by an ex-SAS officer and staffed by a lot of ex-SAS guys who are the instructors or trainers. It started life at the Swanbourne army base, but moved to a building near the Matilda Bay Brewery in North Fremantle, which is where I joined. It is a pretty intense place with an intense approach, which suits me. They are really strict about who they will take on; most of their clients are SAS or hoping to be accepted into it and there are also a lot of serious athletes there. There are no mirrors, no televisions and none of the carry-on you get at a normal gym. Their philosophy is pretty simple and it was just what I needed considering where I was mentally and physically. Their web site sums it up this way: 'Psyche and performance potential is intrinsically reliant on your mental conditioning. To train the mind is to train the body. Fortitude and an indomitable spirit are paramount for success.' Did I say it was intense?

To be honest with you, I got nervous driving there. I knew I was going to be absolutely smashed, but I loved it. I am really hard on myself when I train. Sometimes I can be gasping for air at the end of a session but not satisfied because I think I might have been able to give a little bit more. I am not one for throwing up when training, which a lot of people do when they really push themselves, but I came close there every time. Still, most days I felt really good about myself at the end of a session. Mostly I did work by myself and I was doing four sessions a week.

Dennis insisted I get fit before I went back into the nets and I did what I was told. When I started cricket training again I had to cut down to three visits a week. If I did a net session and a Mill session on the same day I would be absolutely cooked. As I got closer to touring again I was down to two sessions a week. It was great, I felt strong and fit and when I had to go back to the squad I was really confident. Training on your own is a lot harder but it made me really enjoy training with the team because as a group we really push each other. I have to admit I have always preferred doing weights to aerobic stuff. I actually got up to about 100 kg from all the strength work at The Mill then had to run about 6 kg off because that's too heavy to be bowling at my best.

I made some new mates around this time and they had a significant impact on me and my cricket. I met Ben Roberts Smith and Mark Donaldson at a one-day game in Brisbane. Ben had been awarded the Victoria Cross and Medal for Gallantry in Afghanistan for acts of bravery that defy the imagination. In the battle he was decorated for, Ben had drawn fire so that his mates could take out one of three enemy machine guns, and then he'd taken out the other two. He says you have to use the power of fear, that it can bring out the best in people, especially when they don't want to let their mates down. Mark got his Victoria Cross in Afghanistan when he crossed open ground in a firefight to save an interpreter who was wounded. We went out to the pub after the game. Brett Lee was with us, too. It was a funny night. Some guy started mouthing off at me as soon as I got there. Ben is one of the biggest men I have ever seen and I am not small, but this guy didn't seem to care, he was really having a go, claiming he was a Jujitsu expert or something.

I just said, 'Yeah, whatever, mate, I hope you have a good night' and kept walking. Ben said, 'Does that happen all the time?' I said, 'Yeah, pretty much every time we go out,' and he said he couldn't handle it. I said, 'No shit, you could take out every bloke in this pub, it would never happen to you.' He is built like a tank. He was really annoyed that somebody would speak to me like that. Three hours later he was still saying I can't believe that crap happens. It was bizarre that a guy who has been fired on in battle could let something like that annoy him.

We had lunch a little later. Ben was asking me about how to handle the media and I was quite honoured (if a little embarrassed, I was no expert). He handles himself really well when I have seen him speak in public. We chatted and he invited me to come and do some sand hill runs with the SAS near the barracks, but I was still in the moonboot. I was thinking there is no way I could keep up with these blokes. It would be great, but I would just embarrass myself.

These guys are unbelievably fit. Ben would train twice a day privately on top of everything else he did. It put our sad fitness stuff into perspective, but it was the mental strength those soldiers have that really impressed me. They would tell me stories about the situations they found themselves in. They are athletes who have to compete while being shot at, they have to think on their feet, wear that uniform and carry all that gear in incredible heat. There is no 12th man to run a sports drink and a towel out to you when you are under fire in Afghanistan. No lunch or tea breaks in a battle. When people talk or write about elite sport they often compare it to war, but Ben was against that and I agree totally. The difference between winning and losing for them is often the difference between living and dying.

Spending time with these guys at this point was so important to me because it put everything into perspective. Here I was letting drunk members of the Barmy Army get to me and feeling sorry for myself while staying in a luxury hotel room on a cricket tour because I missed my family. Wives and girlfriends don't get to visit when you are in some hole in the desert somewhere and people are trying to kill you. There's no buffet breakfast in the dining room. I had it easy. They were seriously tough guys and you cannot believe the stuff they go through. It really stuck with me. I gained strength from being with them. From then on whenever cricket felt like hard work I thought about what those guys had to go through.

Ben and I became pretty tight and he invited me out to the base at Swanbourne. I got to 'play' with some of the weapons, which was a bit of a buzz, but it was in conversation with those guys that I learned the most. It was the mental approach to things that fascinated me, the way they would work as a team and the thought processes behind being a leader of a unit and the whole structure of it all.

I think it also indulged that part of me that considered signing up when I finished school in Townsville. I remember how the army, navy and air force used to come to school and try to recruit us. I was always interested in the option before cricket intervened. I wondered if I had given the SAS a crack, would I have made it. I must admit I loved it when we had the boot camp all those years before. I am not sure what Warnie was complaining about. I'd watched a series on television about a group of guys training to join the SAS once and I couldn't help wondering if I would have been up to it. Probably not, but I guess I will never know.

It was during this time that we did a live-fire exercise at the base. It started with us sliding down a rope from a mocked-up helicopter onto a rooftop. It was a fair height and they were a bit concerned about that because there'd been a few accidents. If something had gone wrong I am not sure how I would have explained breaking my leg while in the middle of rehab, but I wasn't going to let that stop me. I doubt Cricket Australia would have been keen on me doing stuff like this; I think there are clauses in our contract about avoiding extreme activities, but I am sure it's in the fine print bit that I haven't read.

We then had to force our way into a locked room using explosives and I got to set off the charge before they stormed in. I was hanging back with the instructor who was telling me what they were looking for as they cleared different rooms and obstacles. It's all very high-pressure stuff; they have to make instant decisions about who is a danger and who isn't. They have to be sure not to shoot each other, which can happen easily with bullets that pierce walls like they are paper. Shot selection is critical!

You wear these headphones that block out the explosions and rifle fire to some extent but let you communicate with each other, but it's still hard to hear. They did another exercise where they did a VIP mission on me. We were in the back of a car that came under attack and Ben basically had to get me out of it. He just said, 'Do as I say,' and he was pushing me this way and that as they came for us.

In that scenario I ended up as a prisoner in a room and the team had to come in and save me. That was when the guys burst in and shot the two hostage takers, who were probably an arm's length away from me at the time. It was incredibly exhilarating and these SAS guys were just amazing at their job. I wasn't scared because I had learned to trust them. They are total professionals, but I did feel a bit strange when they burst through the door waving a gun that seemed to be pointing at me as they fired.

I got to throw a few stun grenades and be the shooter myself as well and rescue a hostage, but they made sure there were no live hostages for me to shoot. I was as nervous and excited as a schoolboy. It was good fun and a door to another world. I got a bit obsessed at this stage and read the book *Lone Survivor*, which is about an incident in Afghanistan, after watching the movie. It might not seem such a big deal to read a book, but it was the first I had ever read in my life. My time with the army boys was really important to me ahead of the next stage in my cricket career.

Obviously, determination and not giving up are key to what they do, but it is all the stuff about not leaving anyone behind that also made an impact. I suppose it was the commitment and the mental strength they have that I concentrated on the most. I spoke to them about the stuff that happened in the Ashes and about blocking out the distractions and focusing on what the group needs, about understanding what works for your mates and being able to help them the best that you can. When bad situations did happen on the field, it might just need someone to just say the right thing – a trigger word or something like that. The next time I played cricket I wanted to be the one helping out, not the one who needed help. By approaching my cricket with that mindset I could stop obsessing about myself.

One of the tricks I learned was to turn the crowd targeting me into a positive. If they were all concentrating on me then they were leaving my mates alone. I was taking one for the team. Of course, it was all good in theory, but I was a long way from putting it into practice. There was a very real chance that I would not be wanted back in the team again. A new group of fast bowlers with names like Starc, Pattinson, Hazlewood and Cummins were making names for themselves.

Before I started my rehab I had met with Dennis Lillee and he'd told me to go away and get fit before even trying to bowl again. I was jumping out of my skin by the time he agreed to work with me in the nets. It was mid-2012. I was fitter than I had been in all my life. My body felt great and I was enjoying the act of bowling again. I was not sure, however, if I was ready for the big time straight away. The work I did with Dennis was invaluable. He fixed up my approach to the wicket and gave me the TUFF mantra to hang on to if I started to have any doubts about my action. Pretty soon I reckon I was bowling 10 km/h faster than I had been for the past 12 months. There had been talk about slowing me down and extending my career. I listened, thought about it and thought no. If I was going to bowl I was going to bowl fast, otherwise I couldn't see the point.

John Inverarity had come on board as a selector in South Africa and was a guy who took a personal interest in me. He'd been standing next to Rod Marsh at the academy the day Dennis called him from Brisbane back in 1999 and had given me some batting coaching in those early years. There is nowhere decent to bowl in Perth mid-year so John pulled some strings at Hale School where he'd been Headmaster in a previous life and they prepared a fantastic strip for me with a net in the middle of one of their ovals. Invers has a rounded approach and was as interested in my wellbeing as he was in my cricket and managed me carefully over the following seasons. He must have put in a good word for me, too, because I was picked for the ODI and Australia A squads that were touring England in June and July.

I played a tour game in Leicester and when Pat Cummins was injured they called me into the side to play the second ODI.

My first and third deliveries were no-balls; the free hit from the second was belted for four by Alastair Cook. I bowled another one in the next over that went for four, too, and I had 0–20 from two overs, not a good start in anyone's books. I was taken off. I bowled another no-ball later when I came back on.

They didn't pick me again, which was fair enough. On paper it looked like I'd had a shocker and was no different from the bowler who was there three years earlier. The crowd certainly let me know what they thought, but I knew I had made some headway. When I overstepped and they got up me, I didn't drop my head, I toughed it out and that was a significant step. The other thing was I had my speed back.

After that I joined the A Team for a series against the England Lions. We played Derbyshire first up in a four-day game. I bowled without success again in the first innings but had a bit more in the second where I picked up three wickets, including a bloke called Usman Khawaja who was playing for them that winter.

It was a good A Team – we had Michael 'Max' Klinger, Tim Paine, Steve Smith, Pete Forrest, George Bailey, Ed Cowan, Mitch Starc, Phil Hughes, Nathan Lyon, Joe Burns, Jon Holland, Tom Cooper, Liam Davis and Jackson Bird in the squad. They had some handy players too, including Joe Root, Jonny Bairstow and Eoin Morgan.

Touring with an A Team is a lot different. You go from spending time in five-star hotels to sharing rooms with teammates. They had us sleeping almost next to each other in single beds. I am happy to share rooms as long as I am not right next to some snoring bloke. It was like a 19s tour – which is fine when you are that age. We got it done, though. Some of us might have spent our own money and upgraded to our own rooms. It sounds precious, but trust me you don't want to be sleeping right next to a teammate after a day in the field (I can almost hear my army mates scoff as I write this). We played at Derby, then moved to Manchester and finished in Birmingham, but that game was cut short by rain. My performances were solid, nothing better. I was reasonably pleased, though, with how it had gone given those conditions are not exactly right for me. From there it was over to the United Arab Emirates (UAE) in August for a one-day series against Pakistan that kicked off with a one-off against Afghanistan in Sharjah.

James Pattinson and Mitchell Starc bowled really well there, particularly Starcy who got man of the series. It felt good to play with the younger guys; they were great bowlers who were starting their journey while I was a bowler who was re-starting my journey and I felt like I could help them. I came back from there and played a couple of Shield and one-day games for WA to kick off the 2012–13 season. We took on NSW in the first 50-over game at the WACA where I got to show the Australian captain that I was still a force to be reckoned with by getting him out for one. Sorry, Michael, I had to bring that up.

I found myself back on the treadmill pretty quickly, but I was not in contention for a Test return. Because I was on the outer, I thought I might try the IPL. I had the time and had to start thinking about putting away a bit of money for the family while I could. I had signed on to play with the Mumbai Indians and they were in the Champions League in Johannesburg that year so I flew over in October for four games. The first match was against Perth, so I was playing against a lot of my current teammates. Shaun Marsh should have known me better than to be trapped in front on the first ball of the game. His brother missed a straight one in my next spell. It didn't matter that much, though, as the Scorchers won the match. We didn't have a win while I was there, but I couldn't hang around as the Shield season was underway.

I wasn't taking a lot of wickets around the place but I was feeling pretty good about my cricket and bowling fast. South Africa came to tour and played two Tests against us without me in the line-up. If you read stories from this time you will see I was well down the pecking order according to the journalists. They weren't wrong. I was told that I was the sixth- or seventh-ranked bowler in the country by the selectors. Hearing things like that always encouraged me to work harder and make sure whoever said it was proven wrong.

Fast bowlers break easy and when James Pattinson broke down during the second Test it caused a bit of a chain reaction. Poor old Pete Siddle and Ben Hilfenhaus were bowled into the ground and then the powers that be decided that they would be too tired to play in the decider in Perth. Guess who was up? They named me, John Hastings and Mitchell Starc. Watto had missed the first couple with injury and was back, too. I bowled better in the second innings than the first but we were chasing the game the whole time because South Africa batted brilliantly.

It was good to be back around the boys because Ricky Ponting had announced it would be his last game. I was nervous about returning to the big time and also excited because I wanted to be there for him. He had been a big part of my career and a big supporter and I always felt he wanted the best for me so it felt right to be there. It was a really emotional time. He told us at the team hotel before we went to training and we were all in a state of shock. You couldn't imagine an Australian team or dressing room without Punter. As a sign of respect, we all sat in on his press conference as he told the journos.

It was a significant moment for Australian cricket. He was the last of the giants from that amazing era. It was going to change when he left, I knew that; the team would be different and I was a bit worried about that. I was not sure which way it would go. Even when he wasn't captain Ricky steered things and kept them on the straight and narrow by force of his presence. He was a strong guy and would always speak up. He was the last of that era to say what was on their minds and be happy for others to do it. After that, people got more reluctant and bit their tongue a little bit more. Punter was inspirational, even when he was captain he was a live wire around the fielding drills and he somehow found time to help everyone with their batting. He gave me throwdowns for hours and I wasn't alone there. It was a selfless thing to do when you think of all the commitments the captain has (they are always being dragged here and there) and they also have to do their own work as well. I don't think there was ever a time that he wasn't the last one out of the nets. I can't think of a time when he wasn't the most energetic guy in our drills. There was enormous respect for Punter and his attitudes. He was intimidating because he was so mentally tough and had achieved so much, but he would give his teammates the shirt off his back. All the guys were pretty gutted. He told us not to worry about winning the game for him; we had to go out there and win it for our country. It would have been nice to win for him, though.

With Punter gone I had lost one of my biggest supporters. I had played a lot of cricket under him and learned a lot from him about the way to play cricket, like I had learned from the older guys at Queensland. The Test went okay for me, but we lost it and the series. I picked up six wickets, which wasn't too bad after 12 months on the sidelines.

We all went in to the South African rooms and played a drinking game after the match and that was also special. I remember it was a great dressing room to walk into; you knew they were a good bunch of guys and they played for each other and they knew how to celebrate a win. They made us feel really welcome. Jacques Kallis was leading the whole drinking game. It was a good experience to witness a tight, stripped-back unit that had achieved something away from home.

We used to joke about what the England team were doing with so many support staff, but we had become the same. It always seemed over the top, but all the teams followed that trend. It was how it was and people often commented about how many people we have on the field before or after a match.

Somehow we are like a '70s rock band with our physio, doctor, masseurs, media managers, head coach, batting coach, bowling coach, assistant coach, analyst, team manager …

To me the support staff are part of a team. It is special for everyone when we win because they have contributed. I know that as a player we are all focused but the guys off the field have a role that helps us do a job. If guys want to have throwdowns for four hours you need someone to do it. There have been many times when players would not have got on the field but for the hard work of the physios and doctors – as we learned a few years later when Ryan Harris was struggling on the last day in Cape Town.

I wasn't picked for the first Test of the Sri Lanka series that immediately followed the South African series. It was alright by me. Our first child, Rubika, was about to be born and I wanted to go home and be with her and Jess and that's what I did the moment they told me I wasn't needed. I treasure every minute with those two. Our family life is so special and I hate not being there for them. I've missed so many little milestones in Rubika's life. Being at the birth was absolutely fantastic! I was fascinated by the whole thing, and while I was nervous about what sort of father I was going to be, I was just so happy and proud to be a dad that I managed to shut out those doubts. Holding her for the first time I was more nervous than I have ever been. I didn't know you could be that happy.

There was a picture of Michael Clarke breaking the news to me about not fitting into their plans and you would assume I was annoyed at missing out, but I just wanted to be at home for the birth so it was not a big deal. They brought back Hilf and Sidds and opted for Mitch Starc instead of me. There were articles written at the time saying I was the pick of the bowlers in Perth, but if the selectors were going to focus on the future they had to go with the younger Mitchell. I wasn't the future according to some. Things went badly for the team in Hobart even though they won the match. Ben Hilfenhaus broke down and moved onto the injured list along with Pat Cummins, James Pattinson and Josh Hazlewood. They had to bowl a lot of overs in that game, with Shane Watson bowling more than he had in any game and Mitch Starc bowling a heap, too.

To compound matters it was decided that Mitchell Starc – who was bowling well – should be rested from the Boxing Day Test in Melbourne. I was called in to the side again. As I was getting ready to leave Perth and fly across the continent, things started to go wrong.

Rubika was 16 days old on 21 December, which happened to be Jess's birthday. She calls it the worst birthday of her life and I can't disagree. Rubika started to get sick and they thought she had a urinary tract infection. That meant a lot of needles and procedures that really upset Rubika, Jess and me. She was screaming, Jess was crying and I wasn't going all that well myself. Then they put a drip in her arm, which doesn't sound so bad, but when you are a couple of weeks old you're not very big and the needle is enormous. I felt sick. She didn't have the infection they thought she had so now they announced that she was in danger of getting meningitis and they would have to stick a needle in her spine to draw some fluid. Things seemed to be going from bad to worse. They wouldn't let us stay in the room while they did the procedure and we had to sit outside. They assured us that babies were resilient but I wasn't so sure. We could hear her screaming. They were torturing her (with good intentions) with all this stuff and we felt so frightened and helpless.

The joy of having a baby had turned into a nightmare. I couldn't bear the thought of her being taken from us. I couldn't even think it.

We had gone in at 9.30 pm and it dragged on and on. Eventually Rubika's health started to improve, which was an enormous relief, and Jess sent me home. I was supposed to fly to Melbourne in two days, but I just couldn't leave them. It was hard enough being away from the hospital. It dragged on through the following day as well as they tried to find out if she had meningitis or not. I told Jess I wasn't going to Melbourne. It was hard enough without Rubika being sick but it was out of the question with her like this. Jess insisted that I had to go. I still didn't know what to do and so I sent a text to her mum and she spoke to her dad. He said that if Jess says go, you go. I should have known that!

I was due to fly the next morning. Jess said to push the flight back and we should know how things were by then. Eventually I left, but I felt so guilty. Jess's family had booked a holiday on Boxing Day so they were all going to leave town and she'd be alone. Even her brother was going. It was a pretty tough few days for both of us, but on Christmas Eve they announced that she didn't have meningitis and we were in the clear.

It's events like this that put into perspective just how self-centred you have to be to play elite sport. When people talk about sacrifices they aren't just talking about things that affect them. More importantly it put in perspective just how lucky I was to have Jess. Fans, the press and the game don't make allowances for the private lives of athletes and I guess they shouldn't have to. If you cross the line you are fit to play and judged against everyone else out there, but occasionally there are things that go on in the background that can intrude.

The next time we went to England, Brad and Karina Haddin had to rush their daughter, Mia, to hospital and in the end he couldn't play. He'd already played many times when people didn't know what was going on. I have seen guys go through so much behind the scenes that nobody ever knew about. Ricky and Rianna Ponting went through a lot of struggles to have their first, most of which they kept to themselves. There were often small things that just got bigger because we were on the road. Kids got sick, relatives died and you couldn't make the funeral. I knew that Jess had the worst birthday and the worst Christmas ever, so I had to make sure it was worth her while. I wanted to win for Jess.

The boys thought the visitors didn't like the short ball in Hobart and when I got to Melbourne they told me that was my job. That suited me. Bowling short sharp stuff is what I love doing. I really enjoyed having a bowl. My short ball was surprising batsmen. In the first innings I got Tillakaratne Dilshan early and was going alright, but Kumar Sangakkara climbed into me.

Kumar is one of the great batsmen; he finished his career with 12,000 runs in Test matches and an average of 54. I loved bowling to him because he was so aggressive. If I gave him a sniff he leapt on me. Trying to take him down was the sort of challenge I craved. He started our battle with a pair of fours and then went one better by hitting three in a row in my next spell. He brought up his 10,000th run with a drive wide of point for four. It wasn't my best ball.

Jackson Bird was playing his first Test for Australia. He was a good state cricketer who got his chance because of some excellent performances at Shield level. He'd carried that form into the Test arena by picking up two top order wickets to keep the visitors on the back foot. Then, I managed to pick up Prasanna Jayawardene and Dhammika Prasad in consecutive balls, which put us right on top. In the following over, I got one big on Sanga, and Matthew Wade ran almost to the boundary to take the catch. It was my 200th Test wicket and it was good to bring it up by taking down one of the big names.

In the second innings, Davey Warner and I combined to run out their opener Dimuth Karunaratne and then I had Dilshan out caught at short leg the following ball to give us two wickets in the first over. In my second spell, I hit Sanga on the hand and he had to retire hurt, which was the last thing they needed as they already had two bowlers who couldn't bat in that last innings because of injuries. You don't mind intimidating blokes. To be completely honest you don't mind hurting them a little bit, but you don't like to see them suffer significant injuries. I don't like to admit this, but I am a bit of a softy and I paid a visit to the Sri Lankan rooms in the break to make sure that Sanga was okay. He's a lovely bloke and I hoped I hadn't done too much damage. It turned out he had broken his hand and was out for the series.

I ended up taking 4–63 and 2–16 in the game and hit 92 not out with the bat in the first innings. That was a healthy return by any measure. Jess's sacrifice hadn't been in vain. We'd won by an innings and 201 runs in three days.

We played a one-day series against the West Indies after that and then I was picked in the Test squad to tour India in February–March, but to be honest I don't think I was among their first choices for the team even after that effort in Melbourne. That was alright; maybe if I had got back too easily I wouldn't have been so determined. The feeling that some people didn't rate me anymore was the sort of motivation I thrived on.

A lot of things had changed in a relatively quick time in our cricket set-up and I wasn't that comfortable with some of it. Tim Nielsen had been replaced as coach by Mickey Arthur, and Ricky Ponting had not captained for a while, and as I said earlier, when he left Test cricket he took something with him. There were a lot of new people around the set-up. Old hands like our team manager Steve Bernard had been replaced and he took a lot of knowledge out the door with him. There were new media people, new selectors and there had been a complete shake-up of the way things worked, with Pat Howard coming in as high-performance manager. A lot of the structural changes were driven by the Argus review, which they had after we lost the Ashes at home. They called us all in to ask us what we thought, but I don't think they really cared what a fast bowler thought. The corporate side of cricket wasn't my thing anyway, but the team was and things were changing faster than I liked.

There were a lot of new people and I couldn't help but feel that we had lost something. We got hammered in the first two Tests in India. I have always avoided the behind-the-scenes stuff. I don't like any politics or backbiting or anything like that; I want to play cricket and get the job done. I had mates but I don't think that I had enemies or moved in cliques. When they were looking for a coach I told people they needed to get Mickey Arthur. He'd done a really good job with WA. But it was a bit disappointing how it all turned out. I am sure there was more to it, but there were too many different groups within the team at that point. I think it was apparent from the outside; it was from the inside. People had formed factions. It seemed like there was a young clique who were the 'in' group and the rest of us were outsiders.

I remember pretty clearly the day it all hit the fan. We were beaten in Chennai and then smacked by an innings in Hyderabad. I hadn't played either game because I wasn't in favour. After that second Test we were told that we needed to write down a few things about how we could do things better ahead of the third Test in Mohali. At that moment I thought I should just go and tell them instead of writing it down. I wasn't much good at doing assignments. I should have gone with my instincts but I just left it. We went to Mohali the next day and had a couple of days off and it wasn't on my mind. I wasn't in the team and I didn't have the focus I should have – it was probably a bit selfish, it wasn't deliberate – but I was trying to manage my way through a long tour of India when I wasn't playing. I just forgot about it ...

One morning before training I got a call to come up to a meeting with Mickey Arthur, our new manager Gav Dovey and Michael Clarke. As I was walking in, Usman Khawaja was walking out. I had no idea what was going on, but he didn't look too happy. That's when they told me I would not be picked for the game because I hadn't done my homework. I was absolutely stunned. I didn't know what to say or do. I think I was in a bit of shock. Usman, James Pattinson and Shane Watson were given the same message. Perhaps the worst part of it was they told me I would have played in that match if I hadn't done the wrong thing. Why would you tell me that?

By the time I got to training I was furious and I took it out on the batsmen, particularly Phillip Hughes. Watto decided he'd had enough and left training. His wife, Lee, was about to have their first baby and he figured he may as well go home for that as hang around. I think everyone was cool with that. He was back in time for the fourth Test anyway. That night I spoke with Gav for about three hours; it was quite intense. I don't think it achieved anything. I told him that it was ridiculous to miss a Test match for something so trivial. He tried to explain their point of view.

I had a chat with Mickey as well, for maybe an hour. I had lost respect for him and told him and he didn't like it; he was gutted by it. I had to tell him. I was really disappointed in the whole situation, but I took my punishment and moved on. I copped it a little bit because I was mates with Watto and we would talk a lot. Watto is an honest bloke and that is what I love about playing with him. He speaks up and says what he is thinking and you respect that. He was carrying the torch for the old school. It was the same with Matty Hayden, Justin Langer and Ricky Ponting. When we came into the team, people spoke their minds and were strong in their points of view. They would speak up when it was needed and that was how it had always been, but at that point in time it became almost frowned upon.

Mickey told me I spent too much time with Watto and that was the real issue here. I was told we were too close, like we were a faction or something. I am sorry but you can't help but be close to a bloke you have been playing cricket with since you were 19. Usi and Patto got caught in the crossfire. Watto was being punished for speaking his mind about some of the things that were going on and we all went down with him. The problems between him and Michael Clarke were well known and it just seemed to get out of hand on this tour. There were other minor disciplinary issues with different blokes, but for some reason it all fell on us.

It should have and could have been handled so much better.

It was a new era and to be honest I wasn't sure I wanted to be part of it. I certainly felt that way in India and what happened with Huss drove it home. You could see in the summer that things weren't quite right in the team. It came to a head after the Sydney Test, which was Michael Hussey's last. I loved Huss; he was a passionate team man, a good teammate and the person who led us in the team song after a win. He is one of the best guys in cricket and an absolute nuffie with it. After the match we had a bit of a celebration in the rooms, but then we were told to go back to the hotel and get changed as we were going out on the harbour on James Packer's boat, which sounded alright to me. I didn't care that much. Michael Clarke had organised it and it seemed like a great idea. When we got to the boat Huss wasn't there, neither were Peter Siddle or Shane Watson. I found out that Huss and his wife hadn't been keen on the idea and so the others had bailed out, too. If I had known I would have stayed with them. It was a real bummer and it played on my mind for a long time afterwards. I was really annoyed that we had been split up like that and it reflected how fractured the team had become. People made calls to Huss to get him on board, but he wouldn't come and then there was talk about us getting off early to go back and join him, but we were trapped on board.

When Watto was still angry and on his way home from the Test in India he'd told the journos that he was going home to consider his future as a Test player and I am sure he was. I was in the same boat. I was thinking that if this was what the team was like, I had wasted my time trying to get back into it. This was not the sort of environment I wanted to play in. I eventually moved past that thinking and I am glad I did because it would have been an awful note to end my career on. I guess it was easier to do nothing and that was what I did. I just put my head down and worked on proving that I was a better bowler than people gave me credit for.

The next big thing on the radar was the Ashes in England in 2013. I was not named in the squad and it was emphasised to me that I was still a fair way down the pecking order. Without doubt an element of it was that they didn't have faith in me on English pitches and maybe they didn't have faith in me for a big series. I was really disappointed at the time and found it pretty hard to be left out when that first Test was played. I can say now that I guess it was the right decision; I didn't feel like I was quite ready and that was a sure sign I wasn't.

I wonder now if I had played in those Tests I would have been alright to back up for the next clash. We had two Ashes series back to back that year and if I had gone badly again it might have been curtains for me. I was in the one-day squad for the series against England after the Ashes, though, and keen to prove myself. I was 31 years old and many considered me too old to be worth backing, so I had plenty to prove. I think I did. I bowled really fast in that series and I used the short ball better than I ever had in England. I got inside their heads and it was glaringly obvious that Jonathan Trott really didn't know what to do when I pitched it short. I got him out with one in the second match and we made sure he knew about it in our own special way. When we played the third game at Edgbaston and he came on strike, Michael Clarke stood beside him at the batting crease and moved in a leg slip just to make sure he knew what we had in mind. It was a trick that Michael used a fair bit. He was good at standing next to the batsman and moving the field in place for the short ball. It was an aggressive act to stand in their space and one that could unnerve the batter.

Trott hung on a bit in that match but never looked comfortable. At one point he copped one right in the grille and that rattled him. He was wearing one of the older helmets and you could see that the grille had smashed into his face when the ball hit. It looked nasty and while he wasn't hurt, it made an impact. It was a warning bell and he heard it loud and clear. He didn't play the last match and there was talk that he'd lost his nerve and couldn't face me again. I don't know about that. I do know I felt like I was in control when he was at the crease. We put that in the back of our minds for down the track.

I didn't get a lot of wickets in the series but I bowled with real aggression and everybody could see that the batsmen didn't like it. The other thing I was really pleased with was my body language. I had learned to accept it when I bowled a bad ball, not to drop my head, and while the Barmy Army did its best to rattle me I handled the crowd a lot better. The work I had done with the psychologists and the lessons I'd learned hanging around with Ben and Mark had paid off.

George Bailey led the team during a one-day series in India in October and we had a bit of fun. He is easy-going and has a very dry sense of humour, but he is also very competitive. Playing under him I understood why the Tasmanian boys rated him so highly. I was released early so I could play a Sheffield Shield match and get some red ball cricket before England arrived for the Ashes. The press at the time noted I was bowling well, but there was widespread scepticism about whether I would be any good in a big Test series.

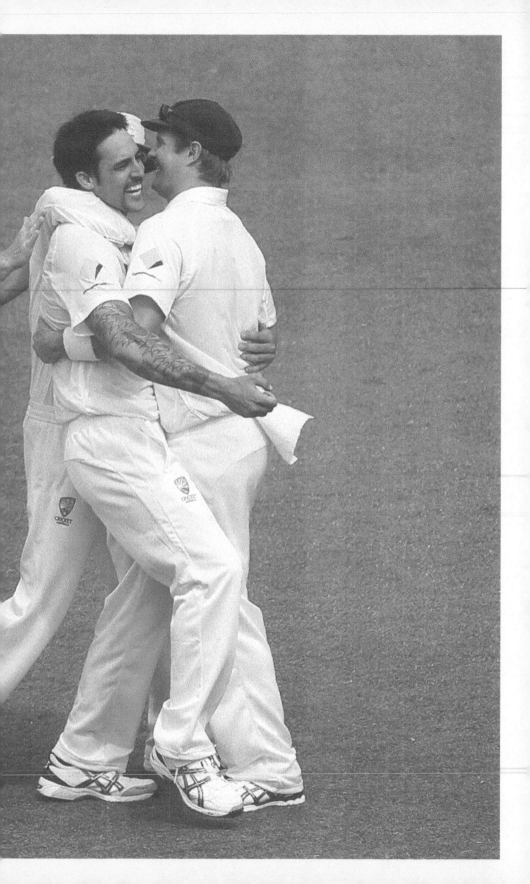

2013–14 Ashes series, Australia v England, First Test,
Day 2, the Gabba, 22 November 2013.

9

Rising Out of the Ashes

SOMETHING FELT RIGHT ABOUT the group in the lead-up to the 2013–14 Ashes. All the stress around in India earlier in the year had gone. We traditionally gather in Brisbane before the summer and work at Allan Border Field and when we arrived ahead of this series everyone was in a good place. I don't think I've ever been involved in a better build-up.

Darren Lehmann had come in as coach and really changed things – he told us to get out there and enjoy ourselves, that this was supposed to be the best time of our lives. Nobody was walking on eggshells anymore. It felt like the approach we had when I started with Queensland and I was good with that.

We weren't the most experienced team going around, but Michael Clarke, Shane Watson, Brad Haddin, Ryan Harris, Nathan Lyon and Pete Siddle had played a few Test matches.

George Bailey was also set to make his debut. George is the nicest guy in cricket and was in no way wet behind the ears. He'd been captaining Tasmania for a while, playing in the Australian one-day team and was captain of the T20 side. Chris Rogers only had six Tests under his belt, but was one of the most experienced first-class cricketers in the world. Dave Warner was moving into a good place and Steve Smith was a cricketer with unlimited potential. It looked and felt like a pretty balanced group and there was a sense that while they'd fallen short in England they were not really that far away.

Still, England's side did look better on paper. Alastair Cook is a brilliant batsman and had carved us up here last time. Kevin Pietersen could do anything. Graeme Swann was a good spinner in the right conditions. Ian Bell, Jonathan Trott, Stuart Broad and James Anderson were all great players too.

I remember Michael coming out to talk to me, Sidds and Ryno when we were sitting on the grass at Allan Border Field before the first Test. We chatted through the bowling plans and what he said sat right with me. When I came back I had said to myself that I was here to bowl fast and to intimidate batsmen. All the talk about slowing down and finding a middle way was well intentioned but it didn't interest me. Guess what? They wanted me to bowl fast and hard. They wanted me to rough-up the Poms, especially the tail. Sidds and Ryno had their own roles. Ryno was obviously one of the smartest seam bowlers in world cricket. He had an incredible record. The idea was I would get them on the back foot and then Ryno would bowl that relentless line of his, tempting them to free the arms a bit, which was always dangerous. He was tight and effective. Sidds was just enormous – he shoulders the load, bowls with the older ball, digs in when nothing is happening and gets a lot of key wickets. You can't have an ego when you do that role; you have to keep it dry and make sure the batsmen don't get a chance to score. I just had to wang it down as fast as I could. It was a plan I was happy to follow.

When the first Test rolled around I was pretty nervous. I think we all were. England arrived as favourites. The experts had locked them in, and that was fine, we didn't care. There is so much tension around the first Test of a series. And it's no coincidence you see people cramp up in Brisbane. The heat, the lack of air in that ground and the stress really takes it out of you. There's a corner of the ground to the left of the dressing rooms that is always in the sun. We called it cancer corner when I was at the Bulls. The Gabba's a gruelling place to play cricket. I've learned over the years to hydrate well in the days leading up.

We won the toss and batted. The best time to bowl in Brisbane is on that first morning and they made the most of it. By the time I was wandering out into the heat we were 6–132 and it wasn't even tea. Nerves got to our batters and I think all of Australia had that 'oh, no, here we go again' feeling. All of our batsmen were out and Brad Haddin was waiting for me when I arrived in the middle, just as he had been in South Africa in 2011. We were down to the keeper and a fast bowler with not many runs on the board. The funny thing was I wasn't nervous at all. My first thought was that it was way too early to have to bowl. I really didn't want to have a crack on the first day, so I thought I would do my best to stall them. It's strange the way your mind works. Hadds and I are good mates. We are both extremely competitive cricketers, but we try and keep it on the level. We got into trouble on the field a few times, but I think that's because he leads me astray. Anyway, I just decided to get my eye in and see how it went. I noodled around for a while and had only scored four runs after 31 balls.

Hadds and I both like to play a big shot if it is there. He is a much better bat than me, but we both like the lofted drive. Before tea, Graeme Swann came on and there was really only one thing to do with him – smash him back over his head for a six. My first attempt came right out of the middle and felt pretty good and at least I was in double figures when the tea break came. We were having fun despite the situation, but were happy to get out of the hot sun and have a breather in the rooms.

For some reason we didn't score a lot of boundaries in the partnership and I remember saying to Hadds that I wasn't into all this running business. I never was, to be honest. I always tried to keep my legs as fresh as possible. There was talk around the place that if I batted well I bowled well but I never thought that way. Hadds and I kept going after the break and put on 114. I was proud of that partnership. I'd gone after Swanny a bit and hit him for a couple of sixes. When they took the new ball, that was it for me. Stuart Broad got one to go right through the gate. I would rather not have got out, but there's no shame in falling to the new ball. Even the best batsmen struggle against it.

I didn't see out the day, but I got us close and we managed to push on into the next morning and make 295. Some people thought it was below par, but we hadn't bowled yet so it was hard to know. It didn't look like a lot of runs, but it gave us something to bowl to. The tension went up another notch when I had to bowl. I talked about that right at the start of this book. Everything was down to this moment – my life would have been so different if it didn't come off. I started shakily and then things fell into place in a way I could only dream about. Jonathan Trott's wicket looked a bit scrappy, but it was the plan and it paid off. It was right on the stroke of lunch and I got a chance to take some deep breaths, cool down and think about things. He wasn't keen on facing me and I reckon it sent a shiver down the spine of the team. The tailenders were going to have a lot more trouble because I was not going to spare anyone.

After the break, I started to bowl at Michael Carberry and rattled him. Another message to those waiting to bat! Joe Root chased one trying to relieve the pressure. Another one down. Ryan Harris was collecting scalps at the other end. Swann waited for the short one and was hanging back to a ball pitched up and they had lost 8–91. We were riding a wave. England was all out for 136, but, more importantly, they knew that we were hunting them.

It was time for some payback to them and to everybody who questioned me. And, I suppose I have to include myself in that.

When I was dropped after the last Brisbane Ashes Test, I realised I was trying to please too many people. When I came back from my injury, one of my resolutions was to play cricket my way. My way involved bowling fast and using the short ball to set batsmen up. I never want to be taken off when I am bowling, but the short spells obviously worked for me. When you bowl longer spells you try to maintain a rhythm. If you only have 18 balls you go hell for leather. At the same time it took as much out of me, especially because I was bowling a lot of bouncers, which take extra effort.

There was another distinct change to my bowling by this time and that was I had no real interest in swinging the ball. I had always wanted to bowl with the new ball, but when I had got it in the past I think there was too much expectation that I swing it. When I had the mindset of trying to swing the ball was when I floated it up and put it in the spot. I bowled my best when I had the good mindset of hitting the wicket hard with the new ball. You only have to swing one ball to a batter and it brings you into the game. That changes everything. That's when they start to play balls outside off stump because they aren't sure if it is coming back at them again.

If it happened it happened, if it didn't bad luck; I was just going to have to target them with short stuff. I took only 4–64 in that innings, but it was the way I took them that was the most important thing. It laid down a marker for the series.

Davey Warner and Michael scored centuries in our second innings, Hadds got another half-century and I was denied one when we declared at 7–401. I was 39 not out at the time and having fun at the crease. I was particularly proud of a little paddle sweep I played off Swanny for four and a straight shot that put Chris Tremlett in the stands.

I was enjoying cricket again!

We had a big lead going into that last innings and we rode that wave. We had our foot on their throats and they didn't like it. Ryno got Carberry early and it only took me five balls to get Trott to spoon a short one to Nathan Lyon at backward square. They were 2–10 already. Trott just didn't know how to handle the ball coming at his body and was in deep trouble. I fixed up my old mate KP next, who was well caught by the sub Chris Sabburg off another short ball. It was his hundredth Test, but it hadn't gone well for him. They were 3–72. Wickets came regularly after that. Sidds got Ian Bell. Nathan Lyon finally got rid of Alastair Cook, who'd been out there for nearly four hours and scored just 65. Nathan then knocked over Prior and it was my turn again.

Broad showed no interest in getting behind the ball after the first innings and nicked off early, then Swanny nicked off and then Ryno got Tremlett. I was having a bit of fun with the Barmy Army by now. They were trying to wind me up but I was smiling and keeping it light-hearted with them. When I got Swann I let them know that I was thinking of them by giving a little wave in that direction. I kept that up for the rest of the series. They were nine down, we were closing in on a big victory and I was hunting my fifth wicket for the innings when things got heated between George Bailey, Michael Clarke and Jimmy Anderson.

I have to say I played no role in this. It started when Jimmy and George had an exchange on the side of the wicket between overs. I don't think Jimmy thought George was good enough to be out there and he stood over him. There was talk later about threats of violence. I don't know what was said but Shane Warne, who was in the commentary box and could hear through the on-field microphones, says he knew. Pup stepped in and told Jimmy to get ready for a broken arm, although he may have expressed it a little differently.

Normally, nothing would have come of it, but this time, for some reason, the stump mike was on and everybody heard what was said. Jimmy and I have had our run-ins through the series. I always enjoyed that competition and the chat, but it stayed on the field. When you play club cricket in Queensland you hear a lot worse. The problem with this exchange was it was broadcast to the general public. If it wasn't, nothing would have happened.

Pup regrets the fact it was heard in lounge rooms because we know how that sounds to young people and it shouldn't have been heard. There was no real intention of breaking anyone's arm; he was trying to make Anderson feel nervous because I was coming around the wicket and digging it in. He wanted him to think about the possibility of getting hurt so he would make a mistake. I'll give Jimmy his due – he survived a pretty testing over, but then we took the new ball and when he tried to fend off my first delivery he only managed to hit it up in the air. Anyone could have caught it, but I insisted. I almost pushed George away. Sidds gave Jimmy a special send-off. He really wasn't that popular with opposition sides.

Me? I was more interested in acknowledging my mates in the Barmy Army. It felt good and we went straight into the rooms to sing the team song. It's hard to describe the relief I was feeling. Relief and joy at going one up in such convincing fashion. It was a little after 6 pm on the fourth day. We had won by 381. I'd picked up nine wickets and Alastair Cook admitted they had not done well against me. 'We've played him well in the past and that's something we'll have to look to do in the next game.'

There was certainly an expectation that England would go better in Adelaide, which is traditionally a track that doesn't suit me as much. It was important to me to back-up. I'd done that in the second innings and I needed to do it in the second Test because historically my performances were erratic. Still, it was going to be hard to match a haul of 9–103 in a convincing win ...

It was an Ashes tour and a bit went down between Tests as it always does. The tension creates strange situations. Jonathan Trott went home between games and there were mixed messages about why, but it seemed apparent his mind was in no place to carry on. I could see in Brisbane that he didn't know what to do when he was batting and David Warner had seen that, too, and made that statement about fear in his eyes. You have to be careful what you say about opponents and, when Trott left, the media came down hard on David, but he didn't know what was going on and I really don't think he'd said anything wrong. He'd made an observation and it was true. England tried to make out it was a lot worse than it was. They were playing games; they always did. Their media always seemed happy to play along. Davey apologised as soon as he realised Trott was struggling.

I had some sympathy for Trott, who seems like a nice bloke. During the previous one-day series we had run into each other in a shop in Birmingham and had a bit of a chat. I remember him asking about my family. He had always seemed a bit different from the other guys in the team. I liked him whenever I had anything to do with him. Having been there myself to some degree I think I had some understanding of his situation, but I couldn't really know what he was going through. I respected his decision.

Pup copped a fine for the incident with Anderson and that became a big drama, too. Everyone wanted to carry on about the ugly Aussies and the ICC stepped in and leaned on the umpires to get involved more often when players clashed on the field, which seemed to me to be an overreaction. Sure there were exchanges, but did they ever amount to anything more than angry words? After this and for the last years of my career, umpires started intruding too often. If I stood for an extra second staring at a batsman they would tell me to get back to my mark, which was annoying. There's no need for it. A bit of theatre never hurt anyone. I don't think it hurts the game's image either. I have never seen it get to the point where someone was going to get hit on a cricket field. Most of us have reasonable self-control; we know the rules, we know in the back of our minds that people are watching. What Michael didn't know – nor should he be expected to – was that everyone was listening.

Perhaps the most bizarre report after the first Test was that the England board had complained about the fans and media in Brisbane taunting their players and had threatened not to return to the Gabba. Really? It was terrible to think that somebody could be abused by a home crowd. Of course, it wouldn't happen in England ...

We planned to do well in Brisbane because the conditions suited us and it paid off. The heat kills a lot of teams; it hurts us, but we are a bit more used to it. Adelaide can be hot, too, but we thought the drop in wicket would suit them more. I was a bit annoyed before the second game. I was trying to have a session off my long run and like Brisbane I couldn't do it in the nets. That frustrated me and that can turn out badly, but I managed it and moved on. I get like that before games, I need to know I have done all I can to prepare and I get obsessive if a box isn't ticked. I can't understand why nobody ever fixes that. Is it so hard to give bowlers a decent run-up in your nets? It seems a sensible thing to do.

Cook wasn't the only one who thought I wouldn't be as effective in Adelaide. Jason Gillespie had said something about how I needed to change my lengths for this game and I didn't know how to take that. If he was having a go at me, I used it as motivation. We won the toss, batted first and put on 570, thanks to hundreds from Pup and Hadds, who deserved one after missing out in Brisbane (he was run out on 94). Then Ryan Harris did his bit with a nice half-century just to rub it in.

That left 20 overs to bowl at England in the last session on the second day. I wasn't half as nervous as I was in the first Test, but I was twice as determined. Remember how Alastair Cook thought I wouldn't go as well in this game? I remembered it, too, and in my second over I bowled a fast straight one that looked like it might come in, but actually drifted away a little. He tried to block it, but was late and on the wrong line and the ball hit his off stump. I often visualise what I want to do before a game and that was one of those deliveries I see in my mind. It doesn't come off very often and even less often against a batsman like that, so it is a happy moment when it does. The best ball of the series was yet to come, but it wasn't bowled by me: it was an effort by Ryan Harris to bowl him in Perth. That was the ball of the century in my opinion. Still, I was pretty happy with that nut. Getting Cook like that was so satisfying because he is a really difficult batsman to get out. He puts a high price on his wicket. There are better batsmen around, but few who are as hard to get out.

Joe Root and Michael Carberry hung on after that, but I should have had Carberry last ball of the day. I hit him in the pads and got turned down on the appeal; my instinct was that it was out but I was talked out of it by the others. The replay showed the decision would have been overturned if we had gone upstairs. I should have spoken up.

We shared the load the next morning. Nathan Lyon got Root, Pete Siddle got Kevin Pietersen and Shane Watson got Carberry thanks to a sensational catch by David Warner. Carberry pulled hard and got pretty much over the top of it, but Davey dived and threw out a hand at square leg. They were 4–117 when I started the 51st over. It was just after lunch and they were in trouble, but there was more to come. A lot more.

Marais Erasmus gave Ben Stokes not out lbw first ball, but I wasn't going to be robbed of this one. There were two noises for sure, but I thought it was pad first. I'd done him for pace and the replay showed the ball would have hit middle. Michael wasn't keen on the referral but Brad backed me up. It was lucky they overturned it because he'd gone off for a single and then we'd given away four overthrows in the confusion.

By now the ball was reversing and I was in a really good place with my bowling. It was coming out of the hand just right. Matt Prior hadn't scored a run in the first Test and was under pressure when he came out. I gave him two short balls to push him back, then one that slides across; he nibbled at it and was caught behind for a four-ball duck. He was lucky to last that long. I was bowling with great rhythm and in that place where I was almost ahead of the game.

When the ball is reversing like that and you are in the zone you almost get too excited. Broad came out next, but before he faced a ball he complained about some bit of glare on the sightscreen and I had to wait for what seemed like ten minutes at the top of my mark before he faced up. The crowd was giving it to him and I was getting agitated. Sidds came over and said, just take a deep breath, calm down and make sure you make the first ball count. I ran in with no doubt in my mind that I was going to bowl him middle stump or have him trapped lbw if he got in the way. My visualisation was a little bit off. The ball slid a little and knocked over his leg stump. I had 3–0 from the over and England was 7–117. The crowd and the team were going berserk. I can't tell you how good this felt.

I had to wait to see if I could get the hat trick as that was the last ball of the over, but Swanny survived the first ball of my next one and they held me out for the next five balls. Then he went searching for the fourth ball of my next over, nicked it and Michael Clarke hung on to a screamer. It's funny how the catches stick when you are on top. I had five by now and it felt like nothing could stop us.

We couldn't do anything wrong and now it was time to reacquaint myself with Jimmy Anderson. I had my tail up and you could tell I was in their heads. Broad had been anticipating a short ball – that was why he jumped across and exposed leg – so was Anderson. I pitched it up, it reversed in and he was edging back in the crease when he should have been coming forward. The ball took out his middle stump. I gave my old mate a good long stare to go on with. You can't get in trouble when you say nothing. Warner and a few of the others had some things to say to him, though. It's not everyone that gets treated like this and it's always for a reason.

I was on a hat trick again, but the over had ended. Ian Bell was facing when I went for it and I managed to get him to scoop it up but it hit the ground just in front of short cover. It was about the closest I have ever come to a hat trick. I was taken off for a rest as I'd bowled five straight, which was a little more than we'd budgeted for. When I came back on a little while later I picked up Monty Panesar, bowled, with my first ball. Job done.

England was all out for 172 and I had 7–40 from 17.2 of the best overs I have ever bowled. The wicket wasn't doing anything, I just tried to hit it hard and it had paid off. From a purely selfish point of view this was the highlight of the series for me and it might be my favourite day as a bowler.

I have to admit it was a bit emotional walking off. I felt like I had achieved what I needed to, that I had proved myself. I'd copped lots of shit over the years about not being able to back-up, I'd missed the Adelaide Test on the previous Ashes tour, people thought I'd never come back from where I was ... Lots of things were going around in my mind and all of that hit me as I walked off. The appreciation of the crowd and my teammates was really special. I had a tear in my eye. It was a good moment. It was my best mate Dylan's birthday and he was there with his brother Dave, so it was great to share an experience like that with them and we had a fair celebration at dinner that night.

We were almost 400 in front so didn't have to bat long before putting them in again. Things didn't go as well for me in the second innings, but Ryan Harris put in a good effort to catch Cook on the boundary in my second over. There was no luck for me after that. Stuart Broad came out and tried to hit a few around and then he started to mouth off. He was saying, 'You are not here, mate, you're gone again.' He was implying I was mentally broken, the same as I had been in the past. That stirred the fire a bit. I targeted him after that with a few short balls that he didn't enjoy.

In the Perth Test I hit him on the foot with a yorker. He was given out lbw and had to spend a bit of time on crutches, which was a real shame. Anyway, Ryno and Sidds got the wickets I couldn't and we belted them, winning on the fifth day. I was certainly in a good place. I felt like I was intimidating some of them, especially the tail (I'd picked up the last five batsmen in the first innings at Adelaide), but, to be honest, nobody looked very comfortable facing me.

This time I was inside their heads and I knew from the feeling in the team that we weren't going to let up. I think they hoped we would, but that aggressive cricket was what worked for us. There were definitely English guys who did not want to be out there batting. Broad was a guy who we talked about in batting meetings; he was a bowler who could score a hundred and get away from you quite quickly, but his batting changed dramatically through that series. He was brave in the first dig in Brisbane but lost his heart the longer it went on. He didn't get behind the ball and didn't look like he wanted to be part of it, and that was our aim. We didn't want their tail scoring valuable runs.

Swann was the same. He could get away and score a quick 50 and frustrate you, but we put a stop to that. He was another who went home early and he copped a bit for that. I shouldn't say much, as I retired after two Tests a few summers later, but we were winning and we were at home. It was a sign of weakness in the whole team to leave when you are not winning. He left after the third Test in Perth. It definitely would have affected their group. I am sure there was a bit going on behind doors and they seemed divided into cliques. Swann seemed to take a swipe at KP on the way out, which confirmed things. You could see they weren't having any fun. Swann's departure was a victory for us on some levels, but we weren't concerned by his bowling; he rarely did anything in Australia and we might have preferred he kept going.

The great thing about the 2013–14 Ashes was the balance we had in the side. Our fast bowling cartel, me, Sidds and Ryno, had spent a lot of time together and the chemistry was right. They can bowl a relentless line and length, which kept the pressure on and allowed me to bowl short, sharp spells. There were no clashing egos and nobody fighting for their spots. When I missed out, like in the second innings at Adelaide, they stepped up. Nathan Lyon was another who was emerging as a really good finger spinner. He is one of the guys I admire the most. He's a nervous character and not too sure of himself, which probably wasn't helped by me bullying him, but I adopted him as my little brother when he came into the team so that meant he had to put up with a bit of rough stuff. That's what older brothers are for where I come from! A country boy, he is honest, hard working and straight up and down. There is no bullshit with Nathan Lyon. When Michael Hussey retired, he handed over our team song duties to Lyno. Naturally, he was petrified; he just isn't the sort of bloke to make a loud noise in front of the group, but he embraced it. Huss and Lyno were so close that Huss would invite him around for dinner when we were in Perth. No one else got a look-in, so we used to rib them quite a bit about their bromance.

Lyno is a really good bowler, who doesn't have a lot of tricks, but he has great shape and when he gets his speed right it makes up for not being able to turn it both ways. In 2015, he took his 142nd Test wicket, passing Hugh Trumble to top the list of Australian off-spinners. Brad Haddin announced that from now on Nathan was to be known as GOAT (Greatest of all Time). He absolutely hated it, which ensured that from then on that was his nickname. In all seriousness, I think he is a great cricketer who will go on to take a hell of a lot more wickets.

We won the third Test and the series in Perth early on the fifth day. I remember that while it was inevitable by then it was nerve-racking. Achieving something this big was almost frightening. It was so important for us older guys like Watto and Hadds and Pup and Sidds. We'd lost in England and we'd lost at home last time, but this was going to make up for that. We were bowling in the last innings and I wasn't sure how to react or what we were going to do when we won the match. When they were eight down, Chris Rogers caught a good one off me to get rid of Tim Bresnan and was running around like a goose. It was a good catch, but there was an added edge to his celebration. They were nine down and we were on the precipice. I walked back to my mark and got really nervous; I had to stop myself and take a deep breath.

I got Jimmy in the next over and I didn't know what to do. I ran down the wicket and just stood there. Everyone got in together and it was crazy. This was another level of happiness. I took a backward step as it broke up so I could take in what was going on. I could see the raw emotion of all the boys and I wanted to watch it from a bit of a distance rather than be a part of it. It was stuff I hadn't seen for a long time on a cricket field.

This was a big moment in our careers, some of which had just begun and some that were winding down.

The team had a great feeling that series – we were really tight. It was hard for the guys on the sidelines, but they were part of it, too; they were there at training and supported us. It takes more than 11 people to win an Ashes series. It was a long, enjoyable afternoon in the dressing room before we wandered onto centre wicket at twilight to sing the song. I'd taken six wickets, and Steve Smith picked up man of the match for his century in the first innings. Watto and Davey got centuries in the second innings, but by far the highlight of the game was George Bailey.

Playing his first series, George had not made a lot of runs, but he was a key member of the team. He's just one of those blokes you want around. He gives his all with a smile on his face but is as tough as nails. His grin while Jimmy Anderson stood over him in Brisbane said it all. He might have been on debut, but he wasn't taking a backward step. In Perth, George got his own back by smashing 28 runs off one of Jimmy's overs as we pushed towards a declaration. That he did it to Jimmy was fitting and we all enjoyed it with him. Friends and family came in the rooms afterwards. Dylan was there again and a couple of his mates. One of them said he didn't really watch much cricket but that it was one of the best moments of his life to be in the room.

We kicked on that night and old mate Ryno got himself into trouble by venting some drunken thoughts after they wouldn't let him in to the casino. It was nothing serious; he just got a bit lippy about not being allowed in because he'd had a few. There's one in every crowd. And then it was back across the continent for the Boxing Day Test. Christmas is a good time in Melbourne with the families all around and this was our first one with Rubika, which was sweet, and I was in a much better place than the same time the previous year when she had been in hospital.

The lunch is enjoyable but there's cricket to play and you can't relax too much. We were determined not to let England off the hook by arriving with a belly full of food and beer. We bowled on the first day and it was an enormous buzz. It wasn't the first time I have bowled on a Boxing Day at the MCG, but with 91,000 people in the stands and the series in the bag it was exhilarating. I didn't get a wicket until we took the second new ball and then I took five in my next eight overs.

Things just seemed to happen quickly that summer. We would be motoring along and then everything would speed up. The highlight of the day was Watto's dismissal of Carberry. My good mate from the academy days played the two-card trick perfectly, bowling an outswinger and then deceiving the opener with one that came back in next delivery. Carbs shouldered arms and lost his off stump. It was a fair effort against a good batsman.

I took care of Stokes, Bairstow, Bresnan, Pietersen and Broad. Three of the five were bowled, which is always nice. It was the tenth time I had taken five in an innings, but the first time at the MCG. The crowd was so loud all day it was fantastic. You watch those big stadium shows with rock and roll bands and see the guys strutting around in front of an audience and think that must be pretty cool. Getting a bag at the G on a day like that is as close as I will ever get and it feels great. Even for a shy lad like myself! I was pushing toward 150 km/h when I got the outside edge of Stokes' bat and old mate Watto took the catch in slips. The noise was awesome. Bresnan got one of those effort balls I bang in short. It was the first ball of the spell and it was unplayable. He skied a catch but saved himself from some serious damage. If he hadn't hit it, it would have hit him. Four balls later KP, who'd made 71 from 161 balls and been more patient than ever, just lost it. He stepped back, swung wildly and was bowled.

The Barmy Army had been getting a bit chatty before I started to take wickets, so when I did I celebrated one by advising them to shoosh up a bit. I made sure they knew when I got my fifth by giving them a special wave. When I'd got Bairstow I didn't bother giving my teammates a high five because I was so keen to let the English blokes on the other side of the fence know.

I'd been having a running conversation with their fans through the series. I wanted to share moments with them. I reminded them regularly how many games we were up in the series, but it was done without anger. I was enjoying the interaction and their press were calling me a 'pantomime villain'. I had to look up what it meant. They were a lot easier to like in circumstances like this and I think we were getting on pretty well.

It was late on the third day that I lost it with KP. I was tired and hungry and can get a bit cranky when that happens. It was really windy and that can be irritating at the MCG. Rubbish blows around and it's quite hard to settle. KP had pulled out on us a few times when we were running in to bowl and when he did it a third time I just threw the ball in his general direction. It wasn't aimed at him, but it was a bit provocative. He said someone was moving behind the sight screen, but there is an exclusion zone a mile wide behind the wicket and batsmen get so bloody fussy. I let him know that at the time and when he got a single and came up my end I let him know again. It was pretty heated.

We actually trailed them at the end of the first innings of the game, but again won the match easily. It was now 4–0 and we were one game away from something remarkable. The Melbourne and Sydney Tests are almost back to back and that makes the fifth match of the summer the hardest to get up for, especially if you are a bowler. We headed to Sydney and celebrated New Year in the team hotel as we always do. It has good views of the fireworks, but most of us just watch the 9 pm show and go to bed.

We batted first and were dismissed for 326 (Smith got a century). It wasn't a lot, but we got them fast and so we had a bowl late in the day. Nathan Lyon thought we should have a leg slip in for Carberry. It seemed a bit mad, but he thought if I could get one around his ribs he would fend it wide of the keeper. I gave it a crack in the fourth over. The ball didn't bounce like it should have and he played it off his hips straight into Nathan's hands at leg slip. Good plan, that!

The next morning we just tore through them again. They were 5–61 at lunch and all out for 155 by tea. The fast bowling cartel shared nine wickets equally among us and we had a 180-run lead. That stretched out, thanks to a century by Bucky and we had them 3–87 by tea on the third day after I picked up both openers and Ryno got Bell. All the fight had gone out of England and most of it had gone out of me, to be honest.

I was absolutely exhausted in the rooms during the break and thought I wouldn't be able to bowl another over as long as I lived. And there was still a session to go! I never usually drink those caffeinated energy drinks, but this was one occasion when it had to be done. I remember looking at Nathan Lyon and noting that he looked equally tired. We were both shattered. England hadn't made us work that hard but you can't underestimate the grind of bowling fast for five Tests in a row – even spinners can get worn down doing it. I think our bodies had decided we were over the line before the scorebook agreed. We'd not relaxed for a minute on the field. We had put everything we had into winning this series. We vowed to go out there and get this series over and done with and we did, thanks to a great spell by Ryno, who finished with five wickets.

And that was that. It was a special moment and it was great to go around the fence and share it with the fans. There were 42,000 spectators there that day and I think the only ones who had left were English. After the presentations, when Ryno won man of the match and I got the gong for man of the series, the fast bowling cartel sat at the back of the dressing room and had a drink together. We let Watto join us, which goes to show we were in a pretty good mood as he is a batsman and sweatband swinger, not a fast bowler. I think he got a temporary pass for knocking over Carberry. We all shared a pretty strong bond and one that is stronger for having got through those five Tests.

We had the right attack in that series; our batters don't get mentioned by me much, but they did well, only I just can't get past the bowling attack. It just clicked; it was the best bowling group I have been involved with. It's easy to say that, when you win, but we all worked well together, we are all really good mates, we enjoyed each other's successes and we were playing for each other. It was definitely the best time of my career. We were all at our peak in a way.

The cartel had claimed 75 of the hundred English wickets on offer between us. Nathan Lyon got 19, Watto four and Steve Smith chipped in with one. I'd taken 37 at an average of 13.97 and excuse me if I am a little proud, but that's a fair return from the place I had found myself before that summer. We often get judged only on how many wickets we get but that can be a shallow measure. If it wasn't me getting them then one of the other guys would have and I would have been happy for them. Ryan got a fair share and Sidds did the job that he was asked to do without complaint or ego. I never saw him get frustrated; he never spoke about not getting wickets. He knew he was doing his part and that was important. I could retire happy now. Not that I was in any mood to waste this form I was in and the way the bowling unit had gelled – we'd worked way too hard to get here to throw it away now.

I was standing in the corner with Jess at one stage and there were people everywhere and I said I don't think I am going to last tonight. It is an enormous emotional and physical let-down at the end of a series. I don't know if it would have been more special to win in England, but it is hard to imagine anything better. I had played cricket the way I wanted to play, with that aggressive brand, and that was really important as others had wanted me to change. Maybe this was the first time I had lived up to everybody's expectations. The journey had started that day in 1999 when I went down to Brisbane and Dennis anointed me as the best bowler since Brett Lee. A lot of people had seen my potential and there had been times when I had displayed it, but I guess this time I had fulfilled it.

Michael Clarke had some nice things to say about me at the presentations.

'Man of the Series, who would have thought, except me and probably Mitch? He's been an amazing bowler for a long time. He's bowled with a lot of aggression. To be able to bowl at that pace is one thing; to be able to do every single innings and back it up is an amazing achievement.

'Mitch has bowled a couple of spells through this series that are without doubt as good a spell as I've ever seen in my career. I've been lucky enough to play with Glenn McGrath, Jason Gillespie, Brett Lee, Shane Warne … Mitch's spells certainly match the greats I've seen, if not better.

'He's copped a lot of criticism through his career – he's been dropped – and no one in the world can doubt Mitchell Johnson's character ever again. He's as tough a cricketer as I've played with. To have the attitude and hunger to say, "No, I'm not giving up, I'm going to come back" is a credit to him.'

I'll take that. There was a fair celebration over the next few days, perhaps the highlight of which was Chris Rogers missing the bus to the public event at the Sydney Opera House. I don't know where he was when it left, but he was in such a loose mood when he got to the event that he did a few dance moves on the stage. Typical batsman. They're all show-offs.

Of course, the summer wasn't done yet. There was a one-day series to play but I was excused from all but two matches. There was no chance to empty the suitcase when they were done, though, as we had a three-Test series to play in South Africa, so I kept it by the door.

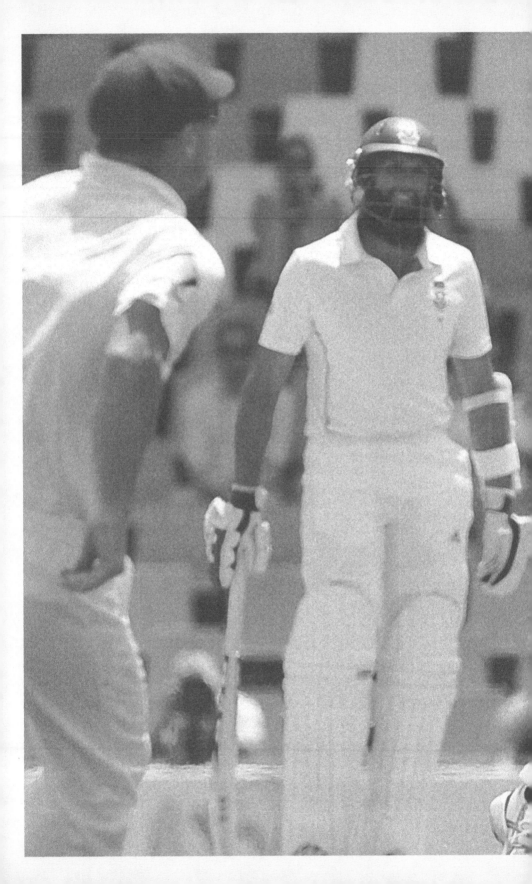

10

Unfinished Business in South Africa

IF I HAD TICKED boxes by returning to cricket and playing well against England, I still had another on the checklist. We love touring South Africa. The conditions are familiar and they play a hard brand of cricket like we do. We generally play well there, it's always competitive and although we were tired we were keen to continue what we'd started against England. I had some butterflies about returning to South Africa. It had been a very dark experience when I was there two years earlier, but this time I was in a far better place.

The first match was at Centurion, outside of Johannesburg, so we stayed in town and commuted. Johannesburg is a pretty intense city and we were advised against going out. However, we usually stayed at a hotel in Sandton that is connected to an enormous shopping centre and restaurant strip. Basically, you never really go outside. The shops are connected to the restaurants, built around Mandela Square, which features a huge statue of the great man (this year someone had made him an equally huge African shirt that looked pretty cool) and you can sit in the open but you are never really outside as such.

It was emphasised to us just how hairy it can get when we were staying there in 2009 and there was a gunfight on the footpath outside the hotel. And this is in the best and safest part of town. On the way to games you drove through the nice suburbs and all the homes were behind enormous walls with security guards posted at the driveway. It was a strange way to live. Anyway, we were here to play cricket.

I knew things had really changed for me when somebody pointed out that kids in the crowd at the first Test were wearing Mitchell Johnson moustaches. South African crowds can give the Barmy Army a run for their money. I remember in one game at the Wanderers one guy was so offensive security escorted him out and the people around apologised to me for it. So to have young fans in a foreign country was amazing. I guess it showed the impact I'd had in that Ashes series and how many people had watched it. I hadn't planned on growing the moustache that summer. I'd been doing it for years for Movember, a charity for testicular cancer. With the big series coming up I just didn't want to draw any attention to myself, but Jess said not to be silly, so I did it.

It became a thing. I looked like a serial killer. Some people said I looked like Ivan Milat or a bad guy in a Western movie.

I was a bit self-conscious of it at first, but came around as it seemed to help give me an aggressive edge. I did look like a psycho! It was never going to stay but I've had a thing for not being clean-shaven when I play ever since.

I definitely arrived in South Africa feeling confident. Graeme Smith had said they knew what to expect from me and were prepared for it, which was interesting to hear. He didn't mind adding fuel to the fire. It was the South African way. They were a bit like us in that regard. Michael wasn't above a bit of talk, too, and let it be known at the start of the series that he thought he had the best bowling attack in the world. This was pretty provocative because they had Dale Steyn, Morné Morkel and Vernon Philander.

They sent us in at Centurion and our batters did well, knocking up 397. I enjoyed my innings, crashing a few fours from my opposite numbers on the way to 33. There was good bounce and pace in the wicket and I was going to have some fun by the look of it.

Graeme Smith said he was ready for me, but on the second ball I bowled to him he used his bat handle to protect his face and looped a simple catch into the slips cordon. I'd trapped him on the crease and he couldn't get out of its way. That was an absolute statement. I was still bowling as well and as nastily as I had at home and Smith was always going to be in trouble. He has heavy feet and he puts himself in bad positions to the short ball. It's always nice to have one over the opposition captain.

Ryno and I tied Hashim Amla and Alviro Petersen down for the next couple of overs, then Petersen cracked and had a slash at one he was in no position to play. Hadds took the catch. Faf du Plessis is a bloke who'd caused us some trouble at home on the previous tour and one we liked to wind up. For some reason he hates wearing a shirt and is always walking around bare-chested. Some of the boys thought this was a bit much and would really get stuck into him for his vanity.

There wasn't a lot of time to chat because five balls into his innings he found himself in the same position Smith was in a few overs earlier. Again he found a ball rushing at his face and he had no way of getting out of the way so he had to throw the bat up in front of his face and was caught in the slips like his skipper.

The South African top order was having as much trouble with me as the English tail had a month or two earlier. From four overs I had 3–10 and it was time to rest. Sidds knocked over Amla lbw while I was catching my breath, then South Africa rallied a bit before Nathan Lyon got JP Duminy to try and hit one over my head later in the day. I ran backwards, threw a hand up and managed to hang on to the ball. I was pretty pleased with the catch and so were the boys.

It was getting late in the day, but I had my tail up and managed to work one through the gate and bowl Ryan McLaren and pick up my fourth wicket. It was getting pretty rough for the batsmen as the light was fading and there was a thunderstorm rolling in. Africa does the best storms. It feels great bowling in these situations. You feel like you are in a horror movie (and not the victim).

I aimed a bouncer at AB de Villiers after tea that ripped through him and then sailed over Hadds's head for four. Later, he wore a nasty blow on the arm but gritted his teeth and stuck around until lightning and rain forced us back into the shed. It was a pity – I had 4–50, they were 6–140 and we were on top. AB had just notched up his 11th consecutive half-century. He is a remarkable batsman; he just has that time to play you that others don't. I have to admit to even congratulating him on a shot he played during that session.

Our party continued the next day as I picked up three more, including AB who was in the 90s and the only South African to show any resistance. When I bounced Morkel out we had a first innings lead of 191 and I had taken 7–68. They were all out for 206, which was a vast improvement on how I'd gone last time I was in this part of the world.

David Warner and Alex Doolan put on a 200-run partnership, which meant we led by 500 when we declared with two whole days left to play. It's nice to have a new ball in your hand on the fourth morning with that many runs to play with; it means you can just throw the switch to attack and see what happens (pretty much what I'd been doing all summer). I started where I left off, knocking over Alviro Petersen with my fifth ball and bouncing one from Hashim Amla's gloves into his grille the next delivery. Graeme Smith was gone – thanks to a sensational catch by Alex Doolan at a short square leg the next over. The ball came right off the middle of the bat and Smithy just shook his head as he walked off. It was hard work for the batsmen. Ryan McLaren copped a nasty blow to the side of the head from a short ball I bowled that didn't get up as much as he thought. He was bleeding and I was pretty worried about him, but he managed to get himself up to face the next ball, which was the last before the break. I got him with the third ball of my next over. AB made a few but fell short of his 12th consecutive 50 when I got him driving a slower ball for the second time in the match. Vernon Philander hung in there for a while but I crushed his fingers in the first over he faced and broke his bat in the second. We had won easily with a day to spare.

It was a big win for us as the South Africans were the number one ranked team in the world and had lost only one of their last 19 Tests. I had picked up 5–59 in the last innings to finish with 12 for the game – the best of my career. What a difference two years had made. Cricket nuffies informed me that I was the first left-arm Australian bowler since Bruce Reid to get that many wickets in a game. Graeme Smith's comments at the start of the match had given me extra motivation and it was pretty satisfying to pick him up early in both innings. At the end of the Test he put my wickets down to the pitch, which I found laughable. He was making excuses and trying to say my talent wasn't a part of it, but I had the wickets and had done the job. It was a poor thing to say, especially when you have a set of bowlers like he had. Clearly they had every chance to do the same job.

They jumped us in Port Elizabeth. I found it really hard going with the ball and only picked up a handful of wickets for the match (they declared five down in their second innings). Their bowlers got a heap of reverse swing that we couldn't summon. Davey Warner got into trouble for suggesting that AB was doing something a bit tricky with the ball in his keeper's gloves, which he was, but apparently you are not allowed to say such things. There was a big stink over it and he got fined, but that was ridiculous. He didn't say they were cheating. Sometimes the people running cricket treat us like school kids. I know I bang on about it, but why shouldn't we be able to have a bit of a chat or say what we think? It's as if they want the game played by robots who say good shot and applaud politely then go and sit quietly in the corner. You only have to see the things that make highlights packages or listen to crowds to know that they love a bit of spice again.

The South Africans had been in trouble a few times for doing things they shouldn't to the ball. Some think bowlers should be able scuff the ball up a bit to balance up a contest that has become one sided because of flat wickets, big bats and small boundaries. I suspect it went on a bit when there weren't as many cameras. I know people have used their thumbnail, but even if I could grow fingernails I couldn't bring myself to do it. It's against the rules and that's all there is to it. In training I had tried different ways to reverse the ball. I rubbed it on the concrete and loaded it up with lots of spit just to see what would happen, but I could never do it in a game. It felt like I was doing something illegal when I did that. Teams throw the ball from the outfield onto the central wicket square to rough it up and I think that is okay as it is a bit random and can hit either side. I am not sure you should be doing it from the infield.

So it was one-all heading into the final game at Cape Town. We always have a lot of fun in that city. At Port Elizabeth there is not a lot to do, but Cape Town is easier to get around and has some extraordinary food and sightseeing. There are great clubs and restaurants and it is no coincidence that it's the city where the families join us. We have a window for them on every tour, which is paid for by us as part of our pay deal and most come at this time because it usually coincides with a break between Tests. There's nothing to stop partners or kids coming at any other time, though.

The cartel was in trouble going into the last match. Sidds was replaced with James Pattinson for some reason. You don't want to lose someone from a winning set-up, but that's what they did and there is no point getting upset about it. They stuck with Ryan Harris, but, because of his ongoing battles with knee injuries, he was a game to game proposition by that stage. The old man really was in a bad way with his knee; he had a bit of bone or something that used to just float around the joint and would show it to us when it came somewhere you could see. His knees were just bone on bone anyway. The cartilage was worn away. It was amazing he could play cricket at all. If he was a car you'd send it to the wreckers. He declared himself fit for Cape Town, but would have to battle through a bit more pain than usual to get through. Ryno always played in pain but this match was taking it up a notch even by his standards.

The Test went our way and when we declared on the fourth afternoon; we had a lead of 511, thanks to one of the bravest innings you would wish to see in our first innings. Michael Clarke was beaten up as badly as any batsman I have ever seen by the South Africans – Morné Morkel in particular. He was hit everywhere and was constantly being treated by the side of the wicket, but he toughed it out to score 161 not out.

We needed six wickets to win on the last day. Problem was Ryno couldn't get out of bed. Literally. Something had torn in his hip to compound the problems with his knee and he couldn't swing his leg to get off his back. He wasn't in any condition to bowl; they couldn't give him a jab for fear of numbing the whole leg. Our physiotherapist Alex Kountouris did his magic and they decided they might be able to squeeze nine overs or so out of the old bloke. It was a flat pitch and that meant we were going to have to work hard.

The day dragged on. And on. And on. Their lower order just held us out. I bowled and bowled, and bowled some more, and so did everyone else. They weren't interested in scoring runs, but the pitch was so dry and lifeless we couldn't force a wicket. It wasn't really what we needed at the end of a long summer, but it was one of those days that can only happen in Test cricket. It's probably hard to watch and it is bloody hard to be part of, but it turned out to be very special. You find out what people are made of in these situations. It turned out that the old bowler Ryno was made of pretty strong stuff (although I think we knew that anyway).

The boys had in the back of their minds what happened in Adelaide two years earlier when South Africa blocked it out for the day, but we had discussed that and our plan was to keep at it, we knew they would consolidate through the middle of the day and if we kept bowling good balls we knew we might get some at the end. Still, we didn't really expect them to hang on like they did, and it got a bit heated late in the day with Pup and Steyn clashing after Philander wasn't given out caught. It was hot, everyone was tired and frustrated and things were said. Philander had been there for about three hours and we were trying to stay cool but not doing as well as we should.

With five overs left in the game they were eight down and we didn't know where our next wicket was going to come from. I'd bowled 34 overs and was cooked. Ryno had bowled a heap more than he should have, but Pup asked him to go one more time.

The big fella had been hobbling in on one leg and I felt sorry for him, watching him get to the top of his mark for one last attempt at winning the match. He would never give up, but he was absolutely shattered. In three balls, he had wrapped up the game.

Somehow Ryno found the energy to bowl an outswinging yorker first ball to bowl Dale Steyn, who'd been out there frustrating us for more than an hour. God, we celebrated that wicket. Pup especially. Two balls later, he put one right through Morné Morkel and it was the greatest pressure release of all time. We'd done it!

That win was up there with the Ashes. Seriously. I have never seen a braver effort by a bowler. Bowling that day probably cost Ryno his career, but I think he accepted that – he was never going to say no. As it turned, out he never played another Test match.

Neither did Graeme Smith, who had surprised everyone by announcing his retirement midway through the game. We gave him a guard of honour for his last innings, but I wasn't going easy on him, and his farewell innings lasted just three balls. We'd had some history, but I think we respected each other over time. I had followed his career since meeting him at the Under-19 World Cup. It was very difficult for him as a young captain; he got a lot of publicity and a lot of criticism. I saw a change in him over time – he became a really good leader and a good guy. I have respect for what he gave the game even if he got up my nose sometimes with the things he'd say.

We had a lot of battles; Smithy had that unorthodox way and he played the way he played knowing it worked for him. He was quite difficult and frustrating to bowl to at times. Because of his grip we tried to get him to hit through the covers, but he picked up that part of his game as well. He struggled in the end with the short ball. If you got a good one he would seem to lose the ball and throw his hands at it; he couldn't really get underneath it because he was a big man. I remember him coming out to bat at the SCG with a broken hand. We couldn't believe it. We were in shock that he would risk it but it went to show what sort of a person and team man he was. He was trying to save the game for his team. I guess it was just the same as Ryno did in that game.

I finished the series with 22 wickets at 17.36. Smithy had said after the Centurion game that I was picking up all my wickets bowling to the tail, but someone else pointed out that 17 of the 22 were top-order batsman. I'd got him four times and AB de Villiers four times as well.

AB is one of those batsmen you just want to bowl to and do well against because he is so good. As far as I'm concerned we have a massive rivalry. I have always gone hard at him and I have always admired him. He is a class above most other players; he has the ability to wait for the ball, play it under his eyes and he never seems to show any anxiety even on those odd occasions when he is out of nick. It was only after I finished that I had a chat to him about that and he said he was often sweating bullets, but he didn't want us to know.

Ryno wasn't the only bloke struggling at the end of the match. As a fast bowler your feet get hammered and my big toe had been rubbing against the top of my boot for the whole series. The skin rubbed off, which I could live with, and by the end of this match there was a hole on the top of the joint. I remember getting treatment for it in the dressing rooms, but it didn't worry me too much. I was pretty cooked and didn't stay for the one-day series. It was good to get home and see Jess and Rubika. A few days later I went to lunch with Jess and her family and I felt my foot getting hot. I looked down and it was red and swollen. It didn't feel right so we decided to get it looked at. When we were driving to see the doctor I looked down and could see these red lines running up my calf and by the time we got there they were up to the knee. I was sent off to a specialist and by this time the lines had reached my thigh.

Apparently, I had a streptococcal infection. They put me on a drip and started pumping antibiotics into me straight away. The specialist said it was quite serious and that there was no way I could go off to the T20 World Cup, which was really disappointing, but not the worst thing that could have happened, given how rapidly the infection had progressed.

I won the Sir Garfield Sobers Player of the Year award from the ICC for my efforts that year and the Allan Border Medal. I was not one for personal honours in cricket, but those two meant a lot at this point in my career. It was another reward for the effort I had put in. Jess was proud of me, too. I had to record an acceptance video for the international award, but Jess frocked up and accompanied me to Sydney for the AB Medal, and we had a big night that ended up with karaoke singing in a dark bar somewhere. I had something to sing about, but I'm too shy for that business. Jess might have got up, though; it's all a bit of a blur.

Australia v India, Second Test, Day 3, the Gabba,
19 December 2014.

11

Cricket in Perspective

I THINK I WAS in as good a place with my cricket as I had ever been, but my love of the game was put into perspective before the start of the 2014–15 season. Not many people loved cricket as much as Phillip Hughes did. When he died – two days after being struck in the neck by a ball – it was hard to love it or play it the same way I had when he was alive. That horrible tragedy changed so many things. I feel so awful for his family. The impact his passing had on the rest of us is irrelevant by comparison but it's there. I was never the same bowler after Phillip died.

They put his picture up in the dressing room at the first Test against India and I found it hard to look at. He was so happy in his cricket. He would hunker down at the crease and get so focused on batting, but that beaming smile was always just a moment away. When they played those highlight reels on television I cried. I cried a lot at random times. I think everyone did. For some time I wondered if I would ever be able to do what it is I do again.

I wrestled with the fact that it could have been me. I wasn't scared of being hurt; I was terrified that it could have been me that hurt him. Or somebody else. It was my job to intimidate batsmen. To bowl short and fast. To make them play from the fear of being hit by the ball. I questioned all of that. And when I did bowl a bouncer and hit Virat Kohli on the helmet in Adelaide during the first Test match after Hughesy's death, I felt sick. I couldn't drop short with any conviction for a long time after that.

When Phillip died I struggled with guilt because I remembered how I used to pepper him in the nets, how on one occasion I let my anger get the better of me and took all my frustrations out on him. I had no idea the consequences could be fatal – that never crossed my mind or anyone's and the memory of that session filled me with dread. Cricket lost a little bit of its soul when Phillip died. I know I am not alone when I say I struggled to commit to the game again and I don't think it is a coincidence that so many of us finished up after that.

We knew it was only a game, but we fooled ourselves that it was the most important thing there was. Suddenly, it was put into context and didn't matter that much. You get that sense that cricket isn't all there is a bit when you get married and a bit more when you have kids, but it was nothing compared to the way we felt when this tragedy happened. There was a lot of talk about playing the game and doing what he wanted but I can tell you it all felt pretty hollow.

Jess and I were out on 25 November, in Perth, when I noticed alerts coming through that Phillip had been hit while batting at the SCG. It was the last Sheffield Shield round before the first Test in Brisbane, Pup was injured and there was every chance that either Hughesy or Shaun Marsh would get the vacant spot. I learned later that he was playing one of those typical innings where he'd decided no one was getting him out. I'd bowled to Hughesy a fair bit in state cricket and once he dug in like that the only thing you could ever do was to drop short to him. Two seasons before, in a game against South Australia at the WACA, we just couldn't get him out. Nobody was making any runs but he was impossible to remove. I went at him really hard, but nothing I bowled or said flustered him. In the end we ran him out when he was on 92 – it felt like the only way we were going to get him.

I felt bad about the way I'd gone at him and apologised after play. 'Don't worry, bruzzie,' he said, before flashing that cheeky smile. 'It's all good, it's all in the game.' He called everyone bruzzie. Hughesy was one of those guys that nobody could dislike; he always had a smile on his face and he just loved playing cricket. People gathered around him on tours. Before the accident, we were in the UAE together for the series against Pakistan and while he didn't play a game it didn't bother him. He was king of the coffees, always in a café with a group, baseball cap on, mischievous grin …

When the news first came through I wasn't too worried. People got hit all the time; they shrugged it off and my first thoughts were that he would do the same, maybe he was a bit dazed or concussed. I was concerned for him, but there was nothing to suggest how concerned I should be. I had to drive somewhere and Jess was keeping me updated from the passenger seat. She started to get worried and said it looked like it was really serious. We were living with her mum and dad at the time and when we got there Jess went inside and I sat in the car and started to look at the reports myself.

The footage stunned me. It was edited but you could see he was in a bad way. I started texting the boys to find out what was going on. I even texted Phil just to see if he was okay. Batsmen always get up again. Get a few stitches, take a headache tablet, sit down for a while and then get on with it. Messages started to come back saying it was not looking good. I started to really worry. I rang Watto and he told me what had happened. He was fielding at slip and said it didn't look that bad when he got hit, that there was no big noise or anything and that it was only when he collapsed that they realised. He said that they helped him onto the stretcher. Every new bit of information seemed to paint a worse picture.

When I went inside, Jess could see how shaken I was. She was really supportive; she kept saying positive things and tried to ease my mind, but it was hard. I was so far away from everyone and felt really removed from everything. I was supposed to do a pre-arranged live cross to Fox Sports, but it didn't feel right and I cancelled it. I'm glad I did. There was no better news the next day. I didn't know what to do. I went to the gym to try and distract myself. I kept talking to the boys; I remember talking to Ryan Harris about it and then I got a message that night saying that if I wanted to see him I should get on a plane and come to Sydney. The doctor and some of the senior players told us to prepare for the worst. It was the most awful news I'd ever had.

I was all over the place on the flight across the country the next morning. I was anxious about what I would see in the hospital when I arrived, but I knew I had to go. When I was 13, my nan was really sick and I was supposed to go and visit her after tennis training, but I just forgot about it and she died soon after. I felt so guilty and, being young, I sort of blamed myself in a stupid way for her being dead. That bothered me for a long time.

Then, when we were at high school one of the girls, Katie, got hit by a car and was in a coma and I remember going to visit her at the hospital and seeing her on a respirator. We were in Year 11. I couldn't recognise her. They said it would be good if we talked to her, and we did for a while, but the whole situation was really confronting. She died soon after that and the images of her in the hospital stayed with me.

The last time I saw Phillip was when we left the UAE a month earlier, and part of me said that was the way I wanted to remember him. He was so happy on that tour – it was probably the best I have seen him. He was never one to get down, although he had plenty of reason to, but over there he was in a really good place. It was like he had accepted his time would come, that he just had to keep doing what he was doing. He had a real contented feeling about him and it was good to see. Michael Clarke used to say he would play a hundred Tests for Australia and there was no reason to think he wouldn't.

I tried to occupy myself on the plane but I just couldn't stop thinking about him. I don't know if I have ever had a longer trip. I was sitting towards the front of the plane and when we landed in Sydney I turned my phone on and learned he was gone. I couldn't move. I just sat there with my cap pulled down and cried as everybody got off the flight. Some people put their hand on my shoulder and offered their condolences; you could see how shaken up people were. Everybody was feeling it.

Eventually, I got off the plane and headed to the SCG because I knew the boys would be there. The first people I saw when I walked in were his parents, Vinnie and Greg, and you can imagine the state they were in. I'd first met them in South Africa in 2009. I gave his mum a big hug and she wouldn't let go. There was nothing you could say. Seeing his family was the hardest moment. It was very raw.

It was good to be around other cricketers. The guys who were there when it happened were really shaken up but a few of them wanted to talk about it. I really felt for them. I couldn't imagine what they were going through. I was a bit worried about Sean Abbott, who was bowling when Hughesy was struck, and I had a bit of a talk with him. The others said that he was going alright, but we were all keeping a close eye on him. I don't know if I would have handled myself that well if I was in his situation.

From the moment I learned how serious it was I had started thinking about what had happened in India the year before. It was the morning I had been called in and told I wasn't going to be selected to play because of my homework. We had a net session and my eyes were spinning because I was so angry. Hughesy and Glenn Maxwell were in the nets and I just took my frustration out by bowling short. I really tested both of them. He just took it as he always did. I always practised my bouncers when we trained – people knew that if they were in my nets – but that day I really had my tail up.

I just felt really awful about that. Anything could have happened. I think I apologised to Hughesy later. I hope I did. I know I spoke to Alex Doolan when we all got together in Sydney and told him about how I was feeling. They were really good mates. He said Hughesy had mentioned the Shield game when I went at him hard when they were in the UAE and had told him that it didn't worry him at all.

He loved it when people went hard on the field. Funny thing was he never gave anything back. He would smile then put his head down and dig in. He was really level-headed that way. He didn't get angry or take things personally.

It was strange being at the SCG. As night fell, they turned the lights on and a lot of us wandered out onto the wicket. I had a chat with Dools and Ed Cowan. I know Watto was really uncomfortable being there – it brought back memories of what happened. I didn't go out near the pitch; I stayed near the boundary and we talked about happy times with Phillip. It was very, very sad, but we managed a few laughs.

The next day, the Test team met in the dressing room to work out what we were going to do. We were supposed to play a Test against India six days later in Brisbane. To be honest, we were lost, but we had to stick together. There was a bit of back and forth, but we weren't in a place to play and we said we couldn't play the game. There was no real debate about it. Everyone's head was scrambled but we knew the main thing was that we grieve and give him a send-off. Cricket took a back seat, as it should.

I flew home after that for a couple of days. It was hard to leave the group, but I wanted to be with my family. It was good to have that time together with the other cricketers, but most of us needed to get back and be with those we were close to for a few days. Death makes you think about life and if you're making the most of it. It was so unexpected and for it to happen on the field, the place where we love to go and compete and have fun, made it so much more powerful.

When I spoke to Jess about it, I said I didn't know if I could play the first Test. I didn't know if it mattered anymore or if it was worth it. You didn't want to risk your life for a game and I didn't want to risk taking one either. She just said she was comfortable with me playing, that it was what I did, what I trained for. She said it was a freak accident.

Part of me was just so worried about what would happen when we got back on the field. There were so many emotions and thoughts going around that it was really hard to think clearly. They mapped out a few training sessions for us bowlers when we left the group, but it was totally up to us whether we did them or not; there was no pressure. I went to the gym to get some of the tension and the emotion out.

I didn't do any cricket training until two days before I left for the funeral in Macksville. The first session I just went down by myself and bowled in an empty net because I wasn't sure if I could even do it. The next day some of the WACA boys were there and I asked Hilton Cartwright if he was okay to bat. Everyone was in a different place dealing with it. He said he was alright, but I was nervous as all hell. I came off a really short run and just floated the ball up.

The following day we flew to Sydney and then up to Coffs Harbour for the funeral in Macksville. It was the first time I had been to a funeral since school. We walked through Macksville behind the coffin with his family, and the support that turned out for him and them was amazing. At one point Ryan Harris turned to me and said, 'We have got to play', and I said, 'What do you mean?' He said, 'All the support here, all these people, this is why we play, we have to do it.' It was a good point.

Hughesy always talked about that town and his bulls. It was a bit of a running joke, but he loved the place and he loved those animals. He used to say we should all visit and I guess we all did. God, I wish it had been under different circumstances. Afterwards, we gathered at the local RSL and drank with his family and their friends. It was a big show and there were a lot of cricketers there. It felt good to be together again.

The whole time seems surreal. When we said we weren't going to play the first Test, Cricket Australia shifted the game to Adelaide and we all flew there after the funeral. And then we had to face up to the business of playing cricket again. It felt too soon. We had training at the No. 2 ground, a tentative net session, but our fitness coach brought out a music box and got us doing daggy dancing in our warm-up, which was the light touch we needed. We all embarrassed ourselves and laughed a lot.

I then had to try and bowl. I was really nervous and half-hearted. There was no way I could bowl a bouncer. Then I had a bat and was extremely tentative batting. I could only face the spinners. I had a few throwdowns, but when the ball dropped short I cringed like a turtle, pulling my head in between my shoulders. I was spooked in the nets in Adelaide, but I wasn't alone. Most guys were. Watto was struggling big time, Davey Warner walked out after half-a-dozen balls.

In the second session of the day, Darren Lehmann got Billy McDermott to urge me to bowl a short ball. I kept saying to myself you have to do it at some point, get it out of the way now, but I couldn't do it. Watto and Shaun Marsh were batting and I would normally bowl short to Shaun. I always pick the guys I think can handle it. He was one, Hughesy was one of them, too.

Pete Siddle and Ryan Harris dropped a few short, but the batsmen couldn't handle them. Watto couldn't get his feet going to get under the ball. It was like we'd developed this phobia about the short ball. It felt really tense, or that is how I felt. Right near the end I sucked it up and dropped one short to Mitch Marsh, and it only came through at chest height. I didn't feel right about it, but nobody got hurt and it was a small step forward.

It was the same the next day when we moved to the main nets. I can't fit my run-up in there either and that really annoyed me this time. I think I bowled one short ball that session then it was time to go out and play in front of a crowd. At our pre-match meeting the discussion had been about how we would play, if we would play with our trademark aggression. That is what has won us games; it made us the team we were, but the idea of it felt disrespectful. We wanted to go there and give it everything to win that game and do it for the team and him and his family.

I knew I would have to do it; it is what fast bowlers do. I was not as much of a bowler without it. It had been part of the game since it started, or that is what I told myself. There was all this debate going on around it: some were saying it should be banned, some speculated we wouldn't bowl any in the match. I remember Ricky Ponting said the first ball should be short so we can get it out of our system and not make a big deal of it.

I was still nagged by doubts. I kept thinking, what if I get out there and I can't bowl? It wasn't like we were playing a club game. Millions were watching; I think they wanted us to get out there and do it to start the healing process. We were heading into the unknown – nobody knew what would happen. We didn't want to let anyone down.

It was pretty hard when we lined up for the anthem and tribute at the start of the match. I could see how much it was affecting my mates and I was really worried for the guys like Davey Warner, Steve Smith, Watto and Nathan Lyon. You could see in their eyes how much they were struggling. Poor

Davey had to break from the ceremony and pad up to be out there for the first ball with Chris Rogers. He was one of the guys who we weren't sure would be able to play in the lead-up to the game. He was the one who was holding Phillip as they took him off the ground. I don't know how he got through the week. What happened when he got out there was amazing. Davey just launched into the bowlers. He just pasted them to all points from ball one. He hit seven fours from the first 14 balls and the game was on. The Indian bowlers dropped a few short and that was good. Warner, Pup and Smithy got centuries and they were all extraordinary innings. They each marked the milestones by acknowledging Phillip and that was very touching.

We kept India in the field for two days and on the third day I had to face the moment I had been dreading. I stood at the top of my mark and was relieved when I got to the wicket and let the first one go. I dropped one short in my first over but it didn't feel right. It was like I was going through the motions; there was no aggression in it. Later on I got Murali Vijay's wicket and Virat Kohli came out to face up. I had my tail up and a bit of that old aggression back, but not for long. I dropped a short first ball to Virat and he ducked straight into it. It collected him right on the badge of the helmet.

I felt sick. I went up to see if he was okay and he seemed to be fine. Michael Clarke grabbed me and steered me back to my run-up, tried to get me to think about the next ball. He said it was just part of the game, get on with it. I think it was a difficult moment for him as well.

It took me a long time to get my focus back on what needed to be done after that. I couldn't summon up any aggression and I don't think I bowled a whole-hearted bouncer for the rest of that game. I struggled in the following game, too, and I am not sure if I have ever bowled one in the same way since. You have to mean it when you do it. You bowl the short ball to intimidate people. You want them to take evasive action and you want them to be frightened of getting on the front foot after that. Those are the facts of the situation and in the aftermath of what happened to Hughesy it seemed almost impossible or irresponsible to have that intent.

We had to work hard to win in Adelaide, but we did and I am really proud and happy about that. We had to overcome a lot and it was a victory not just for us as a team, but one that meant something to a lot of people. So many of the guys stepped up and I am sure they did it for Hughesy. Pup's, Smithy's and Dave's hundreds were special and Nathan Lyon's seven wickets to win us the match was a breakthrough moment for him. These were the people who were feeling it the most, but they found a way to perform.

In the second Test in Brisbane, the Indians came hard at me; they were giving me a working over verbally when I came out to bat, or one of them was. Both their quicks were dropping short but it stirred up something in me. It got my blood pumping and I took them on, pulling a couple to the boundary early. I hit 13 fours and a six on the way to 88 before they got me. That felt good and I bowled much better too. It must have freed me up a bit. I hadn't got a wicket in the first innings of the game but after having a hit I came back and took four. We won that game and were 2–0 up.

There was a bad moment in Brisbane with Chris Rogers being hit hard on the helmet when fielding in close during their innings. It sent a shiver through us all and you could see he was rattled. He said later that it was when he started to think about retirement. I understood.

Things almost seemed back to normal after that, particularly after an incident in Melbourne where I hit Virat Kohli with the ball while trying to run him out. He'd hit the ball towards me and taken a step down the pitch. Naturally, I hurled it back and it was going to hit the stumps, but he'd pulled out of the run and turned the moment he saw me raise my arm. It struck him hard in the back of the leg. I apologised to him. It wasn't on purpose but he wanted to ignore that. He was in his 80s at the time and we'd just taken the new ball. He flashed at the next one and it went to where third slip would have been. He came up to me and started accusing me of this and that. I replied as best I could but the umpires led him away.

The next over I had him dropped in slips by Watto and then a top edge fell short of Hadds. He was pretty fired up; so was I. He went on to make 169, so I don't know what he had to complain about. I was legitimately trying to run him out, but he didn't like what I did. When he made some comment in the media that night about having no respect for me as a player, that's when I got really annoyed. It was a bit rich for him to go out and complain, as he did, about things that are said on the field. Having said that, Virat is the kind of player you'd want in your team. He's a real fighter and to be honest he's a bit like most of us in the Australian team. We go pretty hard on the field, and he's got that about him as well. The fact he plays the game like us is probably why we've rubbed each other the wrong way. He's a fiery character and he pushes the boundaries, just like I've always tried to do. Maybe that's why we've clashed so often.

One thing that helped me emerge from the fog of Phillip's death was the contest. Taking on blokes like Virat helped distract me, and focusing on the game was therapy of sorts. After the series I had two clear goals for 2015: the ODI World Cup at home and the away Ashes.

2015 ICC Cricket World Cup, Australia v
New Zealand, the MCG, 29 March 2015.

12

On Top of the World

THE BIG EVENTS KEEP you going and give you clear goals. The 2015 World Cup came first and it was at home (except for one match in New Zealand), which was really special for us. I had been a tourist at the 2007 series when the giants of that era won in South Africa. In 2011, we didn't even make the finals in India. I wanted one of my own. I also wanted to make the most of this one knowing it would be my last. I didn't think I was going to be around in another four years so I really wanted to enjoy it on and off the field.

Our World Cup campaign was almost perfect. I was in a good place to enjoy it and the whole team was on the same page. It was a credit to Darren Lehmann's coaching that we could be so relaxed. We didn't put too much extra pressure on ourselves, which can happen when you play in a big event at home. It's funny how you realise all these things in the twilight of your career and a crying shame you can't know them from day one.

The tournament had a strange rhythm. There was a week between games where there would be one game every three or four days on a usual tour. There was no point staying on. That would have been a short cut to burning out. I remember cracking a beer open on the plane to Brisbane after one match, which caused a bit of chat from the boys. They had never seen me do anything like that before. There was a bit of talk that I was going back to the good old days when boys didn't mind a beer or ten, but it was symbolic as much as anything. I just wanted to relax and enjoy it and part of that was to have a beer. A few of us made a point of going out and having a couple every time we arrived in town for a new game. Sometimes the guys went home between games if there was a chance, so it was pretty casual. I think that's why we did so well. It was just a calm approach. Anxiety, as I well knew, can trip you up pretty quickly.

On reflection, having the odd beer in later years was another sign that I was getting the balance right. When I first played Test cricket I liked to enjoy myself and probably overdid it sometimes. I know I used to come home from a tour and get stuck into it every night trying to get over jet lag by drinking myself to sleep the first few days. I'd also discovered that if I went out for a big night on tour it affected me for two days. I would be really lazy the next day and do nothing, whereas a lot of the guys might sweat it out in the gym. Those experiences, combined with my determination to get the very best out of myself, meant I became a bit of a wowser for a while. I think I over-corrected. I remember going six months without drinking at one point and that was probably a bit overboard. There is nothing wrong with having a drink and enjoying yourself; you need to relax a bit. It impacts on everything you do. At a certain point I became robotic. I wasn't playing my game, and the one thing I was really happy with at the end of my career was that I was playing the way I wanted to play and bowling the way I wanted to bowl.

It was the same with food. My diet wasn't great in the early days when I lived in Brisbane. I would smash the takeaway – cooking wasn't my strong point – but that changed when I lost my contract and had to think about my approach. Coming back from my toe injury I think I found a good place with what I ate and what I drank. Sometimes I would have a blow-out, but most of the time I was just having the odd drink to celebrate a win or relax between games. Jess and I are really careful about our nutrition but I am not into diets as such. I tend to eat high-fat low-carb foods but I am not strict about it. Jess is half Italian and she loves her pasta, but these days we might have it once a week instead of four times. It's all about a balance and what works for you. Some regimes work better for some than others, so I would never advocate people do what I do. These days I do a lot of health and fitness advice for Blackwoods, whose customers are tradies and the like. I'm not telling anyone to flog themselves or be strict about this or that, but even if I am fairly qualified to suggest ways to look after yourself, I'm never going to preach.

I guess part of the difficulty cricketers have is that it is such a unique sport. I had watched the Olympic athletes back at the academy and always been interested in their discipline, and Jess was the same in the lead-up to a big tournament herself. These people are so strict and so focused and I really respected that. The difference with us is that we are on the road almost all the time so we need to relax and cut loose every now and then. You can't be full-on all the time otherwise you go insane. I actually think if you are too strict you will burn out and not be at your best. Believe me, I know.

Elite sport is a strange thing. When you first play it is for fun and then after a while it becomes more of a task; there is more pressure. I enjoyed cricket when I first played it, there wasn't that pressure from the outside and I didn't have too many expectations myself. I reckon you get a year early in your international career where you are left alone to do your thing and then people start expecting things of you. That was why Boof [Darren Lehmann] made a difference when he came in and said this should be the best time of your lives. It's true. Yes, you have to train hard but you have to go out and enjoy yourself. It is easier said than done, but it was what I tried to do in the last part of my career.

Winning helps relax you and we did a lot of that in our World Cup campaign, starting with a warm-up match against India at Adelaide. Our batters did a great job in that game. Dave Warner hit a solid 104 off 83 balls and set it up so Glenn Maxwell could do his magic. His 122 off 57 balls was stunning. You can't bowl to him when he gets in one of those moods.

He seems to invent shots and you are just helpless. The Indians were chasing 372 and really didn't have a hope. We then played the UAE in Melbourne in another warm-up and won by almost 200 runs.

The tournament proper kicked off in Melbourne with a game against England. I had played one game in the tri-series against them after the Tests and we'd beaten them easily. Their team was not in a good place and seemed to be playing a dated form of one-day cricket. We batted first and set up a big total thanks to a hundred from Aaron Finch and half-centuries to George Bailey and Glenn Maxwell. They fell about a hundred runs short and we were off to a good start in the series. I was on a hat trick in the game when I had Moeen Ali and Eoin Morgan (the captain left one that swung back and bowled him) out on consecutive balls, but it wasn't to be. Again.

The match in Brisbane against Bangladesh was washed out. So we took off to Auckland for the match against the Kiwis, who were in a good place and probably the biggest threat in the tournament. Trent Boult and Tim Southee bowl beautifully in their conditions. Batsmen like Brendon McCullum, Martin Guptill and Kane Williamson were all dangerous if they got going. Eden Park is an intense venue. It's small and designed for rugby and it feels like the crowd are sitting on your shoulders. They are a passionate mob the Kiwi supporters; they hate us with a passion and they let us know.

We panicked when we batted. We let the crowd get to us, we got caught up in it, they got on a bit of a roll and we just needed to bat out a few overs and get through that adrenalin rush. Nobody did that; we went with it for a bit and it was pretty disappointing. They were bowling well but all we needed was someone to calm things down. They had us all out for 151 and even that was thanks to a bit of sensible batting from Brad Haddin down the order. They got to 1–78 and it was obvious we had lost the game, but when Pat Cummins got rid of Brendon McCullum in the eighth over (50 from 24 balls) things changed.

Mitchell Starc bowled one of the best spells you will ever see. He got James Taylor and Grant Elliott with successive balls at the start of the next over and it was on. He almost won the game for us; he just needed one other bowler to go with him, but even without us he almost did it. It was like he was possessed. He had this focus and determination; he thought he could win the game. The crowd was completely silent in the middle of this and it had been deafening for most of the match. He had 6–28 at the end of nine overs. They were nine down, but Williamson hit the winning runs and that was that.

We didn't let the loss get to us. Sometimes in those big tournaments when you lose a game you can panic, but we just accepted it and moved on. We just thought it was a one-off and knew that most of the games would be at home and so we were pretty confident. We went from one extreme to another, flying from Auckland to Perth for the game against Afghanistan. Somebody worked out we covered 11,000 kilometres to play the Auckland–Perth–Sydney games. Davey Warner hit 178, Steve Smith 95 and Glenn Maxwell 88 as we put on 414 batting first. I picked up 4–22 and we won by 275 runs. We were told later it was the second highest winning margin ever.

It wasn't as easy against Sri Lanka in Sydney, but a century off 50-odd balls to Maxi set us up and Jimmy Faulkner took three wickets as we got home by 64 runs. Michael Clarke had come back from the injury he picked up during the first Test of the summer and scored a solid half-century, which was a fair effort considering how much cricket he had missed. Unfortunately, his return meant George Bailey had to give up his spot.

In Hobart, we put Scotland in and they could not handle Starcy (4–14) or Pat Cummins (3–42). We were three down in the 16th over when we'd scored the 131 runs to win. All good so far. In Adelaide we took on Pakistan and it was Josh Hazlewood's turn to set us up this time. He took 4–35 and they were out for 213. The best part of that game was watching Wahab Riaz bowl to Watto. He had my old mate ducking and weaving and in all sorts of trouble. It was an incredibly hostile spell of bowling and all the funnier because Steve Smith seemed to be provoking the situation by pushing easy singles at the other end to put Watto back in the firing line.

Shane won the battle, finishing with 64 not out. It was a good comeback after being dropped early in the tournament. You need experienced players in a World Cup and Watto brought that to the table. We watched the semi between New Zealand and South Africa while we were in Sydney waiting for our semifinal and we weren't sure who to go for. I think the feeling was that if South Africa won they might be harder to beat because their conditions are similar to ours and they play the game differently from New Zealand. It was a tight finish and looking back you wonder if the Kiwis had played their final in that game.

India was no match for us in the semi. We batted first, Steve Smith got a century and Aaron Finch 81 as we put on 328. I had a bit of fun swinging for a nine-ball 27 not out at the end of the innings and then got the important wicket of Virat Kohli (one off 13 balls) and Rohit Sharma (34 off 48 balls). We beat them by almost a hundred runs.

And then we had to face New Zealand in the final. We had one goal in the big game and that was to get Brendon McCullum early. If he stayed in he could destroy us. We knew that. The Kiwis hadn't played a game in Australia for a while and they hadn't played any during the tournament. A few of their players hadn't played in a ground as big as the MCG and certainly not in a match as big as the final.

McCullum swung hard at the first ball he faced from Starcy, charged the second one and got bowled by a screamer on the third. They'd won the toss and batted and they were on the back foot before the end of the first over. It was a sensational delivery from a bowler at the top of his game. We didn't give them a chance after that. I was really happy with the way I bowled. I was fast and aggressive, picked up Kane Williamson caught and bowled for not much with one I held back, and finished with 3–30. We won by seven wickets with 16 overs to spare and it felt awesome.

Starcy won Player of the Tournament for his 22 wickets at an average of ten. He played with a lot of confidence and he was definitely our strike bowler. It was good to be around him at a time like that. He is still young and was still asking questions and wanting advice, but it felt like he was really coming into his own. I think his one-day stuff had always been pretty good, but some of his spells in the World Cup were unbelievable. I would like to have spent more time with him in Tests, although he was getting pretty close there, too.

It is fair to say we celebrated pretty hard, but it is not every day you win a World Cup and it was going to be the only one I would ever win.

A Humble Champion

If you had a bat in your hand I reckon Mitchell Johnson would be about the last bloke on the planet you would ever want to see coming towards you, but I can tell you that the Mitchell Johnson who walked into our business and our lives a decade or so ago is one of the most genuine, friendly and gentle men I have ever met. I can only tell you that now that he's retired – I don't think he would want it to have got out when he was snarling beneath that moustache and laying into opposition batsmen.

Our organisation, Blackwoods, is an Australia-wide industrial supply business. We heard about the unique emerging young quick before he even played a Test, and were keen to partner with someone who our customers, particularly the younger generations, could relate to.

When I was in my previous role as National Marketing Manager, Mitchell's manager set up a meeting and I was expecting a young sports nut, with spiky hair, piercings and an aggressive swagger to turn up. Mitchell came into the room with a crisp shirt, hair combed, no jewellery in strange places and a big smile. I was almost disappointed, but he explained, in his disarmingly honest way, that his manager told him he needed to make a good impression if he was to land his very first corporate sponsorship. He's been doing that with us, customers and suppliers ever since.

You see and hear some stories about arrogant sportsmen who are so focused on their own environment that they have no time for anyone, but Mitchell is so far from that. His genuine interest in other people always amazes me. One day in Sydney we organised for him to appear at our NSW Head Office and Trade Store in the Western Suburbs. When we arrived together in the morning there was a man in the car park with his young son waiting for an autograph. Mitch had a chat to them both and then went inside to do his thing.

He came out hours later to go to another function and they were still there. The man had taken his boy out of school in the hope of seeing his hero and they were obviously big fans. Mitch had met a couple of hundred people that day but saw them still standing in the car park. Incredibly he remembered the boy's name and went out of his way to speak to him again, and gave him a signed cricket ball. Can you imagine the impression that had on a young cricket fan?

Our customers, many of whom work in heavy industries, relate to Mitch. One of our most effective campaigns involved Mitch filming customised instructional safety-related video clips featuring hydration messaging for those working in the mining, oil and gas, and construction industries.

Mitch knows a thing or two about bowling and performing at his best in the heat in places like India. The workers and OH&S teams loved the videos and the messages, and their delivery received positive feedback from across the country. The thing about Mitch is he is just a casual guy who puts people at ease.

We had a small reception once with managers and key customers and he was asked to sit at the middle of the table so he could talk to and engage with everyone. When he learned that one of the guests was formerly an SAS paratrooper he stopped everything, insisted that the guest take his chair, and then pumped him for stories in front of everyone, saying his line of work was far more important and interesting than a fast bowler's.

The next day that man sent us an email to say how special he had felt and how wonderful it had been to meet such a humble champion and what a good job we'd done having Mitch represent our brand.

Not that it is always so smooth. At one of the very first Blackwoods branch appearances at Carole Park in Brisbane, Mitch met customer service and warehouse team members and signed numerous items for invited customers who lined up with bats we supplied. Some cricket tragics brought their own treasured things in.

Mitch personalised each message and autograph.

'Bowl Fast Nathan ... Best wishes Mitchell Johnson'

'Go Queensland, all the best Richard Mitchell Johnson'

One customer strode forward and said, 'Just put your moniker on this, it's my favourite bat.'

He then turned away to speak to someone while Mitch signed, then was flabbergasted when he walked away reading the bat, which said, 'To Monica, Best Wishes Mitchell Johnson.'

The devastated customer was quickly reassured when he was provided with a brand new top-of-the-range bat.

Once we filmed Mitch for a hydration video in a private box at the WACA with a Shield game going on in the background. Mitch stood on the balcony to recite his lines and a couple of young men in their 20s had taken the day off and were sitting just behind Mitch, and in camera shot. They were politely asked if they could move 10 metres away out of shot and happily complied, but kept watching us work. The boys were increasingly amused by the number of takes required when the hydration message became complex. At one stage they crept back into camera shot and then became hysterical, laughing at Mitch trying to get the technical words and emphasis just right. One of them then took off his jacket to reveal a Mitchell Johnson Number 25 Aussie One Day shirt and said, 'Maybe you should just stick to bowling fast, Mitch!' Mitch signed two balls and tossed one to each of the guys. They stopped heckling and everyone ended up happy!

Having watched and been part of the Mitchell Johnson journey there is not a single moment I have regretted in our association and in the friendship that has emerged from it. I am comfortable introducing him to managing directors and to junior cricketers knowing that he treats everyone with respect and is genuinely interested in their story.

If you know anyone called Monica who is a cricket fan, give me a call.

Barry Hoare
Wesfarmers Industrial and Safety
Indigenous Strategic Business Development Manager

Australia v New Zealand, Second Test, Day 5,
the WACA, 17 November 2015.

13

A Big Decision

ENGLAND WAS A DISAPPOINTING tour for the team, disappointing and frustrating. On a personal level I wasn't unhappy with my performance and I was content with the way I dealt with things when it got rough over there, but that is not what we went there for. I know I didn't get 1000 wickets, but all things considered I gave myself a pass mark. In the first Test at Cardiff I thought I bowled alright. I controlled my nerves and all the baggage that came with me being back where it all went wrong six years earlier.

The ball was swinging a lot and I started off a bit wide. In the second innings I got the line right, but I just didn't get the breaks. I might have held back a little bit, the wicket was slower and with the ball moving in the air it is not really ideal for bowling flat-out. I got 1–150 odd in the first innings. I wasn't fussed by it. The crowd tried to let me know, I definitely copped it. They carried on when I got a hundred runs against my name, but I dipped my baggy to them and played it up a little and didn't let them or my performance get to me, which was important.

I came into Lord's not worried about how I was going on that level. Still, it's hard not to tighten up a little about bowling there. We had midwicket practice the day before the game and I was really unhappy with the way I was bowling from the members' end. It was the left-handers I was most concerned about, particularly Alastair Cook because I knew I would be bowling to him and he is really good at cutting. The slope there really does complicate things. If you don't get it right there with the ball going down the hill it can be disastrous. It's a fine line because he can clip you off his pads if you get too straight. I knew this because I had been taken apart here in 2009.

I was trying to get it right and I didn't normally bowl that close to the game. I certainly wouldn't have bowled as much as I did. I think I was out there for about 45 minutes or so and that's a lot longer than I should have. I remember Ryan Harris was watching and telling me to stop worrying, that I had it right and to give it a break. I just wanted to get it perfect so that I would be calm when the game started. I nailed it in the end, something clicked and I went home knowing that I had done all I needed to do.

We had one issue going into that second Test, which became apparent during the training session. Brad Haddin's wife, Karina, was on tour with his daughter, Mia. It was the first time Mia had been well enough to travel. The family had gone through so much with her; she'd been in and out of hospital for years and it amazed me how well they handled it. Karina and Hadds have been so strong I just marvel at them. Unfortunately, Mia had to be admitted to hospital when we were in Cardiff and by the time we got to London Hadds realised he was in no state to play the game. We could see him on the dressing room balcony with the team psychologist, Michael Lloyd, while we were training and knew something was wrong.

Everyone respected his choice and what he did. I think we all would have done the same thing in that situation. He didn't want it to affect the cricket and just told us to get on with it. Peter Nevill came in for him, which was great for Pete. They were teammates in club and state cricket. Brad and Karina sent him a bottle of champagne to congratulate him on his selection, which was a nice touch.

I tried not to think about it too much, but Brad had put his family first and that had been a mantra since Darren took over as coach. It was a good principle: if your home life was out of whack it would affect your cricket.

Pete is a fine keeper and a good batsman, but in terms of personality they couldn't be further apart. Hadds is the enforcer, he loves a scrap and if he finds an opening in an opponent he is in there digging around straight away. I came to miss that in the following Tests. Davey Warner had taken a vow of silence or something. He'd copped a lot of criticism for his scraps on the field, including from the chief executive at Cricket

Australia and the ICC, so now he was a vice-captain he backed off. It wasn't a great thing for the rest of us. Test cricket is a long game and conflict boosts your energy. Sometimes when we've been in the field all day a clash gets my adrenalin running again. You can tell everyone is a bit sharper if something has gone on. There definitely wasn't enough conflict that winter. Sometimes I looked around for somebody to start a war of words but nobody did. Hadds was absent. Davey was silent. Punter, Haydos, Symmo and the old boys were all gone. Oh, well, I just had to get on with it.

We raced out of the blocks at Lord's. Batting first, Chris Rogers (173) and Steve Smith (215) put on the best part of 300 for the second wicket and we declared at 8–566. It was great to see those two do well. Bucky waited forever to get his chance in Test cricket and must have thought it would never come. He'd got a taste in 2008 when we'd played India at Perth as a fill-in for Matty Hayden and then had to wait until the 2013 Ashes for another go. He was the complete professional cricketer who spent half the year playing in Australia and half of it making runs for County teams. He made the most of his second chance, but he was 37 and this was his last tour. It was also his last hundred. He was in some seriously good form and had scored 50 or more in eight of the last night innings. Unfortunately, he got a nasty blow and had to retire on 49 not out in the second innings. He had a delayed reaction, too, fainting a few days later and scaring a few of us. We were all so spooked by these things now. Earlier, Bucky had been hit in Brisbane in the second match we played after Phillip was killed. He was also concussed in the West Indies and missed two games before we got to the UK.

Smithy's innings was also important. He had been in amazing form since the start of the summer, scoring centuries in each of the four Tests against India. He'd got 192 in Melbourne and 199 against the Windies in the following series, so it was nice for him to break through the 200 barrier. He was a bit like Katich and Chanderpaul in that he was one of those batsmen who moved across their crease as you bowled. He confused your lines and had a great eye. Making 200 at Lord's is something else and he managed to do it with his mum and dad in the stands, which was pretty special for him.

We batted into the last session of the second day before putting them in. Mitch Starc got Adam Lyth with the third ball of their innings. Pete Nevill took the catch, which was a good start for him. I was brought on in the ninth over. Gary Balance hit my first ball for four, but I got one full and under his bat two balls later and he was out bowled. Josh Hazlewood got Ian Bell next over. Then I got Root and they were 4–32 and in deep trouble. Cook was hanging around but not doing any damage. He just wasn't that interested in playing shots, but that didn't bother us too much. He and Stokes hung in until stumps. Mitch Marsh got Stokes in the first session, but they were in a good spot by then and went to lunch at 5–181. Still, our 566 was up on the scoreboard to remind them that there was a long, long way to go. They were out for 312 before the day was over. I picked up one more wicket and finished with 3–53. It was pointed out to me that I was on 1999 runs when I got out in the first innings, but I didn't get a chance to bring up my 2000th at Lord's because we declared at 2–254 on the fourth day, thanks to half-centuries from Rogers, Warner and Smith.

They had to chase 500-plus and we were pretty sure they weren't going to get it. Starcy got Lyth again and when Michael asked me to bowl the ninth I knocked over Cook with my fourth ball. Wickets kept tumbling and when Stokes and Root went for a quick single after lunch I saw a chance and pinged it at Stokes's end. For some reason he didn't ground his bat and the replay showed his foot was in the air when the ball hit the stumps.

We knocked them over for 103 runs in 37 overs, I took 3–27 and we all went away pretty happy with our performance. It was one-all and we felt like the tour was back on track. England had other ideas and I am pretty sure they decided we wouldn't get a decent wicket again on this tour.

I also fell one run short of getting my 300th wicket at Lord's, which would have been nice, but I will take the win any day over a stat. The Test finished a day early so we had an extra day in London. Jess and Rubika had arrived and her parents had come to help us with Rubika, which was great. It can get pretty intense when it's just us three in a hotel room. You have to tiptoe around if the baby is asleep and everyone starts tripping over each other. Most of us with families get two attached rooms – it's that selfish thing again, but you need your sleep when you are playing. That said, there is always someone with rings under their eyes on a tour because their wife or baby is sick, or has jet lag, or things aren't going so well. An Ashes trip sounds pretty romantic, but you can spend a lot of time in some pretty ordinary places. I won't name them, but I will say that London is great and our hotel is right next to Hyde Park and close to the palaces so it's great for families.

It was off to Derbyshire for a tour match after that. The timing was a bit odd. You don't really need it, but I suppose it is good for blokes like Pete Siddle and Shaun Marsh who hadn't had a game yet. I got lucky and was allowed to stay in London. Brad Haddin came back for the game and I suppose everyone was expecting him to get the gloves back. There were some confusing messages about him and Pete Nevill sharing the role, but then Pete ended up doing the job and Hadds played as a batsman. It looked like they had decided Brad wouldn't get his place back and that was confirmed before we played at Edgbaston. There were a few raised eyebrows at the decision. We'd been told that family came first and when Brad did that he lost his spot. The papers reported that there was a division between the players and Darren Lehmann over it and it bubbled away for a while, but I am not convinced it was a distraction.

We won the toss at Edgbaston and all but lost the game before it was 40 overs old. We batted and at drinks were 3–43. The only thing that stopped the tumble of wickets was a bit of rain in the first two sessions. Bucky Rogers scored 52 but the next highest score was Adam Voges's 16. It was a disaster, we were all out for 136 in the 37th over and bowling before tea. Jimmy Anderson bowled beautifully and bagged six wickets. It should have been the best bowling performance of the series, but there was more in store. It was a cold and miserable day in Birmingham and the weather suited our performance. By stumps they were 3–133.

Day two didn't exactly start with a clean slate, but I got to bowl the second over and found something in the pitch. The third ball rose up at Jonny Bairstow and he gloved it through to Pete Nevill. He was my 300th scalp but that meant absolutely nothing in the context of the contest. Two balls later another short one did the same thing to Ben Stokes and he was gone in much the same way. England was 5–142 and we had a sniff again. It was strange how the ball took off like that. It had been dead the day before. I don't know what happened after that, but there were a few questions about the way I bowled. People wanted to know why I didn't keep bowling short, particularly as this had worked so well to their tail in Australia. I guess I just felt like I needed to bowl line and length. When I did drop short it didn't go through like it had when I got the wickets, and I was discouraged. Looking back, I guess my mind wasn't clear about what to do and maybe that reflected where we were at as a team at the time.

Root got a half-century and so did Moeen Ali and they had a lead of almost 150 by the time we bowled them out. We went a bit better in the second innings with Dave Warner, Pete Nevill and Mitchell Starc all getting half-centuries, but they only needed 120-odd to beat us and that's what they did. The game was over in three days.

We were 2–1 down and things just weren't going that well. Our batsmen were struggling. Michael Clarke couldn't get a run and nobody else was picking up the slack. I'm not making excuses or pointing the finger, but as bowlers you need something to bowl to if you bat first. You need more than 133 and you definitely need more than 60.

We moved to Nottingham for the next match. The ground is next to Nottingham Forest's stadium where the famous football manager Brian Clough has a stand named after him. There's a statue in town, too. They might put one up for Stuart Broad after what he did to us. I was extremely disappointed by what happened in the fourth Test. We had to win to keep the series alive and we had our plans in place and then just before the toss everything changed. We'd had our bowling meeting a day or two before the game and were ready to go. Then everything changed. Just after the warm-ups on the morning of the match it was obvious something was going on. We saw the two Marsh boys running around and then Rod Marsh came up to me and said, 'I hope you guys are ready to bowl for a long time.' That's when I learned they'd dropped Mitch for Shaun, which meant we were a seamer short. I was stunned. It might have been okay if Pete Siddle was in the side because he is a workhorse and can take on a heavy load, but he wasn't given a start either. Sidds didn't carry on but I know he was really frustrated by this. I was confused. I went to Watto, who'd been dropped after the first Test and said I really don't know what my role is now. Was I supposed to bowl in short sharp spells or line and length? I think everyone was confused, to be honest. Being a professional sportsman you have to adapt and it is no excuse for the way we performed, but it's not the sort of thing you want to happen just before the game.

In the end we didn't have much of a total to bowl to, so I suppose it didn't matter that much. I'd like to say I haven't seen anything like what happened, but unfortunately I had been there when we made 47 in Cape Town. Somehow this seemed worse. Going in with the three seamers was a gamble and it seemed to rely on us winning the toss and bowling. We lost and England sent us in. It was damp and overcast and just the sort of conditions English bowlers like.

Chris Rogers lasted three balls. Steve Smith three more and Broad had two in the first over. Dave Warner survived two deliveries and it just kept getting worse from there. There was an endless procession of batsmen going in and out of the dressing room door. I was fuming. I couldn't believe what was happening, guys getting out to balls that they could have left. It looked to me like we were panicking and letting the moment get to us. We needed to dig in as a team and we didn't do it. The situation got the better of us. I went out to bat when Pup was dismissed. We were 6–29 and the ball was six and a bit overs old. I wanted to play my game, but the wicket was still doing a fair bit and if our top order was struggling in those conditions how was I expected to cope? I just wanted them to bowl as many balls to me as possible. I reckon we were getting out to deliveries that were never going to hit the stumps, so I was very conservative in my shot selection. I lasted half an hour, faced 25 balls and scored 13. We made 60 inside 19 overs. I was our top scorer, but I say that without any pride. I was really, really disappointed.

The batsmen can't wear all the blame because we had the opportunity to go out there and bowl in much the same conditions. We still had an opportunity. Still, it's a difficult situation. You have to go out there and attack; if it comes off you might get back in the game, but if it doesn't you go for easy runs and they are away. We didn't get to bowl twice, they won by an innings inside three days and the series was over. They were 3–1 up.

Michael Clarke decided it was over for him, too. I wasn't surprised, but I think he took a few others by surprise. He obviously wasn't performing at his best. A few of us at that time were in the same situation; we were the same age and we'd played a lot of cricket together. Watto, as I said, was dropped after the first Test. It was a bit odd to give a guy only one game, but he was the complete professional and kept his chin up around the group even though it turned into a long tour for him following us around. Hadds was in the same boat, too. It was hard to see either of them playing Test cricket again. Michael had been honest; he felt like he was letting the team down and felt he needed to make that decision. He'd been through a lot with his back condition. He'd struggled with it for years and it took a lot just to keep him on the park. That wears you down. Having a child changes you as well and his first was on the way. I know it put a lot of things in perspective for me. For the first time in my adult life, cricket was no longer the highest priority. For the first time, I was an adult with a family to take care of.

We travelled over to Northampton after that for a tour game. One good thing about Ashes tours is that we move around by bus and don't have to bother with airports. The bus becomes like our club room and the cartel takes over the back seats. It's all a bit of fun, but we won't let anyone else down there. You have to be a fast bowler, not a 'sweat band swinger' and definitely not a batsman. Bucky Rogers was a bit put out at one stage that he wasn't let in, but it was Mitch Marsh who moaned the most. He'd carry on about how fast he bowled, but he spent too much time with batsmen for our liking. Up in Northampton there was a bit of a truth session with Darren and Rod Marsh who thought we'd been distracted by a few things and we had it out a bit, but if we were disappointed about anything it was that we were losing. There was a fair exchange of views from both sides. The three quick bowlers were not required, so we headed back to London and waited for everybody to catch up for the last Test.

Sidds finally got his chance at The Oval, which he thoroughly deserved. Josh Hazlewood was worn down and given a break. We won the toss, batted, made a lot of runs and had the game under control from there. We had something to bowl to and did our jobs. Sidds was fantastic, picking up six wickets as we went on to win by an innings. It was nice to have a win. On paper losing 3–2 doesn't look too bad but it felt a lot worse than that.

If you say you had fun on a losing tour you get howled down by critics, but we did do our best, particularly in London. Watto had found a place called Bill's in Notting Hill, which had a good breakfast so we checked it out and invited Ryan Harris and Sidds to join us. The place is owned by an Australian so at least you know the coffee is good. Watto is very particular about his coffee and even has an app on his phone so he can find good places in new towns. When we went back, we had to wait outside because it was full. We noticed a Bentley parked out the front and a photographer waiting in his car. There was obviously someone famous around but for the life of us we couldn't see who it was. We eventually got a table near the back of the place and were looking at the menu when Sidds got excited and started gesturing to the next table. 'It's David Beckham,' he whispered. But it was noisy in there and we couldn't quite hear what he was saying. 'David Beckham,' he hissed. Still couldn't hear him. 'DAVID BECKHAM,' he said loudly and just at the moment when the whole place had gone quiet. Beckham looked over at us with a look of absolute disgust and we nearly died of embarrassment, but Sidds recovered from that and announced he was going to ask him for an autograph. We all said he shouldn't – the man was with his kids and eating. We all hated it when somebody interrupted us in those situations. 'But he's a superstar, it will be alright,' Sidds said. Our mate was a huge fan, but after a while he saw sense and decided not to. I think he was well advised.

Autograph hunters are everywhere, but probably the most persistent are on the subcontinent. Still, it doesn't matter where you are. I was in the supermarket recently and I heard someone say 'Michael!' I had a feeling they were talking to me, but I ignored them and kept shopping. 'Michael!' they said again and I kept shopping. Finally they came right up to me and said, 'Michael, I am your biggest fan.' It was good to know my biggest fan didn't even know my name. It's funny how often things like that happen. Sometimes people think I am Mitchell Starc. Recently, in India, somebody thought I was Glenn

Maxwell and would not believe me when I said I wasn't. That was plain insulting.

Anyway, I like signing autographs for kids because they seem to enjoy it. Probably the people who wear us down the most are the professional autograph collectors who hang around outside every hotel asking us to sign cards and shirts and bats and pictures. They all go on eBay the next day.

The future was in the front of my mind during the England tour and more so when it ended. I reckon I'd almost had enough. An Ashes series is pretty draining, especially on the back of all the cricket we'd had leading in. I had a talk to Michael Lloyd, our psychologist, about the future and what goals I would need to set. The big goals for the season were ticked off with the World Cup and the Ashes. It was a case of where do I go from here?

They sent me home before the one-dayers. If I had stayed on for them it would have sent me over the edge and I probably would have retired. I was pretty cooked, mentally and physically. It had been a big year already. I was pretty happy to be going home but there wasn't really much of a chance to freshen up. I had a week off and then was back training with WA. I didn't play any cricket in September but there were a couple of Matador Cup games in Sydney. Even then I was not really convinced about playing for the summer, but I got five wickets in the second game against Queensland and that weekend I flew back to Perth and had a game with Wanneroo.

One of the good things about being in Perth is that my mate Dave and his brother Dylan from home had moved across and were playing for Wanneroo. It was like the old days when we were kids playing back at home and I enjoyed having them around. I had a great time. I really enjoy playing club cricket; I like the atmosphere. I like the way it is blokes playing the game as hard as they can but without all the added pressure you get when you play for your state or country. The ball was coming out well and I wasn't feeling that tired anymore so I thought I was ready to play another summer.

We went down to Tasmania after the Wanneroo game and played a Shield game. Well, it wasn't a Shield game – in reality it was an experiment with a pink ball under lights. It was pretty ordinary preparation for the first Test against New Zealand, which was soon after, but that is what they wanted us to do. I kept an open mind because I didn't want to let the boys down. I did the best job I could but I didn't enjoy it at all. To me it wasn't Shield cricket; it felt like a shortened version of four-day cricket. Every time night fell, the game would shift and you started another contest. There were too many things going on with the game that I didn't like, but I played it and played it 100 per cent and I bowled a couple of good spells. I got grumpy because Tassie was just blocking it out. The pink ball goes soft so quickly and while it is hard to score with, it is even harder to bowl with. All you do is set a ring field and go through the motions as best you can. George Bailey made half-centuries in both innings, but he took forever and I got really frustrated. I started really attacking him. I bowled really quick and I had a real crack at him. He just laughed at me. Strangely enough, that was a good sign; it showed me I was still competitive.

I was really unimpressed by the situation. I like Test cricket as it is; I don't like the way they are trying to change it. Maybe you could reduce it to four days if they are going to change it – that way they would be forced to make better wickets so it is a fairer competition between bat and ball. That would bring more people to the games. Flat wickets make flat cricket and that's all we seem to get these days. They left extra grass on in Adelaide for the pink ball game. I don't understand why they can't do that with a red ball – that would make for a bit more of an even contest. I understand that they want to get people coming to the game after work, but if Test cricket is held during the summer with quality sides playing and getting a good contest on a good wicket they will come. That's my opinion, but I know a lot of guys feel like that. We have done a lot of player surveys and most people don't like it, but we don't have a choice. It's going to happen no matter what we think.

I headed to Brisbane to catch up with the 'new' Test team led by Steve Smith for the series against New Zealand. Ryan Harris, Chris Rogers, Michael Clarke, Brad Haddin and Shane Watson had not made it to the next series. The journos sensed a pattern and every time I fronted them they asked me if I was next. The wicket in Brisbane for the first match was really disappointing. I'd cracked it at training two days earlier about the run-up, which was not unusual. In the end it was agreed to drive me out to AB Fields so I could get a proper practice. The journos were watching and thought something was going down, but it was all pretty innocent. One of them followed me to the car park to ask where I was going. They should have known by now.

I got 3–105 for the match and I pulled alongside Brett Lee's 310 Test wickets. He was one of my heroes so it was an honour to match him. I did a presser after the Test and when they asked me about retirement, I didn't pull any punches. I was more honest than I suppose you should be. 'I think about it most days,' I told them. 'It is probably getting to be that time, but to be honest I am just trying to play each game and enjoy it like I have said before. It could be after this game. I might just go "I am done", but I'm still enjoying my cricket at the moment and enjoying the challenges. It is a really good time for Australian cricket with these young guys in the team and I want to be a part of that. As long as I am performing well and doing my job in the team, then mentally I am good.'

And then it was back to Perth for the second match where we won the toss, batted and were 2–416 at the end of the first day. There was nothing in the wicket again. Joe Burns nicked the third ball of the day from Tim Southee and it fell short of the cordon. That should never happen at the WACA. When we bowled, there was nothing in the pitch for us. The ball was bouncing twice from the get-go. I was brought on in the ninth over and Kane Williamson was facing. We had one breakthrough already and were searching for another one in the last minutes before tea. The field moved into place, I prepared myself, went through the little checklist at the top of my mark and looked down towards the batsman.

I just couldn't do it. Could. Not. Be. Bothered. I thought to myself: what the hell am I doing here? I felt terrible for being there in that frame of mind. There was a whole Test to play and

I wondered how I was going to get through it. I did my best, but I think it was noticeable to everyone that my pace was down. I didn't squib it, I put in what I had, but it wasn't much. I rang Jess that night and said I'd had enough of this. It wasn't the first time I'd done that. You have those hard days and you get dirty and say I am over it, but this time was a bit different. I was really not enjoying it. Jess calmed me down and said I bowled well, she was really positive and got me up and I sat back and thought about it and I did feel good bowling.

I was in turmoil the next day. My head was all over the place. I kept thinking about what I should do and I reckon the boys could sense it. Nathan Lyon asked me what was wrong and Steve Smith was looking at me funny. I had 0–111 before I finally got a wicket late in the day. It was my 311th and the one that took me past Brett Lee. I was a bit emotional walking off at the end of play and it was obvious that something was going on. I went out the back of the dressing room to call Jess and I was pretty upset by then. That's how I got sprung actually. Brett Lee came around the corner and he had a bottle of champagne for me: Dom Perignon. He just left it in the dressing room and sent me a text later to see if I was okay. He could see that something was going on. That was when I knew it was over. I didn't want to make a big deal out of it, but I rang my family and manager and I told them so they could come if they wanted. I didn't tell the team until the next day.

I was planning to stay around for one-day cricket. When I told Darren I was quitting I began to ask him about one-day cricket, but before he could answer my question I'd changed my mind and said it was all over. It was the right call. The journos were all over it anyway; there'd been a few stories written during the Test saying they expected me to go. Once I told the boys I felt a lot better. My speed had been really down in the first innings, but when I got the chance to bowl again it came out much better. First up, I had to bat and when I went out there Brendon McCullum got his side to form a guard of honour. It was a nice gesture. He said, 'I know you won't like this, but you deserve it.'

I had a bit of a swing and then when they batted again I really cut loose with the ball and I felt really free again. I bounced a few blokes, got my 312th and 313th Test wickets and really enjoyed the last six overs of my career. I hadn't had any fun in that first innings, so it was important for me to leave on the right note. I got my pace up above 140 km/h again, too.

There was hardly anyone there when we decided to end the game as it was obvious there wasn't going to be a result. I was feeling good as I walked off, it was already getting a bit dark and it felt right. Then the boys put me up on their shoulders and I got a bit emotional. Jess and Rubika were waiting for me on the boundary and everyone came out to say goodbye. It was pretty cool. Our families were in the stands and we had a good night when all the fuss on the field finished. We didn't go anywhere, just stayed in the rooms and had a drink.

Not many of the blokes I came into the game with were still playing and with Ryan Harris and Watto gone, two of my best mates weren't around, but in saying that I was enjoying playing with the young guys. It was special to see Starcy progress and to be part of that. I think we had a good relationship. It would have been nice to have been able to play a few more games with Josh Hazlewood. But if your heart's not in it there is no point. Mitch Marsh was another one I was growing close to; he was a bit upset that I was leaving. He was starting to make his mark in the one-day stuff and was learning a lot.

Our team bond was still really good that summer and that made it hard. Everyone trained hard and everything was really good around our cricket. We had freed up a bit around Steve Smith. The younger guys had a good bond from playing together in rep cricket and there was a good energy. Smithy had been under the pump a few years earlier, but had proven himself to be one of the best batsmen in the world and a good leader. He had a bit going on in his career when he took over the captaincy, but he took it all in his stride. He said invite whoever you want into the dressing room after the game but I wanted it to be the same as it always had. Nathan Lyon wanted us to have a barbecue at the team hotel, but I wanted to stay in the rooms.

The Kiwi boys came in. We'd drunk with them after the first Test, too. Brendon McCullum said he was jealous that I had got to go out on my own terms, so he was obviously thinking about getting out himself at that stage. It was nice of those guys to come in and drink with us. Jess was there; my brother was, too. He had a good night. Dad had come over. Dylan and Dave came in.

When the Kiwis left there was a bit of a surprise for me. Boof started speaking and said he wanted everyone to come up with a memory or story about me. That was moving and it made me feel pretty proud, too. To be honest, I can't remember too much of exactly what they said. What I do remember is I felt like I had the respect of the group; I looked at them and it felt like they cared. It was better than any present you could get. It was a little strange when the side left town and went to Adelaide for the next Test and left me behind, but I wasn't too concerned.

I felt like I had ended on a good note. My last spell felt really good, but to be honest I was on the downward slope. I could have got through another year maybe and played a good game here and there, but why would I want to do that? I was about giving 100 per cent for the team and if I couldn't do that there was no point. I would let them down and myself down. I went home and put my feet up after that and I have to say I didn't miss cricket at all.

I was still signed to the Kings XI Punjab in the IPL so I had to get the cobwebs out and in March I went back and played for Wanneroo again. I bowled ten overs. It was six too many. I really don't have the desire to do that anymore. I wanted to bowl four overs and be done. I didn't want to be standing around in the field all day. I enjoyed being with the club, don't get me wrong, but long spells I don't enjoy. I got a kick out of being with the young club cricketers and giving something back. They told me more guys were showing up to training because I was going and I was able to do a bit of coaching, which was rewarding. I even helped a few blokes out with their batting. When we were in the field I discussed tactics with them. I felt like I owed cricket a lot, so it was good to be giving something back.

Even though I was not playing at the elite level I still had to be fully prepared. They'd wanted me to play the weekend before, but I couldn't do it because I felt like I needed to have my preparation right. I can't shake off that perfectionist thing.

It is obvious I retired at the right time. There are no regrets. I am proud of what I have done; I achieved what I wanted to achieve, I don't have any regrets. I had an up-and-down career and I made a lot of mistakes, but I learned from them. I have experienced the whole game and can say I enjoyed it and made the most of it.

One of the things I have really struggled with since retiring is the loss of structure. I have gone from a life of knowing what I had to do, having it all laid out in front of me and being aware that I had to be here, do this, do that. I travelled, I trained, I played. Some days were recovery, but rarely was there a blank in the calendar. It was fast paced but it was reassuring in a way.

I miss it. I am not sure about how to live without those immediate goals and things that have to be done. I love being home; I really enjoy the family time. You'd expect me to say that, but it's just strange to think that there is nothing ahead that I am working for. I stay fit, I eat properly, but it is only for me and I have lost a bit of focus that way.

Australia v New Zealand, Second Test, Day 5,
the WACA, 17 November 2015.

14

A Life in the Fast Lane

IN THE END, I can say that the potential people saw when I was a skinny kid in his dad's golf shoes at the Wanderers and that Dennis Lillee saw that day in Brisbane was completely realised. That last ball I bowled in Perth in 2015 was the 16,001st I had bowled in Test cricket. I was proud to be still going hard when the light faded and happy with the place I had reached, because I worked so hard to get there. I found that place where I was free to bowl fast and ferociously and it was worth all the physical and mental effort that took.

When you are on-song, fast bowling is the greatest feeling you can have. You are The Man. Nobody can touch you. Batsmen want to get out of your way; even the best of them get that furrow in the brow as they dig in. Their eyes open a bit wider. Their hearts beat fast. There are even days in the nets where you can see your teammates standing around jostling to the back of the line so they don't have to come in and face you. To be fair not too many of them were ever keen and some tailenders wouldn't ever do it. In the game you have no choice. There were days when I was angry and letting off steam. On those days you didn't want to cross me.

Bowling is a simple, complicated and slightly crazy business. You can have days when you bowl really well but everything is against you. Batsmen don't get edges. When they do they are spilled or the third slip has just been taken out. Umpires turn you down, catches go to ground and DRS finds millimetres to deny you a wicket.

On other days you just bowl poo and you have no one to blame but yourself. Usually it shows in your figures, occasionally you get away with it. There's not much you can do about it when you are having a bad one. There's nowhere to hide, but as you get more experienced you learn to limit damage.

There were definitely two distinct periods in my bowling. In the first I just bowled without much idea of what I was doing or how to handle it if what I was doing went wrong. I got some big hauls and I went for some big scores. I had a lot to learn even though I was doing it with a baggy green on my head. Even when I had a hundred Test wickets I was still a naïve bowler. Later, I knew myself and my game and things were more calculated.

I am not sure what it is that separates batsmen from bowlers, but there is something that makes us different. When I was young I would watch Brian Lara play and he was brilliant and I didn't mind batting. I reckon I got my big backlift from watching him, but I was never anywhere near his class. I always enjoyed my batting, but I was able to keep it simple. No foot movement. Drive it if it is up, pull it when it's not and just hope there's not too much in between. When it is your job I think it gets a bit more complicated. The good batters make it look easy. Like good bowlers. As a point of honour I always tried to get in behind the short ball and hit it hard. I knew the psychological impact that had on the bowler and I also knew how much better they felt if the batsman was crapping himself and getting out of the way.

Bowling was always the thing I wanted to do when I played. In the backyard I would tape up the ball and try to bowl fast. That desire was always there. I liked fast cars and fast bowling. It was Curtly Ambrose who really got me into it. I remember watching him bowling on television and going into the backyard where I would try and be the left-arm Queensland Curtly. Not that our bowling was in any way similar. He was definitely one of my heroes and he was great to watch. I recall him getting that 7–1 in Perth; it was one of the most exciting things I have ever seen. He was almost unplayable and he got right inside the Australians' heads. I don't think Ian Healy would be too keen on seeing his dismissal that day again. I loved Curtly's bouncers. They were vicious, but what was really cool was his stare. You didn't see him say much; in fact, I can hardly remember him saying anything. He just had this silent threatening thing going on. Someone called it malevolence, but that's too big a word for a fast bowler to use. I tried to do the Curtly stare in my career.

It's pretty embarrassing actually, but it wasn't until I grew a moustache that I realised how pathetic my stare is when I am clean-shaven. I wasn't fooling anybody. I looked like something out of a boy band!

As a shy kid off the field fast bowling was good for me. It gave me a way of getting out some of my frustration in a way that wasn't going to cause trouble. It took me a while to be confident enough to be really aggressive in my entire approach to the game. I eventually got there. It was what worked for me.

I don't see fast bowling as being a bully; it is a competition – bat versus ball. Sometimes on fast and bouncy wickets I got called a bully, but there were plenty of flat track bullies with bats in their hands. It's easy to be a flat track bully when you are a batter. If you can do it with a ball then you are really achieving something, just as it's an achievement to make runs on a lively wicket.

I always felt it was fair to intimidate batsmen. I wanted to scare them; it was part of the game and the way the game was played when I grew up. You can't take that away and when I felt the desire to do that dying in me I knew it was time. The mind games are a big part of being a quick. Most of it is about skill, but part of the skill is that you have to be able to intimidate just like Curtly, Shoaib Akhtar and Brett Lee did. I watched them closely growing up; you could see the look that got into some batsmen's eyes when they bowled.

It's not always about putting the wind up someone, although it usually is. I remember the look Graeme Smith gave me when I swung the first delivery to him in Johannesburg in 2009. He knew he was in trouble, that they hadn't planned for this and his eyes gave it away. Then there was the look Kevin Pietersen gave when I hurried him up with some short bowling in the first Test of the 2013–14 Ashes. I don't know that he was scared, but I could see his mind was racing. Enough has been said about Jonathan Trott, but his experience fits the bill. Some batters were genuinely flustered, but most of them were bowlers and that's okay; it's not their job to make runs.

It was enjoyable and serious while it was happening, but at the end of the day I was able to walk off the field and shake the batsman's hand and say good contest. That was the point of it, you play to win out there, you do everything possible within the rules, sometimes you stretch those rules, but it isn't on purpose – it's because you have that passion and that fire.

Sometimes you get a bit possessed. You could see that with a guy like Dale Steyn when he got those crazy eyes. Most of the time he is a quiet, friendly guy and I think I am too, but in the heat of the moment sometimes you get possessed by what you are doing. It's not something you do for show, it is the emotion that comes out when the adrenalin is up. Sometimes I think it is like a boxing match. You are trading blows from 22 yards. The batsman has the ability to hit back at you – to counter punch. And remember that they get to choose their weapons. Bowlers get a standard ball, same size, same shape, same stitches. Batters get a bat that is as souped up as you like.

I think I was at my best when I had a bit of pent-up anger about something and I could call on that in the middle. It had to be controlled though; early on I would get to the point where

I would lose it for a couple of balls or a couple of overs. No matter how aggressive you were you had to be able to focus it. I did a lot of work with our psychologist Michael Lloyd and before him Ross Chapman. I put a lot of effort into getting to that place where I controlled my mind and my emotions. To be a true professional you have to get to an almost clinical place. If you ride the highs you will also ride the lows so you have to work out a way to rationalise what happens. Control your emotions and don't let them control you.

It's a complex thing trying to bowl fast because often when you try to bowl fast you don't. That desire to do it more often than not slows you down. There were moments when I wanted to bowl really fast and it came off, other times when I thought I was going to rip in and it just wouldn't come out as quick. I learned also that I couldn't bowl flat-out straight away; it probably took an over to get all the mechanics feeling good.

The real key was not to think about it at all. From the start I had my cues, they changed a bit over time, but they were basically the same. The simplest ones for me were three things: relaxed, front arm and finish-off. Relaxed was being relaxed in my run-up, so everything was loose. Front arm was about getting that pull-down. Finish-off was about completing my action and following through. I would say those three things were at the top of my mark all the time in the early days, but on bad days it meant I wasn't thinking about the ball I was going to bowl as much as I should. As I got more comfortable I was able to do both.

Again, it is simple and it is complicated. The best times are when you don't have to think about much at all; your mind is totally clear. It just happens. When I was really on song it was like I was three or four balls ahead. I remember Glenn McGrath talking about that as well, he felt that he pretty much had the over in his head before bowling the first ball on a good day. You would know this one was going to go here, that one there, and so on. It was about setting the batsmen up.

Before games I would visualise how I got wickets. Sometimes I would look at tapes of myself bowling. I would use different things to motivate me. Sometimes it was just something that was annoying me, but a lot of the time it was about coming up against the best players. If a Brian Lara, AB de Villiers or Sachin Tendulkar is waiting 22 yards away with a bat in their hands you knew you had to be on your game or you were going down.

As I said, when you are the bowler you want to be the man. You are like the drummer in the band and you want all the others to feed off the rhythm track that you lay down. You are controlling the way the game is going. If I got the energy going everyone else would feed off it. If I was down you could see that the guys took their cue from you and they would follow. If the bowling was flat so was the whole team.

When you are at your best it is so simple. You feel like nothing. I would feel really light and everything happened easily. I was floating in on my run-up and it felt like there was hardly any effort in letting the ball go. I would get tunnel vision and my thoughts would be really clear and focused. On the best days everything goes right. The ball comes out perfectly. It lands in the right spots. The batsmen do just what you want them to. And the fielders hold their catches.

Of course, those are the good days. There are a lot of times when you are trying to get there and you struggle. You might be a bit sore. There might be a ridge in the wicket approach like the one in Brisbane, or something small like that. A bit of a dip where your foot lands. Sometimes there is no excuse for it at all. You are just off. The ball sticks in your hand, swings when you don't want it to and doesn't when you do. Balls keep pushing down leg side or wider. Others sit up and beg to be punished on the off side.

I actually enjoyed this too once I got my head around it. There is no hiding in these situations, you just have to get the job done as best you can. You have to find a way. There is no hiding; the captain is always going to throw you the ball. Unless you are really stuffing up. If you are a bowler you bowl. It doesn't say in your contract that you only bowl when you are having a good day.

I was never one to worry about the pitch. I wasn't one of those guys who would be out looking at it before we played. I couldn't see the point because we had to play on it no matter what it was like. I remember if somebody asked Adam Gilchrist what a pitch was like he would say it's 22 yards long and has stumps at either end. It didn't worry him when he was batting; he saw the ball and hit the ball and that was what made him good. You meet some batsmen who go on and on about the pitch and how hard it will be. I had no time for this thinking. It is a negative thought before you have even started and it doesn't do the dressing room any favours.

I knew I had to bowl on a pitch no matter what it was like. Even if it was flat I would try to bowl my bouncer because that was an important part of my game. I was always trying to set batsmen up and draw them into a false shot, make them nick off. Sometimes it was easier than others. All I ever wanted from a pitch was that it provided a fair contest between bat and ball. Sometimes we got that.

When kids ask me what to do these days I tell them to be batters because it's easy. I shouldn't as we need more quicks, but you need to be a certain sort of person. I always encourage the kids that want to do it, but I know it's hard work. You are going to get injured, you are going to have really hard days in hot conditions and you have to learn to look forward to that stuff. I actually enjoyed the challenge of flat pitches and heat. It was a chance to test yourself and see how tough you really were. It was one thing to bowl well on a green seamer, quite another to do it on a batsman-friendly road in stinking heat with both batsmen already past a hundred. That is one of the reasons why I said earlier in the book that I was so proud of my seven wickets in Adelaide in the second Test match of the Ashes series 2013–14. I got plenty in Brisbane the game before, but in the follow-up match nobody was expecting me to be as effective.

Early on in my career it was nerve-racking bowling the last over of an ODI or something like that, but as you grow into the game you want to have the ball in your hand at the critical moments. If you don't, you shouldn't be out there.

There were other times when it was great and they were the times when you would get into the zone that I was talking about earlier and you were in such a good place even bad balls got wickets. There was a game against South Africa in Perth in 2008, which we lost and so it wasn't great, but my bowling in one innings was at another level. I couldn't do anything wrong. I bowled a ball at leg stump and it got caught at short fine leg. He was there for the bouncer, but it was one of those days when things just went my way. The thing about the bad balls was you got away with them because everything else you bowled was so good. I took 8–61 in that innings. It was a different story when they batted again, but that was part of the problem with my performances in those days.

That game and the good games in those days felt really different from the way I bowled after 2011, because back then I didn't know why things worked. In the second part of my career I was more deliberate; I had more control and consistency. For that reason, I am more proud of the bowling at the back end of my career. It wasn't luck or chance.

Of course, I was proud of my performance in the Ashes in 2013–14, but even more so when we followed up in South Africa. This time they'd been watching what I did to England; they knew I was going to rough them up with short bowling, but they couldn't do anything about it no matter how prepared they were. That made me really happy.

I didn't get many wickets when we went to the UAE to play Pakistan in 2014, but I thought I bowled well. They were roads over there and if you didn't get a breakthrough with the new ball – when there was just a little bit of swing – it was tough work and you had a long wait for the reverse to kick in. Even when it did reverse the batsmen weren't too worried because they were so used to it. It was hard work, but I used to enjoy those challenges and I was proud of my efforts. I didn't get the best results – I took six wickets in the two Tests at an average of about 30 – but I was proud of how I managed to get the best out of myself and didn't back down. It was extremely hot and it was tough, but it was satisfying to test yourself and not be found wanting.

It was that desire to work hard in conditions that were against me that deserted me in the end. The Test in Brisbane in my last summer was a hard one and when we got to Perth and I was at the top of my mark I just couldn't handle it anymore. I just didn't want to do it anymore. I wondered if I had completely lost it when I retired, but I got angry when I was dropped from an IPL game in May 2016, and the way I bowled in the nets after I was told was a clear indication to me that I still have the fast bowling gene.

I took a while to get to the IPL. I signed a contract to be in the first IPL auction and then I thought about it and it was when I was first starting to play for Australia and I decided not to go ahead. I wanted to get myself a place in the Australian team and then worry about those things down the track. I wanted to play consistent cricket for Australia first. I wasn't in the first auction, but there were always teams asking me if I wanted to come over. I just didn't ever feel like the time was right, but then I had my toe injury and when I came back I thought, what is left? I wanted to make the most of my opportunities; it was just an experience I wanted to have. I thought this might be my last chance as I had said no every other time.

I wasn't being picked for Australia and it's funny, that line about cricket being a business that they'd said to me when they cut me from my contract at Queensland all those years before came back in my head. I then started to think that if cricket was a business I needed to do what I could to look after my family.

So, I went over there and ended up playing for Mumbai in 2013. Ricky Ponting was the captain at the start of the tournament. I enjoyed bowling in short bursts and I really loved the intensity of the contest. It was good, too, to come up against some old mates. Dave Warner tried to take me down one match but I fixed him up with a short ball. I was keen to knock over Watto in another game but was gentle with him.

You get to play cricket with guys from other countries, which is good on a social level and you learn a lot, too. The experience of playing with the Indians is invaluable. I am not sure we take the game that seriously at home, but guys like MS Dhoni and Suresh Raina have enormous experience and they are so good at it. We could learn a lot from them; they see it in a different way than we do and it is revealing. It was pretty interesting to walk into a team with some of the guys we have had a bad relationship with on the field over the years or maybe never got to know. Sachin was intimidating because he is like a god in India. He was really good with me; we share an interest in cars so we could talk about cars and racing. We both have Nissan GTRs.

It never once crossed my mind any of the stuff that happened with Andrew Symonds and the 'Monkeygate' business. I wasn't involved and just ignored it. Harbhajan Singh is a very different bloke off the field. I thought he would be stand-offish but he doesn't mind interacting with the boys off the field and is very easy to get on with. That was quite a surprise.

The IPL might fill a gap now that socialising has gone from cricket. Teams find it hard to socialise now. When I started at Queensland there was plenty of mingling between the sides but part of that was because you went to the other states and stayed for a Shield match and an ODI game. There was a bit of a routine of arriving in town and having a drink and it wasn't unusual for both teams to get together. It wasn't unusual to go out quite a few nights after that either. Even state cricket has lost that a little bit, but it still goes on. Of course, when I first played state cricket I was a bit keener to have a drink than I was later in life.

Then, when I joined the Australian team, there was a bit of mingling, but not much. It became a thing that you didn't have a drink until the end of the series. Even that became difficult as things move so quickly now that as soon as one series finishes you have to get ready to go to the next. There was some fun and games in England in 2015 when they invited us in after the first Test, but to be honest we really don't want to be mingling when the series is on. We invited them into ours when we won the second match just to be a bit smart and they didn't take it up. Having said that, when we do have a drink I have really enjoyed chatting with Jimmy Anderson and Stuart Broad in the rooms when we have done it. We have a lot in common, but I could never let myself like them on the field because I just wouldn't get the best out of myself if I did.

In the Ashes series in Australia when we won 5–0, even if we had shared the ground's dining room or walked past each other in the hallways I would not say hello. I wouldn't say a word. Even if they said hello I would just look at them. I know how rude that sounds, but it became part of the game play. Although it wasn't on the field it was in the stadium and that was where we were in competition. I wouldn't do it in a restaurant or away from the grounds, but if it was a training session I just blanked them. It was a pretty intense approach but we had discussed it. It sounds like I was arrogant and I guess I was, but I was in a bubble and I did what I had to do.

I had been trained from my Queensland days to know that you weren't there to make friends. If you made enemies it was bad luck; it was never meant to be personal and you couldn't do much if people took it personally. If they did it was affecting them more than they should have let it.

I started to lose that a bit at the end. In those last series I got too matey; I just didn't have that mongrel attitude towards the opposition. I even found myself smiling when batsmen played good shots. Australia cops a lot of criticism over that approach to the game but India has embraced that big time these days. Look at Virat Kohli. If he isn't on your side, you think he is a crap bloke, but he is a guy you would have in your team in an instant because he is a real competitor. He will fight for his team as hard as he can. England plays hard when they want to, but are good at complaining if someone else does. South Africa can be a bit the same but they don't complain as much.

I found out in 2016 at the IPL that I still have that fire when the coach came to tell me I was not playing. I was one ball away from a game I reckon. In the previous game I got a wicket early with a no-ball and that would have got me going. I went for 43 off four overs, bowled okay, created a few chances and got a late wicket. Obviously I needed to be getting wickets up front, but I didn't. The coach came in before the next training and said, 'We are going to change the team up,' and started patting me on the shoulder. I replied, 'You are fucking kidding me, just give me my space.' I went to the net session and while I was warming up I was talking to Glenn Maxwell. I was pretty angry and I said, 'Just don't get in my net today.' I was bowling to Manan Vohra and I went really hard. It was almost like I was in a game. Then Maxi came in. There were other blokes due before him – one of them was Wriddhiman Saha, our new captain, and one of our younger players who I had worked over the day before, but neither of them fronted up.

I had warned Maxi, but he'd decided to tough it out. I nicked him off first ball – he was sitting on the crease. Second ball was a half-volley at the stumps and he just pushed it back to me. Third ball he backed away to give himself room. I followed him with one at chest height and hit him right on the end of his thumb. He threw the bat down and the glove off and I thought bugger, I've broken his finger, but luckily it was just on the end and smashed up his fingernail.

It was odd; if I had been bowling like that in a game I would have been right. I just needed to get myself in that frame of mind. Joe Dawes, the Queensland fast bowler, once came up and said, 'I didn't want to say anything, but do we need to slap you in the face before you bowl?' It's true, I need that motivation when I play, I know you shouldn't need that when you are playing for your country or side, but I was driven by a different motivation and that's why I could go out there and bowl like I did. It was letting off steam.

The rest of life is going to be an interesting proposition without cricket.

Jock Campbell, the former Australian team fitness trainer, and I have developed an app called Bowlfit, which is designed to help pass on some of the lessons I've learned along the way. It's for people at every level of the game and includes bits on exercises that will hopefully help bowlers avoid the injuries I had early in the career, but there is a whole lot more to it.

I travelled to a lot of countries as a cricketer and while some were better than others I am glad I had the opportunity. I sometimes wish I could take my mates from home with me to show them what life is like outside the comfort zone where we live. The first trip to Chennai with Dennis Lillee when I was a teenager was a real eye-opener and India continued to challenge me right up to my last visit in 2016 for the IPL.

On one of the first days with Dennis in Chennai we got into a car and when we pulled up at the traffic lights kids came up begging for food and money. They were skinny, dirty and clearly lived on the streets. I felt awful. I didn't know what to do.

The driver said, 'Keep the windows up and give them nothing.' People tell you that drug addicts maim children so people will give the kids money out of sympathy and they tell you if you give money it stops the kids going to school. It is a terrible situation. I rolled down the window and passed out bottles of water and whatever I could find because I couldn't ignore one girl no matter what I was told. It was a pathetic gesture I guess, but she was obviously hungry and I couldn't do nothing.

On my last trip we were at the airport and a family came up to us; they were living under an overpass on the footpath. Again they were all so skinny and dirty. I know it sounds a cliché, but it didn't seem to bother them. They were just so happy to meet a few cricketers. I thought, how can you be happy when you live like that? But I guess that shows how pampered and protected we are. Maybe it is because I have a few kids myself now, but I actually shed a few tears when they left and I haven't been able to shake the memory of those people.

There's a guy called Dharam Veer who follows the Indian team around and is often at our training, too. He had polio as a child, which badly affected his legs, and he scrambles around on his hands like a crab fielding balls. He is surprisingly athletic and has a good throwing arm and somehow we've bonded over the years. He's a good guy and he's a bit of an inspiration. To overcome what he has, and to have so much fun just hanging around cricket, puts my complaints into perspective.

One of the things we took to doing on tours involved hooking up with a local charity and running training camps for underprivileged kids. We've done it in Soweto and all types of places and while the kids all seem to enjoy it, we get as much of a kick out of it as they do.

All these things you see as a cricketer I would never have seen had I stayed at home in Townsville.

Jess and I have two kids now, with the birth of Leo, and I can finally spend more time at home. He was born after I retired and I was there for that just as I had been for Rubika. Being at the birth is non-negotiable, although Jess thinks I am a bit overeager about the whole thing. It still blows my mind that we were out shopping in the morning when Jess was pregnant and that night we had a baby. While I had to go away before Jess and Rubika left hospital, I got to drive Leo home like a real dad. And I got to stay home! Jess is not sure how she feels about this, but I am so happy to be able to spend real time in our home with the family. I'm not sure what I will do with all the competitive urges I have, but one day soon I am going to pack that suitcase away. I might even start to go through all those bits and pieces I have collected over the years.

I can tell you one thing, though. It took a long time to get here, but I am pleased to say that where I have landed is a really good place.

Thanks for being there.

Mitchell Johnson
November 2016

Career Record

of

Mitchell Guy Johnson
(from 2000–2015)

Born: 2 November 1981, Townsville (Qld)
Left-hand batsman and
Left-arm fast bowler

CRICKET CAREER

Summary	M	Inn	NO	Runs	HS	0s	50	100	Avrge	Ct	Overs	Mdns	Runs	Wkts	Avrge	5WI	10WM	Best
Test cricket	73	109	16	2065	123*	19	11	1	22.20	27	2666.5	515	8891	313	28.41	12	3	8–61
Sheffield Shield	27	38	9	737	121*	2	2	1	25.41	4	854.1	177	2851	101	28.23	4	1	6–51
Other first-class games	17	23	6	378	51*	1	2	–	22.24	8	439.5	76	1610	51	31.57	1	–	5–74
First-class total	117	170	31	3180	123*	22	15	2	22.88	39	3960.5	768	13352	465	28.71	17	4	8–61
International limited-overs	153	91	32	951	73*	6	2	–	16.12	35	1248.2	74	6037	239	25.26	3		6–31
Domestic limited-overs	25	13	5	129	27	–	–	–	16.13	3	245.4	21	1133	36	31.47	1		5–31
International Twenty20	30	17	7	109	28*	2	–	–	10.90	5	109.2	2	797	38	20.97	–		3–15
Indian Premier League	43	25	12	131	16*	2	–	–	10.08	12	164.2	1	1345	52	25.87	–		3–27
Twenty20 total	82	46	21	280	30	–	–	–	11.20	18	300.4	3	2360	94	25.11	–		3–15

In all tables in this stats section, * indicates not out. Abbreviations in the headings include: M = Matches; Inn = Innings; NO = Not outs; HS = Highest score; 0s = Ducks; 50 = Scores between 50 and 99; 100 = Scores greater than 99; Avrge = Average; Ct = Catches; Mdns = Maidens; Wkts = Wickets taken when bowling; 5WI = Number of times 5 or more wickets obtained in an innings; 10WM = Number of times 10 or more wickets obtained in a match; Stk-Rt = Batting strike rate (runs per 100 balls faced).

INDIVIDUAL ACHIEVEMENT AWARDS

2008	McGilvray Medal
2009	McGilvray Medal
2008–09	Player of the Series v South Africa
2009	ICC Cricketer of the Year
2013–14	Player of the Series v England
2014	Allan Border Medal
2014	ICC Cricketer of the Year
2014	ICC Test Cricketer of the Year

PLAYER OF THE SERIES AWARDS

Season	Opponent	Venue	M	Inn	NO	Runs	HS	0s	50	100	Avrge	Ct	Overs	Mdns	Runs	Wkts	Avrge	5WI	10WM	Best
2008–09	South Africa	South Africa	3	5	2	255	123*	1	1	1	85.00	1	139.0	28	400	16	25.00	–	–	4–25
2013–14	England	Australia	5	8	2	165	64	–	1	–	27.50	4	188.4	51	517	37	13.97	3	–	7–40

MAN OF MATCH AWARDS: TEST CRICKET

Match Start/Date	Opponent	Venue	With the Bat			With the Ball				
			How Out	Runs	Ct	O	M	R	W	Ct
20/11/2008	New Zealand	Brisbane	c Taylor b Vettori	5		8.0	3	30	4	–
26/02/2009	South Africa	Johannesburg	c Vettori b Elliott	31		17.3	6	39	5	–
			not out	96*		18.1	7	25	4	–
27/03/2010	New Zealand	Hamilton	c Kallis b Ntini	1		34.2	2	112	4	1
			c McIntosh b Vettori	0		16.0	2	59	4	–
			c Patel b Vettori	0		20.1	6	73	6	–
16/12/2010	England	Perth	c Anderson b Finn	62		17.3	5	38	6	–
			c Bell b Collingwood	1		12.0	3	44	3	–
26/12/2012	Sri Lanka	Melbourne	not out	92*		14.0	2	63	4	–
			did not bat	–		8.0	–	16	2	–
21/11/2013	England	Brisbane	b Broad	64		17.0	2	61	4	–
			not out	39*		21.1	7	42	5	1
05/12/2013	England	Adelaide	c Broad b Swann	5		17.2	8	40	7	–
			did not bat	–		24.0	8	73	1	1
26/12/2013	England	Melbourne	c Anderson b Bresnan	2		24.0	4	63	5	–
			did not bat	–		15.0	5	25	3	1
12/02/2014	South Africa	Centurion	b Peterson	33		17.1	1	68	7	1
			did not bat	–		16.0	3	59	5	–

MAN OF MATCH AWARDS: INTERNATIONAL LIMITED-OVERS CRICKET

Date	Opponent	Venue	With the Bat		With the Ball				
			How Out	Runs	O	M	R	W	Ct
26/01/2007	England	Adelaide	did not bat	-	10.0	2	45	4	1
11/10/2007	India	Vadodara	did not bat	-	10.0	-	26	5	-
06/09/2009	England	Lord's	not out	43*	9.0	1	50	2	-
26/09/2009	West Indies	Johannesburg	not out	73*	10.0	-	44	-	1
25/02/2011	New Zealand	Nagpur	did not bat	-	9.1	3	33	4	-
10/08/2011	Sri Lanka	Pallekele	did not bat	-	10.0	1	31	6	-

MAN OF MATCH AWARDS: INTERNATIONAL TWENTY20 CRICKET

Date	Opponent	Venue	With the Bat		With the Ball				
			How Out	Runs	O	M	R	W	Ct
26/02/2010	New Zealand	Wellington	bowled Bond	1	4.0	0	19	3	-

TEST WICKET MILESTONES

Wicket	Batsman	How Out	Venue	Season
1st	TT Samaraweera (SL)	Ct Keeper AC Gilchrist	Brisbane	2007–08
50th	TG Southee (NZ)	Caught A Symonds	Brisbane	2008–09
100th	AN Cook (ENG)	LBW	Lord's	2009
150th	TG McIntosh (NZ)	Bowled	Hamilton	2009–10
200th	KC Sangakkara (SL)	Ct Keeper MS Wade	Melbourne	2012–13
250th	AN Petersen (SA)	Ct Keeper BJ Haddin	Centurion	2013–14
300th	JM Bairstow (ENG)	Ct Keeper PM Nevill	Birmingham	2015
313th	MJ Guptill (NZ)	Caught JA Burns	Perth	2015–16

INTERNATIONAL LIMITED-OVERS WICKET MILESTONES

Wicket	Batsman	How Out	Venue	Season
1st	Khaled Mashud (BAN)	Bowled	Chittagong	2005–06
50th	RV Uthappa (IND)	Ct Keeper AC Gilchrist	Adelaide	2007–08
100th	Shoaib Malik (PAK)	Caught RT Ponting	Centurion	2009–10
150th	Tamim Iqbal (BAN)	Bowled	Mirpur	2010–11
200th	RS Bopara (ENG)	Caught AC Voges	Southampton	2013
239th	MJ Henry (NZ)	Caught MA Starc	Melbourne	2014–15

FASTEST DELIVERIES (km/h)

Speed	Bowler	Opponent	Venue	Season
161.3	Shoaib Akhtar (Pak)	England	Durban	2002–03
161.1	Shaun Tain (Aus)	England	Lord's	2010
160.8	Brett Lee (Aus)	New Zealand	Napier	2001–02
160.5	Jeff Thomson (Aus)	West Indies	Perth	1975–76
160.4	Mitchell Starc (Aus)	New Zealand	Perth	2015–16
159.5	Andy Roberts (WI)	Australia	Perth	1975–76
157.7	Fidel Edwards (WI)	South Africa	Bridgetown	2004–05
156.8	**Mitchell Johnson (Aus)**	**England**	**Melbourne**	**2013–14**
156.4	Mohammad Sami (Pak)	Zimbabwe	Sharjah	2002–03
156.4	Shane Bond (NZ)	India	Centurion	2002–03
155.7	Dale Steyn (SAf)	New Zealand	?	2009
155.7	Lasith Malinga (SL)	New Zealand	Mumbai	2010–11

(Note: The fastest deliveries recorded are based on TV observations and press reports)

LEADING WICKET TAKERS FOR AUSTRALIA IN TEST CRICKET

Bowler	M	Balls	Mdns	Runs	Wkts	Avrge	5WI	10WM	Best
SK Warne	145	40704	1761	17995	708	25.42	37	10	8-71
GD McGrath	124	29248	1471	12186	563	21.64	29	3	8-24
DK Lillee	70	18467	652	8493	355	23.92	23	7	7-83
MG Johnson	73	16001	515	8891	313	28.41	12	3	8-61
B Lee	76	16531	547	9554	310	30.82	10	–	5-30
CJ McDermott	71	16586	581	8332	291	28.63	14	2	8-97
JN Gillespie	71	14234	629	6770	259	26.14	8	–	7-37
R Benaud	63	19108	805	6704	248	27.03	16	1	7-72
GD McKenzie	61	17681	547	7328	246	29.79	16	3	8-71
RR Lindwall	61	13650	419	5251	228	23.03	12	–	7-38

LEADING WICKET TAKERS BY AUSTRALIANS IN INTERNATIONAL LIMITED-OVERS CRICKET

Bowler	M	Overs	Mdns	Runs	Wkts	Avrge	5WI	Best
GD McGrath	250	2161.4	279	8391	381	22.02	7	7-15
B Lee	221	1864.1	141	8877	380	23.36	9	5-22
SK Warne	194	1773.4	109	7541	293	25.74	1	5-33
MG Johnson	153	1248.2	74	6037	239	25.26	3	6-31
CJ McDermott	138	1243.2	99	5020	203	24.73	1	5-44
SR Waugh	325	1480.3	54	6764	195	34.69	–	4-33
NW Bracken	116	959.5	91	4239	174	24.36	2	5-47
SR Watson	190	1077.4	35	5342	168	31.80	–	4-36
GB Hogg	123	927.2	37	4188	156	26.85	2	5-32
JN Gillespie	97	857.2	79	3611	142	25.43	3	5-22

Note: The details for GD McGrath and SK Warne include one game for the World XI.

MOST TEST WICKETS BY LEFT-ARM BOWLERS

Bowling		M	Balls	Mdns	Runs	Wkts	Avrge	5WI	10WM	Best
Wasim Akram (Pak)	Pace	104	22627	872	9779	414	23.62	25	5	7–119
DL Vettori (NZ)	Spin	113	28814	1197	12441	362	34.37	20	3	7–87
WPUJC Vaas (SL)	Pace	111	23438	896	10501	355	29.58	12	2	7–71
HMRKB Herath (SL)	Spin	73	20633	660	9533	332	28.71	26	6	9–127
MG Johnson (Aus)	Pace	73	16001	515	8891	313	28.41	12	3	8–61
Zaheer Khan (Ind)	Pace	92	18785	623	10247	311	32.95	11	1	7–87
DL Underwood (Eng)	Spin	87	21862	1239	7674	297	25.84	17	6	8–51
BS Bedi (Ind)	Spin	67	21364	1096	7637	266	28.71	14	1	7–98
GS Sobers (WI)	Pace/Spin	93	21599	974	7999	235	34.04	6	–	6–73
AK Davidson (Aus)	Pace	44	11587	431	3819	186	20.53	14	2	7–93

361

FIRST-CLASS CAREER

Debut 2001–02 Queensland v New Zealanders, Brisbane

Season	Venue	M	Inn	NO	Runs	HS	0s	50	100	Avrge	Ct	Overs	Mdns	Runs	Wkts	Avrge	5WI	10WM	Best
2001–02	Australia	2	2	2	18	12*	–	–	–	–	–	71.0	17	216	6	36.00	–	–	2-64
2003–04	Australia	1	2	–	26	15	–	–	–	13.00	–	15.0	1	59	2	29.50	–	–	2-59
2004–05	Australia	3	4	1	108	51*	–	1	–	36.00	–	81.0	14	325	9	36.11	–	–	3-23
2005–06	Pakistan	1	2	–	30	24	–	–	–	15.00	–	4.0	–	18	–	–	–	–	–
2005–06	Australia	8	9	1	71	23	–	–	–	8.88	–	231.3	51	733	29	25.28	2	1	6-51
2005–06	Australia	5	8	5	182	54	1	2	–	60.67	2	163.4	34	508	21	24.19	–	–	4-45
2007–08	Australia	9	10	4	248	50*	–	2	–	41.33	2	353.1	62	1172	31	37.81	–	–	4-86
2007–08	West Indies	4	5	1	65	29*	1	–	–	16.25	2	127.5	24	441	13	33.92	–	–	4-41
2008–09	India	5	7	1	72	26	–	–	–	12.00	1	200.4	37	621	17	36.53	–	–	4-70
2008–09	Australia	5	8	1	205	64	1	1	–	29.29	2	225.2	50	594	31	19.16	2	1	8-61
2008–09	South Africa	4	7	3	288	123*	1	1	1	72.00	3	162.0	31	483	17	28.41	–	–	4-25
2009	England	7	8	–	166	63	2	1	–	20.75	1	215.2	19	924	24	38.50	1	–	5-69
2009–10	Australia	6	9	–	125	38	1	–	–	13.89	2	221.2	43	785	29	27.07	1	–	5-103
2009–10	New Zealand	2	2	–	0	0	2	–	–	0.00	1	77.1	20	277	12	23.08	1	1	6-73
2010	England	2	4	–	45	30	1	–	–	11.25	1	53.4	8	217	3	72.33	–	–	1-31
2010–11	India	3	6	–	67	47	1	–	–	11.17	1	95.3	17	339	10	33.90	1	–	5-64
2010–11	Australia	6	9	1	243	121*	4	2	1	30.38	–	200.3	38	767	24	31.96	2	–	6-38
2011–12	Sri Lanka	3	5	–	34	14	1	–	–	6.80	2	101.4	18	313	6	52.17	–	–	2-48
2011–12	Australia	1	1	–	1	1	–	–	–	1.00	–	42.4	12	132	6	22.00	–	–	5-69
2011–12	South Africa	3	5	2	101	40*	1	–	–	33.67	1	91.1	14	367	12	30.58	1	–	5-74
2012	England	3	3	–	27	21	–	–	–	9.00	–	82.1	13	276	8	34.50	–	–	4-47

Season	Venue	M	Inn	NO	Runs	HS	0s	50	100	Avrge	Ct	Overs	Mdns	Runs	Wkts	Avrge	5WI	10WM	Best
2012–13	Australia	8	14	3	291	92*	1	1	–	26.45	6	240.4	38	828	32	25.88	–	–	4–63
2012–13	India	1	2	–	3	3	1	–	–	1.50	–	19.0	3	60	–	–	–	–	–
2013–14	Australia	6	10	2	197	64	1	1	–	24.63	5	226.2	55	679	42	16.17	3	–	7–40
2013–14	South Africa	3	4	–	66	33	1	–	–	16.50	1	126.1	26	382	22	17.36	2	1	7–68
2014–15	Dubai	2	4	–	98	61	2	1	–	24.50	1	75.0	28	177	6	29.50	–	–	3–39
2014–15	Australia	3	5	2	133	88	1	1	–	44.33	1	122.2	26	461	13	35.46	–	–	4–61
2014–15	West Indies	2	2	–	25	20	–	–	–	12.50	–	50.5	8	149	8	18.63	–	–	3–34
2015	England	6	10	2	200	77	1	1	–	25.00	3	170.1	37	609	20	30.45	–	–	4–56
2015–16	Australia	3	3	–	45	29	–	–	–	15.00	2	114.0	24	440	12	36.67	–	–	3–68
Total		117	170	31	3180	123*	22	15	2	22.88	39	3960.5	768	13352	465	28.71	17	4	8–61

FIRST-CLASS CAREER (continued)

Opponent	M	Inn	NO	Runs	HS	0s	50	100	Avrge	Ct	Overs	Mdns	Runs	Wkts	Avrge	5Wi	10WM	Best
Derbyshire	1	1	–	21	21	–	–	–	21.00	–	31.0	3	99	3	33.00	–	–	3–47
ENGLAND	19	29	2	533	77	6	5	–	19.74	5	627.3	117	2246	87	25.82	5	–	7–40
England Lions	3	3	–	53	47	–	–	–	17.67	–	86.1	13	343	8	42.88	–	–	4–47
Indian Board President's XI	2	3	–	11	5	–	–	–	3.67	1	51.3	11	178	6	29.67	–	–	4–75
India A	1	1	1	7	7*	–	–	–	–	1	23.0	4	81	4	20.25	–	–	4–45
INDIA	14	22	6	376	88	2	2	–	23.50	3	554.1	103	1833	50	36.66	1	–	5–64
Jamaica Select XI	1	1	–	10	10	–	–	–	10.00	1	23.0	4	94	3	31.33	–	–	2–64
Kent	1	2	2	59	32*	–	–	–	–	2	30.0	8	85	5	17.00	–	–	4–56
NEW ZEALAND	6	7	–	90	31	2	–	–	12.86	2	216.5	54	771	33	23.36	2	1	6–73
Northamptonshire	1	1	–	14	14	–	–	–	14.00	1	18.1	1	107	1	107.00	–	–	1–65
New South Wales	4	6	2	119	34*	–	–	–	29.75	1	121.0	22	459	8	57.38	–	–	3–50
New Zealanders	1	1	1	6	6*	–	–	–	–	–	39.0	12	106	3	35.33	–	–	2–64
PAKISTAN	13	13	–	214	61	4	1	–	16.46	4	239.4	62	702	21	33.43	–	–	3–27
Pakistan A	4	4	1	87	51*	–	1	–	29.00	–	35.0	3	150	5	30.00	–	–	3–93
SOUTH AFRICA	12	20	5	578	123*	3	2	1	38.53	9	529.0	96	1641	64	25.64	3	2	8–61
South Africa A	1	1	–	0	0	1	–	–	0.00	2	29.0	5	112	9	12.44	1	–	5–74
South African Board President's XI	1	2	1	33	21	–	–	–	33.00	2	23.0	3	83	1	83.00	–	–	1–27
South Australia	7	12	3	229	51*	1	1	–	25.44	1	202.2	42	728	31	23.48	1	–	5–43
SRI LANKA	7	8	2	140	92*	1	1	–	23.33	3	233.4	38	725	23	31.52	–	–	4–63
Sri Lankans	1	1	–	50	50	–	1	–	50.00	–	31.0	6	86	2	43.00	–	–	1–39
Tasmania	4	4	–	21	14	–	–	–	5.25	–	147.4	36	444	19	23.37	1	–	5–69
Victoria	8	11	2	297	121*	1	1	1	33.00	1	238.0	47	779	30	25.97	2	1	6–51
Western Australia	4	5	2	71	27	–	–	–	23.67	1	145.1	30	441	13	33.92	–	–	4–56
WEST INDIES	8	10	1	134	35	1	–	–	14.89	1	266.0	45	973	35	27.80	1	–	5–103
West Indians	1	2	–	27	23	–	–	–	13.50	–	20.0	3	86	1	86.00	–	–	1–86

Innings	Inn	NO	Runs	HS	0s	50	100	Avrge	Ct	Overs	Mdns	Runs	Wkts	Avrge	5WI	10WM	Best
First Innings	70	9	1395	121*	11	7	1	22.87	12	1502.0	267	5340	180	29.67	6	–	8–61
Second Innings	37	8	605	92*	5	3	–	20.86	6	786.4	155	2680	87	30.80	1	–	5–63
Third Innings	48	10	814	123*	4	1	1	21.42	12	955.2	224	3025	118	25.64	6	–	6–73
Fourth Innings	15	4	366	77	2	4	–	33.27	9	716.5	122	2307	80	28.84	4	–	6–51

Venues in Australia	M	Inn	NO	Runs	HS	0s	50	100	Avrge	Ct	Overs	Mdns	Runs	Wkts	Avrge	5WI	10WM	Best
Adelaide	8	9	3	106	39*	1	–	–	17.67	3	296.3	66	970	43	22.56	3	–	7–40
Albion	2	3	–	77	50	–	1	–	25.67	–	51.0	9	172	3	57.33	–	–	1–39
Brisbane	16	21	4	422	88	1	3	–	24.82	2	505.2	106	1731	68	25.46	3	1	6–51
Cairns	1	1	1	7	7*	–	–	–	–	1	23.0	4	81	4	20.25	–	–	4–45
Darwin	1	2	1	57	51*	–	1	–	57.00	–	31.0	3	132	5	26.40	–	–	3–93
Hobart	4	4	–	24	14	1	–	–	6.00	–	156.0	31	483	14	34.50	–	–	4–103
Melbourne	11	15	5	456	121*	2	2	1	45.60	3	397.4	86	1218	47	25.91	2	–	5–35
Perth	15	26	5	457	62	1	2	–	21.76	10	568.5	116	1913	78	24.53	3	1	8–61
Sydney	8	13	3	287	64	1	2	–	28.70	3	279.1	44	999	25	39.96	–	–	4–168
Total	66	94	22	1893	121*	7	11	1	26.29	22	2308.3	465	7699	287	26.83	11	2	8–61

FIRST-CLASS CAREER (continued)

Venues in England	M	Inn	NO	Runs	HS	0s	50	100	Avrge	Ct	Overs	Mdns	Runs	Wkts	Avrge	5WI	10WM	Best
Birmingham	3	4	–	22	14	1	–	–	5.50	–	58.0	8	223	5	44.60	–	–	2–66
Canterbury	1	2	2	59	32*	–	–	–	–	2	30.0	8	85	5	17.00	–	–	4–56
Cardiff	2	2	–	91	77	–	1	–	45.50	1	85.0	11	311	7	44.43	–	–	3–87
Derby	1	1	–	21	21	–	–	–	21.00	–	31.0	3	99	3	33.00	–	–	3–47
Leeds	2	3	–	39	27	1	–	–	13.00	–	52.1	4	211	8	26.38	1	–	5–69
Lord's	3	5	–	115	63	–	1	–	23.00	1	96.5	22	385	10	38.50	–	–	3–27
Manchester	1	1	–	1	1	–	–	–	1.00	–	37.1	8	122	4	30.50	–	–	4–47
Northampton	1	1	–	14	14	–	–	–	14.00	1	18.1	1	107	1	107.00	–	–	1–65
Nottingham	1	2	–	18	13	–	–	–	9.00	–	21.2	2	102	1	102.00	–	–	1–102
The Oval	2	3	–	11	11	2	–	–	3.67	–	56.4	7	215	8	26.88	–	–	3–21
Worcester	1	1	–	47	47	–	–	–	47.00	–	35.0	3	166	3	55.33	–	–	2–48
Total	**18**	**25**	**2**	**438**	**77**	**4**	**2**	**–**	**19.04**	**5**	**521.2**	**77**	**2026**	**55**	**36.84**	**1**	**–**	**5–69**

Venues in India	M	Inn	NO	Runs	HS	0s	50	100	Avrge	Ct	Overs	Mdns	Runs	Wkts	Avrge	5WI	10WM	Best
Bangalore	2	3	–	12	11	1	–	–	4.00	1	77.0	13	240	8	30.00	–	–	4–70
Delhi	2	3	–	18	15	1	–	–	6.00	–	63.0	7	225	4	56.25	–	–	3–142
Hyderabad	1	1	–	5	5	–	–	–	5.00	1	34.4	7	100	4	25.00	–	–	4–75
Mohali	3	6	1	91	47	–	–	–	18.20	–	94.3	15	349	10	34.90	1	–	5–64
Nagpur	1	2	–	16	11	–	–	–	8.00	–	46.0	15	106	1	106.00	–	–	1–84
Total	**9**	**15**	**1**	**142**	**47**	**2**	**–**	**–**	**10.14**	**2**	**315.1**	**57**	**1020**	**27**	**37.78**	**1**	**–**	**5–64**

Venues in New Zealand	M	Inn	NO	Runs	HS	0s	50	100	Avrge	Ct	Overs	Mdns	Runs	Wkts	Avrge	5WI	10WM	Best
Hamilton	1	2	–	0	0	2	–	–	0.00	–	36.1	8	132	10	13.20	1	1	6–73
Wellington	1	–	–	–	–	–	–	–	–	–	41.0	12	145	2	72.50	–	–	1–38
Total	**2**	**2**	**–**	**0**	**0**	**2**	**–**	**–**	**0.00**	**–**	**77.1**	**20**	**277**	**12**	**23.08**	**1**	**1**	**6–73**

Venues in Pakistan

	M	Inn	NO	Runs	HS	0s	50	100	Avrge	Ct	Overs	Mdns	Runs	Wkts	Avrge	5WI	10WM	Best
Rawalpindi	1	2	-	30	24	-	-	-	15.00	-	4.0	-	18	-	-	-	-	-

Venues in South Africa

	M	Inn	NO	Runs	HS	0s	50	100	Avrge	Ct	Overs	Mdns	Runs	Wkts	Avrge	5WI	10WM	Best
Cape Town	3	5	1	181	123*	1	-	1	45.25	-	106.3	22	369	12	30.75	-	-	4-42
Centurion	1	1	-	33	33	-	-	-	33.00	1	33.1	4	127	12	10.58	2	1	7-68
Durban	1	1	-	0	0	1	-	-	0.00	-	49.0	14	115	4	28.75	-	-	3-37
Johannesburg	2	4	3	175	96*	-	1	-	175.00	2	98.4	17	305	10	30.50	-	-	4-25
Port Elizabeth	1	2	-	33	27	-	-	-	16.50	-	40.0	6	121	3	40.33	-	-	2-51
Potchefstroom	2	3	1	33	21	1	-	-	16.50	2	52.0	8	195	10	19.50	1	-	5-74
Total	10	16	5	455	123*	3	1	1	41.36	5	379.2	71	1232	51	24.16	3	1	7-68

Venues in Sri Lanka

	M	Inn	NO	Runs	HS	0s	50	100	Avrge	Ct	Overs	Mdns	Runs	Wkts	Avrge	5WI	10WM	Best
Colombo	1	2	-	12	8	-	-	-	6.00	-	35.0	6	122	2	61.00	-	-	2-122
Galle	1	2	-	22	14	-	-	-	11.00	2	28.0	7	82	2	41.00	-	-	2-56
Pallekele	1	1	-	0	0	1	-	-	0.00	-	38.4	5	109	2	54.50	-	-	2-48
Total	3	5	-	34	14	1	-	-	6.80	2	101.4	18	313	6	52.17	-	-	2-48

Venues in United Arab Emirates

	M	Inn	NO	Runs	HS	0s	50	100	Avrge	Ct	Overs	Mdns	Runs	Wkts	Avrge	5WI	10WM	Best
Abu Dhabi	1	2	-	0	0	2	-	-	0.00	-	32.0	8	104	3	34.67	-	-	2-45
Dubai	1	2	-	98	61	-	1	-	49.00	1	43.0	20	73	3	24.33	-	-	3-39
Total	2	4	-	98	61	2	1	-	24.50	1	75.0	28	177	6	29.50	-	-	3-39

FIRST-CLASS CAREER (continued)

Venues in West Indies	M	Inn	NO	Runs	HS	0s	50	100	Avrge	Ct	Overs	Mdns	Runs	Wkts	Avrge	5WI	10WM	Best
Bridgetown	1	1	–	0	0	1	–	–	0.00	–	23.5	3	113	5	22.60	–	–	4–41
Greenfields	1	1	–	10	10	–	–	–	10.00	1	23.0	4	94	3	31.33	–	–	2–64
Kingston	2	3	–	31	22	–	–	–	10.33	1	59.0	12	169	5	33.80	–	–	2–23
North Sound	1	1	1	29	29*	–	–	–	–	–	44.0	8	142	3	47.33	–	–	2–72
Dominica	1	1	–	20	20	–	–	–	20.00	–	28.5	5	72	5	14.40	–	–	3–34
Total	**6**	**7**	**1**	**90**	**29***	**1**	**–**	**–**	**15.00**	**2**	**178.4**	**32**	**590**	**21**	**28.10**	**–**	**–**	**4–41**

Teams	M	Inn	NO	Runs	HS	0s	50	100	Avrge	Ct	Overs	Mdns	Runs	Wkts	Avrge	5WI	10WM	Best
Australia A	6	8	2	121	51*	–	1	–	20.17	1	140.1	20	507	17	29.82	–	–	4–45
AUSTRALIA	73	109	16	2065	123*	19	11	1	22.20	27	2666.5	515	8891	313	28.41	12	3	8–61
Australian XI	8	11	3	174	47	1	–	–	21.75	7	209.4	35	825	28	29.46	1	–	5–74
Queensland	20	27	8	477	54	–	3	–	25.11	1	611.1	127	2029	65	31.22	2	1	6–51
Western Australia	10	15	2	343	121*	2	–	1	26.38	3	333.0	71	1100	42	26.19	2	–	5–35

RUNS PER BATTING POSITION

Position	Inn	NO	Runs	HS	0s	50	100	Avrge
5	3	–	46	21	–	–	–	15.33
6	5	1	84	30	1	–	–	21.00
7	7	2	69	29	–	–	–	13.80
8	80	12	1710	123*	14	9	2	25.15
9	39	7	739	96*	6	4	–	23.09
10	31	5	491	54	1	2	–	18.88
11	5	4	41	12*	–	–	–	41.00

BEST BOWLING IN A MATCH

Best	Team	Opponent	Venue	Season
10–106	Queensland	Victoria	Brisbane	2005–06
11–159	AUSTRALIA	SOUTH AFRICA	Perth	2008–09
10–132	AUSTRALIA	NEW ZEALAND	Hamilton	2009–10
12–127	**AUSTRALIA**	**SOUTH AFRICA**	**Centurion**	**2013–14**

Best	Team	Opponent	Venue	Season
51*	Queensland	South Australia	Brisbane	2004–05
51*	Australia A	Pakistan A	Darwin	2005–06
54	Queensland	Victoria	Melbourne	2006–07
50	Queensland	Sri Lankans	Albion	2007–08
50*	AUSTRALIA	INDIA	Perth	2007–08
64	AUSTRALIA	SOUTH AFRICA	Sydney	2008–09
96*	AUSTRALIA	SOUTH AFRICA	Johannesburg	2008–09
123*	AUSTRALIA	SOUTH AFRICA	Cape Town	2008–09
63	AUSTRALIA	ENGLAND	Lord's	2009
121*	Western Australia	Victoria	Melbourne	2010–11
62	AUSTRALIA	ENGLAND	Perth	2010–11
53	AUSTRALIA	ENGLAND	Sydney	2010–11
92*	AUSTRALIA	SRI LANKA	Melbourne	2012–13
64	AUSTRALIA	ENGLAND	Brisbane	2013–14
61	AUSTRALIA	PAKISTAN	Dubai	2014–15
88	AUSTRALIA	INDIA	Brisbane	2014–15
77	AUSTRALIA	ENGLAND	Cardiff	2015

BEST BOWLING IN AN INNINGS

Best	Team	Opponent	Venue	Season
5–43	Queensland	South Australia	Adelaide	2005–06
6–51	Queensland	Victoria	Brisbane	2005–06
5–39	AUSTRALIA	NEW ZEALAND	Brisbane	2008–09
8–61	AUSTRALIA	SOUTH AFRICA	Perth	2008–09
5–69	AUSTRALIA	ENGLAND	Leeds	2009
5–103	AUSTRALIA	WEST INDIES	Adelaide	2009–10
6–73	AUSTRALIA	NEW ZEALAND	Hamilton	2009–10
5–64	AUSTRALIA	INDIA	Mohali	2010–11
5–35	Western Australia	Victoria	Melbourne	2010–11
6–38	AUSTRALIA	ENGLAND	Perth	2010–11
5–69	Western Australia	Tasmania	Perth	2011–12
5–74	Australian XI	South Africa A	Potchefstroom	2011–12
5–42	AUSTRALIA	ENGLAND	Brisbane	2013–14
7–40	AUSTRALIA	ENGLAND	Adelaide	2013–14
5–63	AUSTRALIA	ENGLAND	Melbourne	2013–14
7–68	AUSTRALIA	SOUTH AFRICA	Centurion	2013–14
5–59	AUSTRALIA	SOUTH AFRICA	Centurion	2013–14

HOW DISMISSED WHEN BATTING

Innings	Not Out	Bowled	Ct Fieldsman	Ct Keeper	LBW	Stumped	Run Out
170	31	30	69	25	9	4	2

WICKETS TAKEN WHEN BOWLING

Wickets	Bowled	Ct Fieldsman	Ct & Bwd	Ct Keeper	LBW
464	68	207	5	130	54

BATSMEN DISMISSED WHEN BOWLING

Wickets	Opener	3rd	4th	5th	6th	7th	8th	9th	10th	11th
464	109	52	49	41	41	38	40	41	29	24

TEST CAREER
Debut 2007–08 v Sri Lanka, Brisbane

Season	Opponent	Venue	M	Inn	NO	Runs	HS	0s	50	100	Avrge	Ct	Overs	Mdns	Runs	Wkts	Avrge	5WI	10WM	Best
2007–08	Sri Lanka	Australia	2	–	–	–	–	–	–	–	–	1	82.0	14	241	8	30.13	–	–	3–101
2007–08	India	Australia	4	5	3	112	50*	–	1	–	56.00	1	168.1	31	530	16	33.13	–	–	4–86
2007–08	West Indies	West Indies	3	4	1	55	29*	1	–	–	18.33	1	104.5	20	347	10	34.70	–	–	4–41
2008–09	India	India	4	6	1	67	26	–	–	–	13.40	–	166.0	30	521	13	40.08	–	–	4–70
2008–09	New Zealand	Australia	2	3	–	59	31	–	–	–	19.67	–	65.4	21	154	14	11.00	1	–	5–39
2008–09	South Africa	Australia	3	5	1	146	64	1	1	–	36.50	2	159.4	29	440	17	25.88	1	1	8–61
2008–09	South Africa	South Africa	3	5	2	255	123*	1	1	1	85.00	1	139.0	28	400	16	25.00	–	–	4–25
2009	England	England	5	6	–	105	63	2	1	–	17.50	–	162.1	15	651	20	32.55	1	–	5–69
2009–10	West Indies	Australia	3	4	–	54	35	–	–	–	13.50	–	110.2	17	477	17	28.06	1	–	5–103
2009–10	Pakistan	Australia	3	5	–	71	38	1	–	–	14.20	2	111.0	26	308	12	25.67	–	–	3–27
2009–10	New Zealand	New Zealand	2	2	–	0	0	2	–	–	0.00	–	71.1	20	277	12	23.08	1	1	6–73
2010	Pakistan	England	2	4	–	45	30	1	–	–	11.25	1	53.4	8	217	3	72.33	–	–	1–31
2010–11	India	India	2	4	–	61	47	1	–	–	15.25	1	78.4	13	261	8	32.63	1	–	5–64
2010–11	England	Australia	4	7	–	122	62	3	2	–	17.43	–	136.3	22	554	15	36.93	1	–	6–38
2011–12	Sri Lanka	Sri Lanka	3	5	–	34	14	1	–	–	6.80	2	101.4	18	313	6	52.17	–	–	2–48
2011–12	South Africa	South Africa	2	4	2	101	40*	–	–	–	50.50	1	62.1	9	255	3	85.00	–	–	1–61
2012–13	South Africa	Australia	1	2	–	10	7	–	–	–	5.00	4	42.0	4	164	6	27.33	–	–	4–110
2012–13	Sri Lanka	Australia	2	3	2	106	92*	–	1	–	106.00	–	50.0	6	171	9	19.00	–	–	4–63
2012–13	India	India	1	2	–	3	3	1	–	–	1.50	–	19.0	3	60	–		–	–	
2013–14	England	Australia	5	8	2	165	64	–	1	–	27.50	4	188.4	51	517	37	13.97	3	–	7–40
2013–14	South Africa	South Africa	3	4	–	66	33	1	–	–	16.50	1	126.1	26	382	22	17.36	2	1	7–68
2014–15	Pakistan	Dubai	2	4	–	98	61	2	1	–	24.50	1	75.0	28	177	6	29.50	–	–	3–39

Season	Opponent	Venue	M	Inn	NO	Runs	HS	0s	50	100	Avrge	Ct	Overs	Mdns	Runs	Wkts	Avrge	5WI	10WM	Best
2014–15	India	Australia	3	5	2	133	88	–	1	–	44.33	1	122.2	26	461	13	35.46	–	–	4-61
2014–15	West Indies	West Indies	2	2	–	25	20	–	–	–	12.50	–	50.5	8	149	8	18.63	–	–	3-34
2015	England	England	5	8	–	141	77	1	1	–	17.63	1	140.1	29	524	15	34.93	–	–	3-21
2015–16	New Zealand	Australia	2	2	–	31	29	–	–	–	15.50	2	74.0	13	340	7	48.57	–	–	3-105
Total			73	109	16	2065	123*	19	11	1	22.20	27	2666.5	515	8891	313	28.41	12	3	8-61

Opponents	M	Inn	NO	Runs	HS	0s	50	100	Avrge	Ct	Overs	Mdns	Runs	Wkts	Avrge	5WI	10WM	Best
England	19	29	2	533	77	6	5	–	19.74	5	627.3	117	2246	87	25.82	5	–	7-40
India	14	22	6	376	88	2	2	–	23.50	3	554.1	103	1833	50	36.66	1	–	5-64
New Zealand	6	7	–	90	31	2	–	–	12.86	2	216.5	54	771	33	23.36	2	1	6-73
Pakistan	7	13	–	214	61	4	1	–	16.46	4	239.4	62	702	21	33.43	–	–	3-27
South Africa	12	20	5	578	123*	3	2	1	38.53	9	529.0	96	1641	64	25.64	3	2	8-61
Sri Lanka	7	8	2	140	92*	1	1	–	23.33	3	233.4	38	725	23	31.52	1	–	4-63
West Indies	8	10	1	134	35	1	–	–	14.89	1	266.0	45	973	35	27.80	1	–	5-103

Innings	Inn	NO	Runs	HS	0s	50	100	Avrge	Ct	Overs	Mdns	Runs	Wkts	Avrge	5WI	Best
First Innings	44	4	830	96*	10	5	–	20.75	5	1001.3	187	3471	131	26.50	5	8-61
Second Innings	23	4	458	92*	3	2	–	24.11	4	529.1	100	1815	51	35.59	1	5-63
Third Innings	29	4	437	123*	4	4	1	17.48	9	657.3	155	2021	80	25.26	4	6-73
Fourth Innings	13	4	340	77	2	4	–	37.78	5	478.4	73	1584	51	31.06	2	5-69

TEST CAREER (continued)

Venues in Australia	M	Inn	NO	Runs	HS	0s	50	100	Avrge	Ct	Overs	Mdns	Runs	Wkts	Avrge	5WI	10WM	Best
Adelaide	5	5	1	48	23	–	–	–	12.00	3	221.3	48	711	31	22.94	2	–	7–40
Brisbane	7	8	2	236	88	1	2	–	39.33	2	249.2	54	853	34	25.09	2	–	5–39
Hobart	2	2	–	8	8	1	–	–	4.00	–	86.0	13	280	5	56.00	–	–	3–101
Melbourne	7	10	3	223	92*	2	1	–	31.86	2	253.5	56	765	32	23.91	1	–	5–63
Perth	7	14	3	278	62	–	2	–	25.27	7	283.3	53	1025	45	22.78	2	1	8–61
Sydney	6	10	1	216	64	1	2	–	24.00	3	216.1	36	723	24	30.13	–	–	4–168
Total	**34**	**49**	**10**	**1009**	**92***	**5**	**7**	**–**	**25.87**	**17**	**1310.2**	**260**	**4357**	**171**	**25.48**	**7**	**1**	**8–61**

Venues in England	M	Inn	NO	Runs	HS	0s	50	100	Avrge	Ct	Overs	Mdns	Runs	Wkts	Avrge	5WI	10WM	Best
Birmingham	2	3	–	17	14	1	–	–	5.67	–	44.0	6	168	4	42.00	–	–	2–66
Cardiff	2	2	–	91	77	–	1	–	45.50	1	85.0	11	311	7	44.43	–	–	3–87
Leeds	2	3	–	39	27	1	–	–	13.00	–	52.1	4	211	8	26.38	1	–	5–69
Lord's	3	5	–	115	63	–	1	–	23.00	1	96.5	22	385	10	38.50	–	–	3–27
Nottingham	1	2	–	18	13	–	–	–	9.00	–	21.2	2	102	1	102.00	–	–	1–102
The Oval	2	3	–	11	11	2	–	–	3.67	–	56.4	7	215	8	26.88	–	–	3–21
Total	**12**	**18**	**–**	**291**	**77**	**4**	**2**	**–**	**16.17**	**2**	**356.0**	**52**	**1392**	**38**	**36.63**	**1**	**–**	**5–69**

Venues in India	M	Inn	NO	Runs	HS	0s	50	100	Avrge	Ct	Overs	Mdns	Runs	Wkts	Avrge	5WI	10WM	Best
Bangalore	2	3	–	12	11	1	–	–	4.00	1	77.0	13	240	8	30.00	–	–	4–70
Delhi	2	3	–	18	15	1	–	–	6.00	–	63.0	7	225	4	56.25	–	–	3–142
Mohali	2	4	1	85	47	–	–	–	28.33	–	77.4	11	271	8	33.88	1	–	5–64
Nagpur	1	2	–	16	11	–	–	–	8.00	–	46.0	15	106	1	106.00	–	–	1–84
Total	**7**	**12**	**1**	**131**	**47**	**2**	**–**	**–**	**11.91**	**1**	**263.4**	**46**	**842**	**21**	**40.10**	**1**	**–**	**5–64**

Venues in New Zealand

Venues in New Zealand	M	Inn	NO	Runs	HS	0s	50	100	Avrge	Ct	Overs	Mdns	Runs	Wkts	Avrge	5WI	10WM	Best
Hamilton	1	2	–	0	0	2	–	–	0.00	–	36.1	8	132	10	13.20	1	1	6-73
Wellington	1	–	–	–	–	–	–	–	–	–	41.0	12	145	2	72.50	–	–	1-38
Total	**2**	**2**	**–**	**0**	**0**	**2**	**–**	**–**	**0.00**	**–**	**77.1**	**20**	**277**	**12**	**23.08**	**1**	**1**	**6-73**

Venues in South Africa

Venues in South Africa	M	Inn	NO	Runs	HS	0s	50	100	Avrge	Ct	Overs	Mdns	Runs	Wkts	Avrge	5WI	10WM	Best
Cape Town	3	5	1	181	123*	1	–	1	45.25	–	106.3	22	369	12	30.75	–	–	4-42
Centurion	1	1	–	33	33	–	–	–	33.00	1	33.1	4	127	12	10.58	2	1	7-68
Durban	1	1	–	0	0	1	–	–	0.00	–	49.0	14	115	4	28.75	–	–	3-37
Johannesburg	2	4	3	175	96*	–	1	–	175.00	2	98.4	17	305	10	30.50	–	–	4-25
Port Elizabeth	1	2	–	33	27	–	–	–	16.50	–	40.0	6	121	3	40.33	–	–	2-51
Total	**8**	**13**	**4**	**422**	**123***	**2**	**1**	**1**	**46.89**	**3**	**327.2**	**63**	**1037**	**41**	**25.29**	**2**	**1**	**7-68**

Venues in Sri Lanka

Venues in Sri Lanka	M	Inn	NO	Runs	HS	0s	50	100	Avrge	Ct	Overs	Mdns	Runs	Wkts	Avrge	5WI	10WM	Best
Colombo	1	2	–	12	8	–	–	–	6.00	–	35.0	6	122	2	61.00	–	–	2-122
Galle	1	2	–	22	14	–	–	–	11.00	2	28.0	7	82	2	41.00	–	–	2-56
Pallekele	1	1	–	0	0	1	–	–	0.00	–	38.4	5	109	2	54.50	–	–	2-48
Total	**3**	**5**	**–**	**34**	**14**	**1**	**–**	**–**	**6.80**	**2**	**101.4**	**18**	**313**	**6**	**52.17**	**–**	**–**	**2-48**

Venues in United Arab Emirates

Venues in United Arab Emirates	M	Inn	NO	Runs	HS	0s	50	100	Avrge	Ct	Overs	Mdns	Runs	Wkts	Avrge	5WI	10WM	Best
Abu Dhabi	1	2	–	0	0	2	–	–	0.00	–	32.0	8	104	3	34.67	–	–	2-45
Dubai	1	2	–	98	61	–	1	–	49.00	1	43.0	20	73	3	24.33	–	–	3-39
Total	**2**	**4**	**–**	**98**	**61**	**2**	**1**	**–**	**24.50**	**1**	**75.0**	**28**	**177**	**6**	**29.50**	**–**	**–**	**3-39**

TEST CAREER (continued)

Venues in West Indies	M	Inn	NO	Runs	HS	0s	50	100	Avrge	Ct	Overs	Mdns	Runs	Wkts	Avrge	5WI	10WM	Best
Bridgetown	1	1	–	0	0	1	–	–	0.00	–	23.5	3	113	5	22.60	–	–	4–41
Kingston	2	3	–	31	22	–	–	–	10.33	1	59.0	12	169	5	33.80	–	–	2–23
North Sound	1	1	1	29	29*	–	–	–	–	–	44.0	8	142	3	47.33	–	–	2–72
Dominica	1	1	–	20	20	–	–	–	20.00	–	28.5	5	72	5	14.40	–	–	3–34
Total	**5**	**6**	**1**	**80**	**29***	**1**	**–**	**–**	**16.00**	**1**	**155.4**	**28**	**496**	**18**	**27.56**	**–**	**–**	**4–41**

Batting Position	Inn	NO	Runs	HS	0s	50	100	Avrge
5	1	–	4	4	–	–	–	4.00
6	3	–	52	30	1	–	–	17.33
7	5	1	51	29	–	–	–	12.75
8	67	7	1385	123*	13	8	1	23.08
9	18	6	368	96*	4	3	–	30.67
10	14	2	194	31	1	–	–	16.17
11	1	–	11	11	–	–	–	11.00

HOW DISMISSED WHEN BATTING

Innings	Not Out	Bowled	Ct Fieldsman	Ct Keeper	LBW	Stumped	Run Out
109	16	22	44	16	7	3	1

WICKETS TAKEN WHEN BOWLING

Wickets	Bowled	Ct Fieldsman	Ct & Bwd	Ct Keeper	LBW
313	50	131	3	93	36

BATSMEN DISMISSED WHEN BOWLING

Wickets	Opener	3rd	4th	5th	6th	7th	8th	9th	10th	11th
313	68	32	30	32	31	31	24	26	19	20

SHEFFIELD SHIELD CAREER

Debut 2001–02 Queensland v Western Australia, Perth

Season	Team	M	Inn	NO	Runs	HS	0s	50	100	Avrge	Ct	Overs	Mdns	Runs	Wkts	Avrge	5WI	10WM	Best
2001–02	Queensland	1	1	1	12	12*	–	–	–	–	–	32.0	5	110	3	36.67	–	–	2–66
2003–04	Queensland	1	2	–	26	15	–	–	–	13.00	–	15.0	1	59	2	29.50	–	–	2–59
2004–05	Queensland	3	4	1	108	51*	–	1	–	36.00	–	81.0	14	325	9	36.11	–	–	3–23
2005–06	Queensland	7	7	1	44	14	–	–	–	7.33	–	211.3	48	647	28	23.11	2	1	6–51
2006–07	Queensland	3	5	3	118	54	1	1	–	59.00	1	109.4	27	295	12	24.58	–	–	4–56
2007–08	Queensland	2	4	1	86	34*	–	–	–	28.67	–	72.0	11	315	5	63.00	–	–	3–33
2010–11	Western Australia	2	2	1	121	121*	1	–	1	121.00	–	64.0	16	213	9	23.67	1	–	5–35
2011–12	Western Australia	1	1	–	1	1	–	–	–	1.00	–	42.4	12	132	6	22.00	1	–	5–69
2012–13	Western Australia	5	9	1	175	40*	1	–	–	21.88	2	148.4	28	493	17	29.00	–	–	4–103
2013–14	Western Australia	1	2	–	32	27	–	–	–	16.00	1	37.4	4	162	5	32.40	–	–	3–88
2015–16	Western Australia	1	1	–	14	14	–	–	–	14.00	–	40.0	11	100	5	20.00	–	–	3–68
Total		**27**	**38**	**9**	**737**	**121***	**2**	**2**	**1**	**25.41**	**4**	**854.1**	**177**	**2851**	**101**	**28.23**	**4**	**1**	**6–51**

Opponents	M	Inn	NO	Runs	HS	0s	50	100	Avrge	Ct	Overs	Mdns	Runs	Wkts	Avrge	5WI	10WM	Best
New South Wales	4	6	2	119	34*	–	–	–	29.75	1	121.0	22	459	8	57.38	–	–	3–50
South Australia	7	12	3	229	51*	1	1	–	25.44	1	202.2	42	728	31	23.48	1	–	5–43
Tasmania	4	4	–	21	14	–	–	–	5.25	–	147.4	36	444	19	23.37	1	–	5–69
Victoria	8	11	2	297	121*	1	1	1	33.00	1	238.0	47	779	30	25.97	2	1	6–51
Western Australia	4	5	2	71	27	–	–	–	23.67	1	145.1	30	441	13	33.92	–	–	4–56

Innings	Inn	NO	Runs	HS	0s	50	100	Avrge	Ct	Overs	Mdns	Runs	Wkts	Avrge	5WI	Best
First Innings	18	3	368	121*	1	1	1	24.53	–	347.4	61	1278	33	38.73	1	5–35
Second Innings	7	2	63	27	1	–	–	12.60	–	133.4	28	482	19	25.37	–	4–55
Third Innings	12	4	301	51*	–	1	–	37.63	2	227.4	57	688	29	23.72	2	5–43
Fourth Innings	1	–	5	5	–	–	–	5.00	1	145.1	31	403	20	20.15	1	6–51

Venues	M	Inn	NO	Runs	HS	0s	50	100	Avrge	Ct	Overs	Mdns	Runs	Wkts	Avrge	5WI	10WM	Best
Adelaide	3	4	2	58	39*	1	–	–	29.00	–	75.0	18	259	12	21.58	1	–	5–43
Brisbane	8	12	1	180	51*	–	1	–	16.36	–	217.0	40	772	31	24.90	1	–	6–51
Hobart	2	2	–	16	14	–	–	–	8.00	–	70.0	18	203	9	22.56	–	–	4–103
Melbourne	4	5	2	233	121*	–	1	1	77.67	1	143.5	30	453	15	30.20	1	–	5–35
Perth	8	12	2	179	38	1	–	–	17.90	3	285.2	63	888	33	26.91	1	–	5–69
Sydney	2	3	2	71	34*	–	–	–	71.00	–	63.0	8	276	1	276.00	–	–	1–121

Teams	M	Inn	NO	Runs	HS	0s	50	100	Avrge	Ct	Overs	Mdns	Runs	Wkts	Avrge	5WI	10WM	Best
Queensland	17	23	7	394	54	–	2	–	24.63	1	521.1	106	1751	59	29.68	2	1	6–51
Western Australia	10	15	2	343	121*	2	–	1	26.38	3	333.0	71	1100	42	26.19	2	–	5–35

INTERNATIONAL LIMITED-OVERS CAREER
Debut 2005–06 v New Zealand, Christchurch

Opponents	M	Inn	NO	Runs	HS	0s	50	Avrge	100	Stk-Rt	Ct	Overs	Mdns	Runs	Wkts	Avrge	5WI	Best
Afghanistan	2	1	1	1	1*	–	–	–	–	100.00	1	16.3	1	56	6	9.33	–	4–22
Bangladesh	9	3	1	67	41	1	–	33.50	–	176.32	–	64.1	2	289	16	18.06	–	3–17
Canada	1	–	–	–	–	–	–	–	–	–	1	10.0	–	43	1	43.00	–	1–43
England	25	15	4	208	57	1	1	18.91	–	96.74	11	210.4	14	1042	37	28.16	–	4–45
India	27	16	8	171	27*	1	–	21.38	–	100.00	3	220.3	11	1121	43	26.07	1	5–26
Kenya	1	1	1	12	12*	–	–	–	–	171.43	–	8.0	1	40	–	–	–	–
New Zealand	22	10	3	86	21*	–	–	12.29	–	92.47	4	181.4	12	951	34	27.97	–	4–33
Pakistan	9	6	1	46	21	1	–	9.20	–	71.88	5	83.0	3	360	16	22.50	–	3–24
Scotland	3	1	–	1	1	–	–	1.00	–	50.00	–	21.0	5	79	6	13.17	–	4–35
South Africa	17	16	3	124	30	1	–	9.54	–	74.70	2	149.4	5	795	26	30.58	–	4–34
Sri Lanka	19	11	2	63	23	1	–	7.00	–	56.76	3	145.0	11	647	29	22.31	1	6–31
West Indies	16	9	6	145	73*	–	1	48.33	–	136.79	5	122.5	5	588	20	29.40	1	5–29
Zimbabwe	2	2	2	27	20*	–	–	–	–	207.69	–	15.2	4	26	5	5.20	–	4–19
Total	**153**	**91**	**32**	**951**	**73***	**6**	**2**	**16.12**		**96.35**	**35**	**1248.2**	**74**	**6037**	**239**	**25.26**	**3**	**6–31**

Innings	Inn	NO	Runs	HS	0s	50	100	Avrge	Stk-Rt	Ct	Overs	Mdns	Runs	Wkts	Avrge	5WI	Best
First Innings	71	30	738	73*	6	1	–	18.00	101.23	15	726.2	48	3583	134	26.74	1	5–29
Second Innings	20	2	213	57	–	1	–	11.83	82.56	20	522.0	26	2454	105	23.37	2	6–31

Venues in Australia	M	Inn	NO	Runs	HS	0s	50	Avrge	Stk-Rt	Ct	Overs	Mdns	Runs	Wkts	Avrge	5WI	Best
Adelaide	6	2	1	9	9*	1	–	9.00	45.00	4	58.0	3	279	12	23.25	–	4-45
Brisbane	9	5	1	34	16	–	–	8.50	61.82	3	62.0	4	296	7	42.29	–	3-11
Canberra	1	1	1	8	8*	–	–	–	160.00	–	9.0	1	59	1	59.00	–	1-59
Darwin	3	1	–	0	0	1	–	0.00	0.00	–	16.1	1	63	6	10.50	–	3-17
Hobart	3	1	1	2	2*	–	–	–	200.00	1	21.0	1	88	5	17.60	–	2-27
Melbourne	13	6	1	43	21	1	–	8.60	63.24	6	114.4	8	532	20	26.60	–	3-30
Perth	13	10	2	105	26	1	–	13.13	86.78	6	109.3	9	492	21	23.43	–	4-22
Sydney	11	9	3	139	57	–	1	23.17	108.59	–	76.0	6	420	11	38.18	–	3-36
Total	**59**	**35**	**10**	**340**	**57**	**4**	**1**	**-13.60**	**85.21**	**20**	**466.2**	**33**	**2229**	**83**	**26.86**	**–**	**4-22**

Overseas Countries	M	Inn	NO	Runs	HS	0s	50	Avrge	Stk-Rt	Ct	Overs	Mdns	Runs	Wkts	Avrge	5WI	Best
Bangladesh	6	2	1	67	41	–	–	67.00	181.08	–	48.0	–	226	10	22.60	–	3-54
England	14	10	4	111	43*	–	–	18.50	119.35	4	113.0	5	558	18	31.00	–	3-24
India	25	13	7	139	25	1	–	23.17	93.29	3	215.0	13	1071	44	24.34	1	5-26
Malaysia	2	2	–	16	15	–	–	8.00	160.00	–	12.0	–	76	6	12.67	–	4-11
New Zealand	9	5	2	52	21*	–	–	17.33	91.23	1	79.3	4	482	15	32.13	–	4-51
Scotland	2	1	–	1	1	–	–	1.00	50.00	–	17.0	4	63	5	12.60	–	4-35
South Africa	14	10	2	144	73*	–	1	18.00	80.90	3	113.5	4	548	22	24.91	–	4-34
Sri Lanka	7	3	–	2	1	1	–	0.67	22.22	1	59.0	3	241	12	20.08	–	6-31
United Arab Emirates	6	4	2	25	21	–	–	12.50	100.00	2	53.0	2	225	12	18.75	–	3-24
West Indies	5	2	2	3	3*	–	–	–	150.00	1	36.5	2	166	8	20.75	1	5-29
Zimbabwe	4	4	2	51	23*	–	–	25.50	196.15	–	34.5	3	152	4	38.00	–	2-30

Highest Score 73* v West Indies, Johannesburg, 2009–10   **Best Bowling** 6–31 v Sri Lanka, Pallekele, 2011–12

DOMESTIC LIMITED-OVERS CAREER
Debut 2003–04 Queensland v Tasmania, Brisbane

Season	Team	M	Inn	NO	Runs	HS	0s	50	Avrge	Stk-Rt	Ct	Overs	Mdns	Runs	Wkts	Avrge	5WI	Best
2003–04	Queensland	2	–	–	–	–	–	–	–	–	–	20.0	2	87	4	21.75	–	4-37
2004–05	Queensland	4	2	–	35	27	–	–	17.50	44.87	1	37.0	2	200	6	33.33	–	4-45
2005–06	Queensland	9	4	3	26	17*	1	–	26.00	108.33	1	87.0	5	424	9	47.11	–	2-30
2006–07	Queensland	3	1	1	23	23*	–	–	–	82.14	–	30.0	3	134	2	67.00	–	1-38
2007–08	Queensland	1	–	–	–	–	–	–	–	–	–	8.0	1	28	–	–	–	–
2012–13	Western Australia	4	4	–	35	16	–	–	8.75	81.40	1	45.4	6	188	8	23.50	–	3-43
2015–16	Western Australia	2	2	1	10	8*	–	–	10.00	62.50	–	18.0	2	72	7	10.29	1	5-31
Total		**25**	**13**	**5**	**129**	**27**	**1**	**–**	**16.13**	**68.25**	**3**	**245.4**	**21**	**1133**	**36**	**31.47**	**1**	**5-31**

Innings	Inn	NO	Runs	HS	0s	50	Avrge	Stk-Rt	Ct	Overs	Mdns	Runs	Wkts	Avrge	5WI	Best
First Innings	4	2	41	17*	–	–	20.50	87.23	1	103.4	10	439	15	29.27	1	5-31
Second Innings	9	3	88	27	–	–	14.67	61.97	2	142.0	11	694	21	33.05	–	4-37

Opponents	M	Inn	NO	Runs	HS	0s	50	Avrge	Stk-Rt	Ct	Overs	Mdns	Runs	Wkts	Avrge	5WI	Best
New South Wales	5	2	1	16	16	–	–	16.00	145.45	1	49.0	4	244	6	40.67	–	2-68
Queensland	1	1	1	8	8*	–	–	–	100.00	–	9.0	1	31	5	6.20	1	5-31
South Australia	4	2	–	11	8	–	–	5.50	73.33	1	41.0	3	168	6	28.00	–	3-47
Tasmania	5	2	1	19	17*	–	–	19.00	90.48	–	46.0	3	218	9	24.22	–	4-37
Victoria	6	4	1	44	27	–	–	14.67	57.14	–	60.4	4	305	4	76.25	–	3-43
Western Australia	4	2	1	31	23*	–	–	31.00	54.39	1	40.0	6	167	6	27.83	–	4-45

Venues	M	Inn	NO	Runs	HS	0s	50	Avrge	Stk-Rt	Ct	Overs	Mdns	Runs	Wkts	Avrge	SWI	Best
Adelaide	1	–	–	–	–	–	–	–	–	–	10.0	–	59	2	29.50	–	2–59
Ballarat	1	1	–	27	27	–	–	27.00	55.10	–	10.0	–	72	–	–	–	–
Brisbane	11	4	2	17	8	–	–	8.50	42.50	1	108.0	7	490	13	37.69	–	4–37
Drummoyne	2	2	1	10	8*	–	–	10.00	62.50	–	18.0	2	72	7	10.29	1	5–31
Hobart	1	1	1	17	17*	–	–	–	130.77	–	7.0	1	30	2	15.00	–	2–30
Homebush	1	–	–	–	–	–	–	–	–	1	7.0	1	26	1	26.00	–	1–26
Melbourne	1	1	–	15	15	–	–	15.00	68.18	–	9.0	1	30	–	–	–	–
Perth	5	4	1	43	23*	–	–	14.33	87.76	1	56.4	8	249	9	27.67	–	3–43
Sydney	2	–	–	–	–	–	–	–	–	–	20.0	1	105	2	52.50	–	1–38

Teams	M	Inn	NO	Runs	HS	0s	50	Avrge	Stk-Rt	Ct	Overs	Mdns	Runs	Wkts	Avrge	SWI	Best
Queensland	19	7	4	84	27	–	–	28.00	64.62	2	182.0	13	873	21	41.57	–	4–37
Western Australia	6	6	1	45	16	–	–	9.00	76.27	1	63.4	8	260	15	17.33	1	5–31

Highest Score 27 Queensland v Victoria, Ballarat, 2004–05   **Best Bowling** 5–31 Western Australia v Queensland, Drummoyne, 2015–16

INTERNATIONAL TWENTY20 CAREER
Debut 2007–08 v Zimbabwe, Cape Town

Opponents	M	Inn	NO	Runs	HS	0s	50	Avrge	Stk-Rt	Ct	Overs	Mdns	Runs	Wkts	Avrge	5WI	Best
Bangladesh	1	–	–	–	–	–	–	–	–	–	4.0	–	28	1	28.00	–	1–28
England	7	2	2	4	3*	–	–	–	66.67	1	24.1	1	179	11	16.27	–	3–22
India	2	1	1	4	4*	–	–	–	400.00	–	7.0	–	54	3	18.00	–	2–31
New Zealand	2	1	–	1	1	–	–	1.00	33.33	1	7.0	–	38	5	7.60	–	3–19
Pakistan	6	6	2	11	5*	2	–	2.75	68.75	1	24.0	1	182	5	36.40	–	2–21
South Africa	1	1	–	10	10	–	–	10.00	100.00	–	4.0	–	20	1	20.00	–	1–20
Sri Lanka	5	3	2	57	28*	–	–	57.00	142.50	–	17.2	–	132	5	26.40	–	3–15
West Indies	5	2	–	13	9	–	–	6.50	92.86	2	17.5	–	138	6	23.00	–	2–22
Zimbabwe	1	1	–	9	9	–	–	9.00	180.00	–	4.0	–	26	1	26.00	–	1–26
Total	**30**	**17**	**7**	**109**	**28***	**2**	**–**	**10.90**	**114.74**	**5**	**109.2**	**2**	**797**	**38**	**20.97**	**–**	**3–15**

Innings	M	Inn	NO	Runs	HS	0s	50	Avrge	Stk-Rt	Ct	Overs	Mdns	Runs	Wkts	Avrge	5WI	Best
First Innings		9	3	64	28*	1	–	10.67	123.08	3	57.2	2	412	23	17.91	–	3–15
Second Innings		8	4	45	22*	1	–	11.25	104.65	2	52.0	–	385	15	25.67	–	3–19

Country	M	Inn	NO	Runs	HS	0s	50	Avrge	Stk-Rt	Ct	Overs	Mdns	Runs	Wkts	Avrge	5WI	Best
Australia	6	3	1	7	4	–	–	3.50	46.67	1	23.0	1	149	8	18.63	–	3–29
England	7	5	2	43	28*	1	–	14.33	148.28	1	22.0	1	199	6	33.17	–	2–36
New Zealand	1	1	–	1	1	–	–	1.00	33.33	–	4.0	–	19	3	6.33	–	3–19
South Africa	7	4	2	24	10	–	–	12.00	141.18	1	28.0	–	173	9	19.22	–	3–22
Sri Lanka	2	2	1	29	22*	–	–	29.00	107.41	–	8.0	–	82	2	41.00	–	1–35
West Indies	7	2	1	5	5*	–	–	5.00	125.00	2	24.2	–	175	10	17.50	–	3–15

Highest Score 82* v Sri Lanka, Nottingham, 2009   **Best Bowling** 3–15 v Sri Lanka, Bridgetown, 2009–10

INDIAN PREMIER LEAGUE CAREER

Debut 2012–13 Mumbai Indians v Bangalore Royal Challengers, Bangalore

Seasn	Team	M	Inn	NO	Runs	HS	0s	50	Avrge	Stk-Rt	Ct	Overs	Mdns	Runs	Wkts	Avrge	5WI	Best
2012–13	India	17	6	2	39	11	–	–	9.75	108.33	7	64.0	–	459	24	19.13	–	3–27
2013–14	United Arab Emirates	5	2	–	4	4	1	–	2.00	57.14	2	19.2	–	143	7	20.43	–	2–19
2013–14	India	9	6	5	52	16*	1	–	52.00	120.93	2	34.1	1	301	10	30.10	–	2–27
2014–15	India	9	8	4	31	13*	1	–	7.75	86.11	–	35.5	1	336	9	37.33	–	2–23
2015–16	India	3	3	1	5	4	1	–	2.50	35.71	1	11.0	–	106	2	53.00	–	1–35
Total		**43**	**25**	**12**	**131**	**16***	**2**	**–**	**10.08**	**96.32**	**12**	**164.2**	**1**	**1345**	**52**	**25.87**	**–**	**3–27**

Opponents	M	Inn	NO	Runs	HS	0s	50	Avrge	Stk-Rt	Ct	Overs	Mdns	Runs	Wkts	Avrge	5WI	Best
Bangalore Royal Challengers	5	3	2	26	16*	–	–	26.00	123.81	3	19.0	–	129	4	32.25	–	2–19
Chennai Super Kings	8	5	2	20	11*	–	–	6.67	111.11	3	31.0	–	276	9	30.67	–	3–27
Delhi Daredevils	4	1	–	4	4	–	–	4.00	33.33	1	14.1	–	146	4	36.50	–	2–27
Gujarat Lions	1	1	1	0	0*	–	–	–	–	1	4.0	–	35	1	35.00	–	1–35
Sunrisers Hyderabad	5	2	1	8	4*	–	–	8.00	66.67	2	19.0	–	155	6	25.83	–	2–26
Kolkata Knight Riders	7	5	2	35	14	1	–	11.67	109.38	1	26.1	–	207	11	18.82	–	2–13
Kings XI Punjab	1	–	–	–	–	–	–	–	–	1	4.0	–	29	2	14.50	–	2–29
Mumbai Indians	4	4	3	12	8*	–	–	12.00	85.71	–	16.0	1	144	4	36.00	–	2–23
Pune Warriors	2	–	–	–	–	–	–	–	–	–	8.0	–	41	5	8.20	–	3–33
Rajasthan Royals	6	4	1	26	13*	1	–	8.67	96.30	–	23.0	–	183	6	30.50	–	2–23

Teams	M	Inn	NO	Runs	HS	0s	50	Avrge	Stk-Rt	Ct	Overs	Mdns	Runs	Wkts	Avrge	5WI	Best
Kings XI Punjab	26	19	10	92	16*	2	–	10.22	92.00	5	100.2	1	886	28	31.64	–	2–19
Mumbai Indians	17	6	2	39	11	–	–	9.75	108.33	7	64.0	–	459	24	19.13	–	3–27

Highest Score 16* Kings XI Punjab v Bangalore Royal Challengers, Bangalore, 2013–14   **Best Bowling** 3–27 Mumbai Indians v Chennai Super Kings, Mumbai, 2012–13

Index

Acknowledgements

There are a great many people who have supported and encouraged me throughout my life and my career – I reckon I could fill a fair few pages with names and anecdotes! But I'm going to keep it simple. To my family, friends, coaches, mentors, sponsors – a big thank you. You all know who you are, and I want you to know I wouldn't be where I am today without you.

There's a special group of people I'd like to thank who have always backed me through good times and bad – my teammates. Whether it's club cricket or international cricket there's no better feeling than being part of a supportive team. I will always cherish the moments we've had competing together on the field, as well as spending time together as mates off the field.

Thanks also to the fans. The atmosphere and excitement at every game is down to you all, and it makes a big difference to our energy and enthusiasm and passion for the game.

A very special thanks goes to Mum, Dad and my brother, Adam. I would never have made it to where I am without your encouragement and support at different times throughout my life – including all that endless driving to and from practices and matches! You made sacrifices to give me opportunities to succeed, and words cannot express my thanks for everything you have done for me.

To Peter Lalor, this book literally wouldn't have happened without you. Huge thanks, mate. I've had the best time working with you and you've done an exceptional job bringing my story to life on the page.

To Dennis Lillee, for your ongoing encouragement, support and inspiration. You're a legend and I'm proud to call you a mate.

To Sam Halvorsen, my manager and friend. My life would look a lot different without your guidance and mentorship. You're not afraid to give me a kick in the bum when I need it, and sometimes I really do! You've been a big part of my career and my life outside the game. I am forever grateful to have you in my corner.

To Jess's family, Branco, Nives, Brian and Michelle. You have welcomed me from day one and it's a real privilege to be part of your family. You are always there for me and Jess and the kids, helping us whenever we need you without a moment's hesitation. I am enormously grateful for everything you do.

To Jessica, my wife. I feel I can do anything with you by my side, Jess. At times it has been tough, especially in the early days when we were apart because of our sporting careers, but through it all you have been absolutely amazing. You put your own career on hold to support mine, and you stuck with me through thick and thin. You fire me up when I need it, and your positive approach to everything in life is infectious. I look forward to the years ahead and a life outside sport with you and our two gorgeous children. Thank you with all my heart.